Israel and Hizbollah

This book examines the local and international dynamics and strategies that have come to define the often violent relationship between Israel and Lebanon.

Since the end of the Cold War, academic debate over the nature of war in the contemporary world has focused upon the asymmetric nature of conflict among a raft of failed or failing states, often held together by only a fragile notion of a shared communal destiny. Little scholarly attention has been paid, however, to one such conflict that predates the ending of the Cold War, yet still appears as intractable as ever: Israel's hostile relationship with Lebanon and in particular, its standoff with the Lebanese Shi'a militia group, Hizbollah. As events surrounding the 'Second Lebanon War' in the summer of 2006 demonstrate, the clear potential for further cross-border violence as well as the potential for a wider regional conflagration that embraces Damascus and Tehran remains as acute as ever.

This book focuses on the historical background of the conflict, while also considering the role that other external actors, most notably Syria, Iran and the United Nations, play in influencing the conduct and outcomes of the Israeli–Lebanese conflict. In addition, it also looks at Hizbollah's increasing sway in Lebanese domestic politics, its increased military cooperation with Iran and Syria and the implications of such developments.

This book will be of much interest to students of Middle Eastern politics, War and Conflict Studies, International Security and International Relations in general.

Clive Jones is Professor of Middle East Studies and International Politics in the School of Politics and International Studies (POLIS), University of Leeds, UK. His books include *Soviet Jewish Aliyah 1989–92* (1996), *Israel: Challenges to democracy, identity and the state* (with Emma Murphy, 2002) and *The al-Aqsa Intifada: between terrorism and civil war* (co-editor, 2005).

Sergio Catignani is Lecturer in Security and Strategic Studies at the Department of International Relations, University of Sussex. He is the author of *Israeli Counter-Insurgency and the Intifadas: dilemmas of a conventional army* (2008).

Middle Eastern Military Studies
Series Editor: Barry Rubin,
Interdisciplinary Center Herzliya, Israel

Israel and Hizbollah

An asymmetric conflict in historical and comparative perspective

**Edited by Clive Jones
and Sergio Catignani**

Routledge
Taylor & Francis Group

LONDON AND NEW YORK

First published 2010 by Routledge
2 Park Square, Milton Park, Abingdon, Oxon, OX14 4RN

Simultaneously published in the USA and Canada
by Routledge
270 Madison Avenue, New York, NY 10016

*Routledge is an imprint of the Taylor & Francis Group,
an informa business*

Typeset in Sabon by Swales & Willis Ltd, Exeter, Devon
Printed and bound in Great Britain by CPI Antony Rowe,
Chippenham, Wiltshire

British Library Cataloguing in Publication Data
A catalogue record for this book is available
from the British Library

Library of Congress Cataloging in Publication Data
Israel and the Hizbollah: an asymmetric conflict in historical and
comparitive perspective / edited by Clive Jones and Sergio Catignani.
p. cm.
Includes bibliographical references.
1. Israel—Military relations—Lebanon. 2. Lebanon—Military
relations—Israel. 3. Hizballah (Lebanon) 4. Asymmetric
warfare—Lebanon. I. Jones, Clive, 1965– II. Catignani, Sergio.
DS119.8.L4I74 2009
956.05—dc22
2009020409

ISBN10: 0–415–44910–3 (hbk)
ISBN10: 0–203–86552–9 (ebk)
ISBN13: 978–0–415–44910–6 (hbk)
ISBN13: 978–0–203–86552–1 (ebk)

Contents

    accommodation and resistance**   124
    MATS WÄRN

10 **The hubris of initial victory: The IDF and the
    Second Lebanon War**   147
    URI BAR-JOSEPH

11 **Conclusion**   163
    SERGIO CATIGNANI

    Glossary   169
    Notes   170
    Select bibliography   193
    Index   199

List of contributors

Hani A. M. Akho-Rashida is a Professor of International Relations and Political Theory at the University of Al-Bayt, Jordan and is a former researcher and lecturer at the University of Jordan in Amman. His research interests focus on the politics of the Eurasian region. Occasionally, he contributes op-ed articles for some Jordanian and Arab dailies. His scholarly articles include: 'Russian-Chechen Conflict: ground realities call for decisive action', *Al-Manara for Researches and Studies*, 4/13 (2007), and his most recent article that is forthcoming 'Dialectics of Modernization and Political Development', *Dirasat*, 37/1 (2010).

Hassan A. Barari is a Professor of Middle Eastern Politics at the University of Nebraska at Omaha (UNO). He is a former Senior Fellow at the United States of Peace (USIP) based in Washington, DC. He was also a researcher and a lecturer at the University of Jordan in Amman. He received his PhD in International Relations from Durham University in England. He has written extensively on the politics of the Middle East and his books include: *Israelism: Arab scholarship on Israel: a critical assessment* (London: Ithaca, 2009) and *Israeli Politics and the Middle East Peace Process, 1988–2002* (London and New York: Routledge, 2004). Dr Barari writes a column for the Jordanian Daily *al-Rai* and has been a frequent commentator on Middle Eastern affairs for key Arab and international media.

Uri Bar-Joseph is a Professor in the Division of International Relations at the School of Political Science of Haifa University, Israel. His books include *The Watchman Fell Asleep: the surprise of the Yom Kippur War and its sources* (2005); *Two Minutes Over Baghdad* (co-author with Amos Perlmutter and Michael Handel, 2003); *Israel's National Security Towards the 21st Century* (ed., 2001); *Intelligence Intervention in the Politics of Democratic States: the USA, Britain, and Israel* (1995); and *The Best of Enemies: Israel and Transjordan in the War of 1948* (1987). He has published numerous articles in leading journals including *Political Science Quarterly, Armed Forces and Society, Journal of Conflict Resolution, Foreign Policy Analysis, Political Psychology, Survival, The Journal of*

Military History, The Journal of Strategic Studies, The Journal of Contemporary History, Security Studies, and Intelligence and National Security. His fields of interest are national security, intelligence and the Arab–Israeli conflict.

Sergio Catignani is a Lecturer in Strategic and Security Studies at the Department of International Relations, University of Sussex. Dr Catignani has also served as a counter-insurgency military advisor to the US Army's 4th Brigade Combat Team (Airborne), 25th Infantry Division. He is the recent author of *Israeli Counter-Insurgency and the Intifadas: dilemmas of a conventional army* (Routledge, 2008) and has published in the *Journal of Strategic Studies*, *Terrorism and Political Violence*, *Parameters* and the *Royal United Services Institute Journal*. His research interests focus on organizational change, contemporary military operations (particularly counter-insurgencies) and Middle East security issues.

Laurie Zittrain Eisenberg is an Associate Professor in the history of the modern Middle East at Carnegie Mellon University. Her areas of research and publication include the Arab–Israeli conflict and peace process and the historical background to Israel's interaction with multiple Middle East actors, particularly Lebanon, Jordan, and the Palestinians. Her publications include *My Enemy's Enemy: Lebanon in the early Zionist imagination, 1900–1948* (Detroit: Wayne State University Press, 1994) and with Neil Caplan, *Negotiating Arab–Israeli Peace: patterns, problems, possibilities*, revised second edition (Bloomington: Indiana University Press, forthcoming, 2010), as well as articles published in the *Middle East Review of International Affairs*; *Israel Affairs*, *Journal of Strategic Studies*, and *Studies in Zionism*.

Clive Jones is Professor of Middle East Studies and International Politics and Head of School in the School of Politics and International Studies (POLIS), University of Leeds, UK. His books include *Britain and the Yemen Civil War* (2004), *Soviet Jewish Aliyah 1989–92* (1996) with Emma Murphy, *Israel: challenges to democracy, identity and the state* (2002), and *The al-Aqsa Intifada: between terrorism and civil war* (co-editor, 2005). He has published numerous articles in leading journals including *Middle Eastern Studies*, *British Journal of Middle East Studies*, *Intelligence and National Security*, *Studies in Conflict and Terrorism*, *Democratization*, *Civil Wars* as well as contributed to *Jane's Intelligence Review*. His research interests are focused primarily on Gulf Security and the Israel–Palestine conflict.

Asher Kaufman is an Assistant Professor of History at the University of Notre Dame. He is the author of *Reviving Phoenicia: the search for identity in Lebanon* (I. B. Tauris, 2004). Among his recent publications are 'Too Much French but a Swell Exhibit: representing Lebanon at the 1939 New York World's Fair', *British Journal of Middle East Studies*, 35/1 (2008); 'Forgetting the Lebanon War? On Silence, Denial and Selective

Remembrance of the First Lebanon War', in Jay Winter, Efrat Ben Zeev and Ruth Ginio, *Shadows of war: the social history of silence in the twentieth century* (Cambridge University Press, 2009).

Hussain Sirriyeh is a Senior Lecturer in the Department of Arabic and Middle Eastern Studies, University of Leeds, UK where he teaches Politics and Modern History of the Middle East. He is the author of *US Policy in the Gulf, 1968–1977* and an Adelphi Paper entitled *Lebanon, Dimensions of Conflict*. He has also published a number of articles on Lebanon, the Gulf, Iraq and the Arab–Israeli conflict. His present research is focused on Lebanon and Jordan.

Daniel Sobelman served as the Arab affairs and Middle East correspondent for the daily *Ha'aretz* (1997–2003) and is currently working toward a PhD in International Relations at the Hebrew University in Jerusalem. His nearly two dozen contributions to the study of Hizbollah have appeared under the aegis of the Jaffee Center for Strategic Studies at Tel-Aviv University, as well as in *Jane's Intelligence Review* and RUSI publications (London). His monograph 'New Rules of The Game: Israel and Hizbollah after the Withdrawal from Lebanon' (JCSS 2004) was also published in Arabic in Lebanon. His research focuses on the issue of asymmetric warfare and conflict management between Israel and Hizbollah.

Mats Wärn is a lecturer at Department of Political Science, Stockholm University, Sweden. He is co-editor of *Globalization, Imperialism and Resistance* (2007). His work has been published in *Journal of Palestine Studies*, *Civil Wars*, *Jane's Intelligence Review*, and *Middle East International*. His main theme of study is Islamist movements in the Middle East.

1   Introduction

Clive Jones

With the end of the Cold War, academic debate over the nature of war in the contemporary world has increasingly come to focus on the concept of 'asymmetric conflict'. It is perhaps worth noting from the outset that all conflicts, conventional or otherwise, are, by their very nature asymmetric – power being a relative concept that can decide the outcome of violent confrontation.[1] Even so, the term has come increasingly to be associated with an imbalance of power and resources between the militaries of developed states on the one hand, and a range of armed actors on the other often located in failed or failing states, and held together by those whose loyalties are often based on a fragile notion of a shared communal destiny. Amid the debate over the impact of globalisation on the very idea of the nation state, religion and ethnicity have come to exercise powerful claims on peoples and resources as mobilising agents that often enjoy the support – both benign and malign – of other actors. Conflicts in Iraq, Afghanistan, the Congo and throughout the Caucasus could all be incorporated within this causal description.

However, relatively little scholarly attention has been paid to an asymmetric conflict that predates the ending of the Cold War, yet still appears as intractable as ever: Israel's hostile relationship with Lebanon and in particular, its standoff with the Lebanese Shi'a militia group, Hizbollah. Moreover, as events during the so called 'Rocket War' or *Harb Tammuz* – the Sixth War – over the summer of 2006 demonstrated, the potential for a wider regional conflagration that could include Damascus and Tehran remains more acute than in the case of the Palestinians. Indeed, while Israel's efforts to curtail the activities of a Hamas-led Palestinian Authority have provoked international opprobrium at the level of bloodshed inflicted upon the inhabitants of the Gaza Strip during Operation 'Cast Lead' over December and January 2008/9 – a campaign ostensibly designed to end the continuous rocket attacks fired from the strip at southern Israel – it is a conflict that to all intents and purposes remains confined in terms of the actors directly involved.

In retrospect, the kidnapping of two Israeli soldiers on 12 July 2006 quickly drew the ire of officials in Jerusalem. Having enjoyed relative quiescence on its northern border since withdrawing unilaterally from Lebanon in May 2000, the attack on the Israel Defence Forces (IDF) patrol was seen not only as an act of unprovoked aggression on the part of Hizbollah, but an attempt to embroil Israel in a two-front war designed not just to force Israel into a process of asymmetric prisoner exchanges, but more fundamentally, to change the strategic balance in the region to the detriment of the Jewish State. To this end, both Hizbollah (and Hamas) remain, depending on your viewpoint, either the beneficiaries of the political and material support of Damascus and Tehran as symbols of resistance or alternatively, regional actors beholden to the dictates of Presidents Bashar al-Assad and President Mahmoud Ahmadinejad.

Explaining the events of 12 July 2006, therefore, is seen in Israel through this realist prism. Given the symbiotic relationship with Tehran, the assumption remains strong among decision makers in both Jerusalem and Washington that both Iran and Syria gave the green light to Sheikh Hassan Nasrallah, the spiritual leader of Hizbollah, to precipitate this crisis. According to this rather circumstantial interpretation, the defence pact reached between Tehran and Damascus on 15 June 2006, ostensibly designed to deter the 'common threat from Israel and the United States' veiled an agreement over increased military support for Hizbollah, though the actual modalities of the agreement remain obscure. For Iran, the gain to be had was to expose the division between Europe and the United States at a time when Tehran faced the threat of UN-backed international sanctions over its nuclear programme. For Damascus, forced to publicly withdraw from Lebanon in the summer of 2005 under UN resolution 1559, following well-founded suspicions of its involvement in the assassination of former Prime Minister Rafiq al-Hariri, Hizbollah remains a potent mechanism through which it can wield influence over the Lebanese political landscape. The continued existence of its military wing *al-Muqawama al-Islamiyya* (The Islamic Resistance) in south Lebanon remains a violation of UN resolution 1559 which called explicitly 'for the disbanding and disarmament of all Lebanese and non-Lebanese militias'.

The continued existence of Hizbollah's military wing is a sober reminder that while the so-called 'Cedar Revolution' – the outpouring of public grief and anger at Syria's alleged involvement in Hariri's violent demise – forced Syria's withdrawal from Lebanon, it was not a popular movement that encompassed all Lebanese confessions. Sectarian interests still dominated the political dispensation. Indeed, seen from the perspective of Damascus, Hizbollah remains a palliative to Washington's attempts to ostracise the Ba'athist regime over its links to Hamas and Hizbollah as well as its apparent indifference to jihadists crossing from Syrian territory to fight alongside the insurgents in Iraq.

But the decision to actually launch the kidnap operation remained with the leadership of Hizbollah alone. The organisation had repeatedly stated its intent to kidnap Israeli soldiers, partly as a demonstration of support for the Palestinians, partly to secure the release of the few Lebanese held in Israeli gaols, but equally, to solidify its dominant position at the apex of Lebanese politics. Since the international opprobrium heaped on Damascus over the Hariri assassination and its subsequent overt withdrawal of its military forces from Lebanon, Hizbollah has found itself at a political crossroads. The largest single party in the Lebanese parliament and with two Cabinet members in the government of Premier Siniora, the relationship of the movement to the state has proved complex. On the one hand, its involvement in a political system still conditioned by a confessional order was at least seen as tacit acceptance of the existing dispensation. On the other, the continued existence of its military wing, numbering anywhere between 8,000 to 12,000 militiamen and Nasrallah's refusal to abide by either the Saudi-brokered Taif accord of 1989 or more latterly, UN resolution 1559, which both call for the disbanding of all Lebanese militias, is seen by some commentators as indicative of a movement which hides a radical pan-Shi'a Islamist identity under the cloak of parochial parliamentary participation.

Such involvement in the political system does not translate necessarily into agreement with its course or direction. Having lost access to direct Syrian patronage, coupled with the emergence of a Western orientated government in Beirut, Nasrallah undoubtedly foresaw the erosion of Hizbollah's influence, a position that would only be of benefit to the United States and Israel. As such, the operation to kidnap Israeli servicemen was as much about reaffirming the centrality of Hizbollah to the political direction of Lebanon as it was about any particular trade in human currency. Nasrallah himself stated that the planning of the kidnap operation dubbed *al-Wa'd al-Sadiq* (The Sincere Promise) had been carefully planned over the course of a year. Undoubtedly too, Hizbollah expected a heavy response initially from the IDF, but a response akin to the heavy if periodic bouts of artillery fire and air strikes that have accompanied previous clashes with *al-Muqawama* members over the disputed area of the Shebaa farms. Then, according to the script, Israel would enter into third-party negotiations for the release of its servicemen, a precedent already set in 2004 when Jerusalem released 400 Palestinian and 30 Lebanese prisoners for the remains of three Israeli soldiers killed in a border clash in the year 2000 and an Israeli businessman and reserve army Colonel, Elhanan Tannenbaum.

But Israel tore up the script. While Hizbollah may have believed its accumulation of missiles would deter the IDF, or at least limit the scope of retaliatory action, such hubris was soon exposed by the magnitude of Israel's military onslaught. Several factors have been used to explain the severity of the Israeli response based upon personal, organisational as well as regional variables. The need for former Israeli Premier Ehud Olmert, given his lack of military experience and expertise, to prove his security credentials and, thus, solidify support for his Kadima-led coalition government that had been badly shaken by events in Gaza has been often cited. Equally, his defence minister, Amir Peretz, leader of the Labour party lacked similar security credibility, thereby creating a situation that has allowed the IDF High Command and the Chief of Staff, Lieutenant General Dan Halutz to dictate both the scope and pace of the operation. Such analyses, while perhaps containing elements of truth, miss the point. Irrespective of background and expertise, any Israeli premier in the shadow of the kidnapping of the two Israeli soldiers, Ehud Goldwasser and Eldad Regev, would have reacted with overwhelming force to a kidnapping which coincidental or not, appears to presage a war on two fronts.

The abduction represented intelligence failures at the operational level at least. Given the declared intent of Nasrallah over the past year to organise a kidnap operation and the clear capability of *al-Muqawama* to execute such a plan, credence must be attached to the paucity of real time intelligence from *Agaf Modi'in* (*AMAN* – IDF Military Intelligence). Equally however, the kidnapping presented the IDF with the opportunity to reassert a deterrent capability widely regarded as having been undermined by unilateral withdrawals from south Lebanon in May 2000 and the Gaza Strip in August 2005. From the *Kiriyah* (the IDF headquarters in Tel Aviv) these withdrawals in the absence of any political agreement only served the interests of those who countenanced armed struggle as the only means to extract concessions from Jerusalem. Psychologically, it also reinforced the belief that both Hamas and Hizbollah are but different sides of the same coin in this two-front war, a view that denies consideration of both the political nuance and religious distinctions that set them apart.

Such reasoning on deterrence goes beyond the two Islamist movements however. Regarded in Israel as extensions of Syrian, but more worryingly, Iranian foreign policy, Hizbollah conflated with an aggressive Iranian foreign policy that sought to take advantage of Washington's malaise in Iraq to reassert its influence and deny the 'democratic project' so beloved of former President George W. Bush in his vision of the Middle East. Thus, while Israel's overwhelming response to Hizbollah was premised on responding to a violation of Israeli territorial sovereignty implicit in the abduction of its soldiers and the re-establishment of a deterrent capability along its northern border, its scale and scope came to be justified as part of Washington's wider struggle over Iran. Seen from this perspective, the acquisition of missiles of varying range and conventional capability by *al-Muqawama* is not just a function of its confrontation with Israel or its need to affirm its hegemony, both political and martial over the Lebanese polity. Hizbollah has in fact become the embodiment of an Iranian view of forward or extended deterrence as it seeks to develop its nuclear programme. According to this logic, Israel and indeed the United States would be less likely to launch any attack on Iranian nuclear facilities given the missile threat Israel would face on its northern border from Hizbollah. Degrading as much of this capability as possible reduced the constraints on pre-emptive action should the time ever come when Washington and Jerusalem concluded that diplomacy alone remained insufficient to curb Tehran's nuclear and regional ambitions.

As such, there can be no guarantee that future conflict between Israel and the Hizbollah can remain limited in scope. This sobering thought, therefore, informs the importance of this edited volume in understanding the underlying dynamics that have come to shape this particular 'asymmetric' conflict. It sets out to examine the causes, conduct and outcomes of Israel's conflict with Hizbollah by examining the key domestic and international actors, strategies and actions that have underpinned this bloody relationship over three decades and more; broadly, Israeli–Lebanese relations since the founding of the Jewish state in 1948. While the book is necessarily historical in its broad methodological approach, it is nonetheless informed by a number of key empirical themes:

1   The extent to which the Lebanese confessional system helps or hinders the pursuit of regional hegemony for key state actors.
2   The extent to which Hizbollah can accommodate itself to a confessional political system while remaining loyal to an Islamist agenda that questions the legitimacy of the nation state.
3   The extent to which domestic drivers such as ideology and civil–military relations have come to determine Israeli national security policy towards Lebanon and the Hizbollah in particular.
4   The extent to which the broader strategy of seeking alliances with minority communities in the Middle East has helped and/or hindered Jerusalem in its attempts to secure a sympathetic political dispensation in Lebanon.

These themes, to one extent or another, inform the chapters of this book. In Chapter 2, Laurie Zittrain Eisenberg, traces the early history of Israel's relationship with the confessional order in Lebanon from 1948 through to the 1970s. Ever since the establishment of the *Yishuv* (Jewish settlement) in Palestine in the early part of the twentieth century, a constant theme in the external policy of all Jewish leaders has been the establishment of relations with minority communities in other states. This need to establish relations with non-Muslim or non-Arab communities has seen Jerusalem forge ties with Kurds in Iraq, the Christian communities of southern Sudan, as well as establishing strong bilateral ties with Iran under the Shah. However, it has been Israel's ties with the Christian Maronite 'confessions' in Lebanon that have attracted most interest.

For the Christian Maronite 'confessions', fearing the loss of the demographic hegemony that had underpinned their political hegemony under the 1943 National Pact, ties with Israel were seen as insurance against the intrigues of Syria with its irredentist claims, as well as claims of Muslim communities, aggrieved at the inherent bias of the confessional order. For Israel, not only did the Christian communities offer a wider window on developments in the Arab world, but also offered a means by which the growing power and influence of the Palestine Liberation Organisation (PLO) in southern Lebanon and Beirut after 1968 could be countered. This chapter explores this often symbiotic relationship, critically examining whether Israel's preoccupation with courting minorities in the Middle East blinded policymakers in

Jerusalem to a longer term political and demographic shift in Lebanon that should have been assessed more objectively: the growing power of the Shi'a.

Chapter 3, by Asher Kaufman explores the period from 'Operation Litani' in 1978, through to Israel's controversial invasion of Lebanon in 1982 and its immediate aftermath. The hijacking of an Israeli Egged bus by Palestinian gunmen affiliated to the PLO in early 1978 led to the deaths of over 30 Israeli civilians. In response, the newly elected Likud coalition government launched 'Operation Litani', a land invasion of south Lebanon designed to push the PLO away from Israel's northern border. Over 500 Palestinian and Lebanese civilians were to lose their lives in this incursion, but it set a precedent for Israel's invasion of Lebanon in June 1982, a far larger venture sanctioned ostensibly in response to the attempted assassination of Israel's ambassador to London, Shlomo Argov. The rationale behind these two invasions has often been presented in terms of assuaging a clear existential threat: the need to remove and destroy the PLO as a military threat, while concurrently, curtailing Syria's military and political influence in Lebanon. But beyond this purely strategic justification, a broader geo-political advantage was being pursued by Jerusalem. This chapter examines the extent to which under the influence of Defence Minister Ariel Sharon, 'Operation Peace for Galilee', was designed not only to reassert Christian hegemony, but equally to destroy the PLO as a symbol of Palestinian nationalism. In so doing, the chapter examines the extent to which military policy towards other confessions in Lebanon was preordained, a process that pushed an already alienated Shi'a population towards a religious radicalism that would result in the emergence of Hizbollah.

It is this ideological and organisational emergence that remains the focus of the fourth chapter in this collection by Hussain Sirriyeh. Prior to the arrival of al-Qaida on the international scene, Hizbollah was widely regarded in the West at least as the archetypal 'terrorist organisation'. Its use of suicide bombings, not least the attacks on the US Marine and French Paratroops headquarters in Beirut in October 1983 was seen as the leitmotiv of an organisation unyielding in its drive to rid Lebanon both of foreign troops and the confessional system.

With its close spiritual and political ties to the Ayatollahs in Tehran, it was widely perceived as an extension of a belligerent Iranian foreign policy, able and willing, as a succession of hijackings and hostage takings revealed, to humiliate the West in general and the United States in particular. Yet, the theological, as well as political emergence of Hizbollah reveals a complex social movement, the progeny of the Vanished Imam, Mohammed al-Sadr whose proselytising among the Shi'a of south Lebanon gave a religious context to the process of political empowerment that their increasing demographic weight demanded. As such, this chapter examines the extent to which the perceived links with Iran, personified perhaps in the figure of Imad Mughniyeh, undermined a sober appreciation among policymakers in Jerusalem of the movement's importance as a social actor amid a failing state, whose pan-Islamic rhetoric disguised a more sober appreciation of Hizbollah's more parochial agenda.

Chapter 5, by Daniel Sobelman takes the discussion of Hizbollah further by examining its evolution from what many regarded as a terrorist organisation to one whose role in organising resistance to the Israeli occupation of south Lebanon gave it an appeal hitherto unknown among Lebanon's fractious confessional order and beyond. Widely credited with forcing Israel into a unilateral withdrawal from south Lebanon in May 2000, Hizbollah enjoyed the regional approbation of the Arab street, claiming a military victory over the Jewish State that had long eluded more powerful state actors. Yet, the extent to which Hizbollah had become part of the fabric of Lebanese politics, able and willing to work with a political system it had previously eschewed, says much about how a predominantly Shi'a organisation accentuated its Lebanese identity over its Islamic credentials. This chapter examines the extent to which this approbation of nationalism helped legitimise Hizbollah in the eyes of Christian and Sunni alike, conferring upon it a cross-communal legitimacy it had hitherto lacked. It also examines the extent to which Israel's withdrawal from south Lebanon in May 2000 posed dilemmas for a movement whose banner of legitimacy across Lebanon remained pinned to the totem of external resistance.

Chapter 6, by Sergio Catignani examines the extent to which the strategies and tactics of the Israel Defence Forces (IDF) helped rather than hindered the development of the movement. In particular, the chapter explores the extent to which counter-insurgency and counter-terrorist methods developed to combat Palestinian militants of the PLO, proved inadequate to countering a wholly different insurgent movement and one whose very existence became part and parcel of the very political DNA of the Shi'a community of Lebanon. The argument put forward here is that while it remained impossible for Israel to accommodate a movement that denies the legitimacy of a Jewish dispensation in Palestine, the very methods used by the IDF against the Hizbollah, methods that often had to balance the competing demands of 'deterrence' with 'force protection' singularly failed to undermine the military capabilities or indeed appeal of the military wing of Hizbollah, *al-Muqawama.*

This is certainly an argument developed further in Chapter 7, in relation to the intelligence war fought between Israel and the Hizbollah between 1990 and 2000. It examines the way in which intelligence was used by Israel in its war against Hizbollah in south Lebanon. By using ideas drawn from the literature on strategic culture, it argues that in trying to replicate methods used in countering Palestinian insurgents, methods that often posited little distinction between terrorism and insurgency, Israel's intelligence agencies, and in particular *Agaf Modi'in* failed to appreciate fully the finite political aims of Hizbollah's guerrilla struggle. As such, the paucity in Israel's collective intelligence effort was as much a result of a faulty appreciation of the context of Lebanese politics as an actual paucity in objective operational intelligence. This in turn allowed operatives of Hizbollah's military wing, *al-Muqawama* to score notable intelligence triumphs over Israel, triumphs that did much to force the IDF into a unilateral withdrawal from south Lebanon in May 2000.

Since the mid-1980s, Jerusalem has claimed that the ability of Hizbollah to function as both a military and social organisation has been contingent upon the financial, material, military and ideological support it has received from Tehran and Damascus. For Israel, that support has not only been consistent with an aggressive intent which denies the very basis of Israel as a Jewish State, but it is a support in which the costs to Syria and Iran have been minimal in pursuit of their own particular foreign policy goals. It is an exploration of these claims that informs Chapter 8 by Hassan Barari and Hani A. M. Akho-Rashida, and in particular, the claim that Hizbollah is nothing more than a proxy of Damascus and Tehran. For Iran, Hizbollah remains a symbol of an Islamic rejection of Israel's right to exist within defined borders in land considered to be a *waqf* (Islamic endowment). For Syria, military and political support for a movement whose religious basis otherwise contradicts the secular basis of the Ba'athist state, has always been directed towards extracting concessions from Israel over the occupied *Jaulan* (Golan Heights). While this blend of realpolitik and ideological affinity has defined the boundaries of sponsorship for Hizbollah, Syrian and Iranian support for the movement has also been dependent upon the eddies of the changing political leadership in the region. This chapter, therefore, explores the evolving nature of support given to Hizbollah and in the process examines the extent to which the movement has managed to remain an autonomous actor despite its logistical and political reliance upon Damascus and Tehran.

It is this sense of autonomy that informs Chapter 9 and the ideological, as well as theological debates that now define Hizbollah. In his insightful essay, Mats Wärn explores the conflicting pressures that have faced Hizbollah ever since the Israeli withdrawal from south Lebanon in May 2000. While bathing in the regional approbation of having humbled the IDF, Hizbollah under Sheikh Hassan Nasrallah faced the challenge of adapting to a post-conflict environment where its legitimacy could no longer depend upon claims to national resistance. In short, Hizbollah faced an uneasy choice between full involvement with a political dispensation it had already begun to work with, or a return to Islamic piety that increasingly antagonised the prevailing social and political order. The failure of Hizbollah to disarm and fold its armed wing into the Lebanese Armed Forces was widely seen as indicative of Hizbollah's desire to retain an autonomous semi-state structure, a position sustained by its claim that Israel continued to occupy alleged Lebanese territory (the Shebaa farms area) as well as hold a number of Lebanese prisoners. Such claims increasingly ran foul of changes in the broader Lebanese political arena. Christian, Druze and Sunni confessions looked to reassert Lebanese sovereignty and remove Syrian influence from the politics of the country. Following the assassination of former Prime Minister Rafiq Hariri and the subsequent Cedar Revolution that looked to usurp the influence of Damascus, Hizbollah once more began to adopt a more belligerent approach towards the confessional order. This chapter examines these issues and the renewed emphasis placed by Hizbollah on its Islamic identity. In so doing, it seeks to examine whether the decision to launch a kidnap operation against IDF troops in July 2006 was merely opportunist, or designed to place Hizbollah once more at the centre of the Lebanese political arena.

Finally, Chapter 10 by Uri Bar-Joseph examines the events of the summer of 2006 from an Israeli perspective. For Israelis, this was a war of *Ein Breira* 'no choice', forced upon Jerusalem by an atavistic organisation that enjoyed the indulgence of a regime in Tehran that actively called for the dismemberment of Israel as a sovereign state. Yet, Israel's conduct of the war has left a bitter aftertaste. While the Air force did score strategic success against Hizbollah's longer range missiles, undue reliance upon air power did little to contain the barrage of Katyusha rockets that fell across northern Israel. When a ground offensive was finally launched, paucity in adequately trained troops, shortages of basic equipment and a failure to appreciate the extent of Hizbollah's military preparations, all exposed an apparent malaise at the heart of the IDF. Moreover, despite the random nature of the Katyusha attacks, Israel's aerial bombardment killed more Lebanese civilians than the Hizbollah attacks killed Israeli civilians; indeed, the majority of Israeli casualties were servicemen. As such, Israel, despite its claims of self-defence, was subject to a barrage of international opprobrium, while internally, Israelis questioned the conduct of the war by the political and military elites. This chapter examines these debates within the context of how Israel has come to view the problem of asymmetric warfare amid two unilateral withdrawals – in Lebanon and Gaza – that are widely believed to have undermined Israel's deterrent capability.

This volume does not seek to be *the* definitive work on the conflict between Israel and Hizbollah and there remain many areas and themes this volume has not explored. For example, the military structures of *al-Muqawama* and their exact relationship with Hizbollah remain the subject of much conjecture, not least in the aftermath of the February 2008 assassination of Imad Mugniyeh, widely regarded as the military genius of *al-Muqawama*. For the most part, however, our knowledge of such structures remains sketchy and academic conjecture remains beyond the realm of this book. Equally, the relationships, vexed or otherwise that Hizbollah enjoys with the Shi'a communities across the Middle East certainly deserve to be the subject of future academic examination, but for the sake of clarity of purpose, they remain outside the scope of this enquiry. Even so, the contributors to this volume individually and collectively, provide an excellent insight and understanding into one of the longest running 'asymmetric' conflicts in the Middle East, and one whose contours continue to shape the contemporary regional order.

2   From benign to malign
Israeli–Lebanese relations, 1948–78

Laurie Zittrain Eisenberg

Introduction

The relations between Lebanon and Israel in the 30 years from 1948 to 1978 were predicated not on the interactions between two sovereign governments, but rather on the largely clandestine associations between various Lebanese groups and Israel, and even more so on the hostility between Israel and third parties active in Lebanon. The weakness of the Lebanese state stemmed from its confessional system, which apportioned political power among feuding sects more interested in dominating one another than in cooperating for a common good. This domestic battle for supremacy sent Lebanese parties in search of external resources, in effect inviting outsiders, such as Syria and Israel, to project their influence into Lebanon. Israel's political isolation in an unwelcoming Middle East made it particularly susceptible to secretive overtures from Lebanese groups professing common cause with it. Even more compelling, however, were the activities of Israel's Palestinian and Syrian enemies in Lebanon. The Palestine Liberation Organization (PLO) set up headquarters in Lebanon in the late 1960s and PLO guerrillas took over southern Lebanon after their eviction from Jordan in 1970. PLO activity eventually contributed to the outbreak of the Lebanese civil war in 1975, which set the stage for major Syrian intervention in 1976. These three factors – Lebanon's weak central government and confessional system, Israel's isolation in the region and the role of third-party players in Lebanon determined the course of Israeli–Lebanese relations during the period May 1948 to March 1978. This period began with a relatively calm border between the two states, witnessed increasingly sharp Israeli hit-and-run attacks against Palestinian and Lebanese targets and deepening involvement between Israeli and Christian Lebanese actors and ended on the cusp of a significant Israeli invasion of Lebanon. Consideration of the roles of Lebanese confessionalism and Israeli isolation in determining Israeli–Lebanese relations requires a brief review of their emergence during what can be loosely called the 'pre-independence' (1943 for Lebanon, 1948 for Israel) period.

Lebanon's confessionalism is derived from the unusual heterogeneity of its population. Carved out of the 'Greater Syria' region of the Ottoman Empire by the European Powers at the end of the First World War, the boundaries of modern Lebanon caught within it a population comprised of many different sectarian and religious communities, primarily Christians (Maronite Catholics, Greek Orthodox, Armenian Apostolic and Melkite Greek Catholics), Shi'a Muslims, Sunni Muslims and Druze. A civil war between the Maronites and Druze in 1860 had provoked French intervention on behalf of their fellow Christians; under French pressure the Ottomans agreed to the creation of an autonomous protectorate (*mutasarifiya*) in Mount Lebanon under the stewardship of a non-Lebanese Christian governor. Advising the governor was a council carefully composed of Maronites, Shi'a, Sunni, Druze, Melkite and Greek Orthodox members, a harbinger of modern Lebanon's system of organizing political power by sect. In 1920 France expanded Lebanon (*le Grand Liban*) beyond the Mount Lebanon region and separated it from its natural Syrian hinterland. Under direct French aegis during the period of the French Mandate over Lebanon (1920–43), Christians, particularly Maronites, enjoyed special power and privilege. Throughout, Lebanon's body politic suffered from a tension between those who looked to Europe for political orientation (many Christians, particularly Maronites) and those who looked to the Arab East, predominantly Sunni Muslims, who agitated for a reunion with Syria.

As the prospect of independence approached, the chiefs of the two leading sectarian communities, Bishara al-Khoury (a Maronite, and future first president of independent Lebanon) and Riad al-Sulh (a Sunni, and future first prime minister) hammered out a compromise agreement designed to reassure the two camps that each one's interests could be preserved through political cooperation. Working from the results of the 1932 census, their unwritten 'National Pact' of 1943 called for institutional power-sharing among the various sects by a fixed ratio of Christians to Muslims in the parliament (to the Christians' advantage) and the distribution of high office by sect, with a Maronite president, Sunni prime minister, and the less influential speaker of the parliament a Shi'a. In its signature catch phrase the National Pact described Lebanon as a nation with 'an Arab face'. Walid Khalidi has explained this unusual description as 'a compromise formulation between the outright description of Lebanon as an "Arab country" and the denuding of Lebanon of any Arab characteristics'.[1] In a nutshell, the Christians were agreeing to countenance Lebanon's natural ties with the Arab world and forego calling upon the Europeans, particularly the French, to bolster their position; for their part the Muslims were recognizing the special European affiliation of a large segment of the Lebanese population, and relinquishing aspirations for Lebanon's assimilation into a greater Syrian or pan-Arab state.

The factionalized nature of Lebanese society had a great impact on the direction of relations between Lebanon and Israel. Although Bishara al-Khoury represented mainstream Maronite inclinations to preserve Christian power via accommodation with the Sunni Muslim majority, there was a competing Francophile Maronite faction which viewed Lebanon as Christian, separate from the Muslim Arab world, and superior to it. Prior to Lebanese (and Israeli) independence, these ultra-nationalist Maronites embraced a vision of an implacable Muslim menace to Christian privilege in Lebanon, and looked to the Palestinian Jews as natural allies. Although this group constituted only a minority within the Maronite community, some of its members held lofty positions in Lebanese political circles, among them President Emile Edde (1936–41) and President Alfred Naccache (1941–43), the highest officials in the Maronite church, especially the Patriarch Antoine Arida and the Archbishop of Beirut, Ignatius Mubarak, and leading cabinet ministers, entrepreneurs, intellectuals and editors. Going as far back as the 1920s, these advocates of Maronite exclusionism repeatedly approached the Jewish Agency for Palestine, the governing body of the Jewish community in Palestine, with proposals for joint entrepreneurial, cultural and political endeavours. Political initiatives generally aimed at achieving a tactical alliance based upon the similar minority positions of Palestinian Jews and Lebanese Christians and their shared fears of a perceived common Muslim enemy.[2] Convinced that President al-Khoury was endangering Christian Lebanon with his wholesale collaboration with Lebanon's Muslims, the politically active Lebanese Maronite Church concluded a secret treaty with the Jewish Agency in 1946.[3] This was a remarkable document, expressing Jewish support for Christian Lebanon and Christian Lebanese support for a Jewish state in Palestine, replete with mutual economic, cultural and security pledges – negotiated by a Church acting in opposition to the legitimate (and Maronite-led) Lebanese government and a non-state Zionist organization operating without the knowledge of the British mandatory authority, a full two years before Israel would achieve independence! Meticulously negotiated, signed and accepted by the respective leaderships, the treaty proved utterly inoperative; once word leaked out, its very existence was adamantly denied by the Lebanese side. Most of Lebanese public opinion, both Christian and Muslim, was firmly on the side of the Arab claim to Palestine. The Church's temptation to draw upon Zionist resources to advance exclusivist Maronite political aspirations in Lebanon was overridden by fear that public disclosure of its 'unholy alliance' would result in its total delegitimization.

The National Pact was intended to be an interim measure to ensure that Lebanese independence got off the ground; once successful self-government was underway, its authors expected Lebanese across the sectarian spectrum to shed their primordial identities in favor of a shared Lebanese identity. Lebanon declared independence in 1943 and for a brief while, the combination of a weak central government and the cooperation of the power brokers of Lebanon's many sects brought prosperity and stability to the country. But few Lebanese relinquished their sectarian sense of self for an identity rooted in the Lebanese state. The concept of an 'Arab face', designed to help merge Christian and Muslim sensibilities into a Lebanese whole, instead proved to be more of a mask, ultimately unable to disguise the persistent distrust and competition among Lebanon's factions.

The alliance of minorities

For much of the pre-state period, however, some individuals in the Jewish Agency for Palestine allowed themselves to be fooled. Acutely aware of their minority status as Jews within a vast Arab-Sunni Muslim sea, some Zionists hoped to find allies within Lebanon's unique constellation of communities. Lebanon did not immediately disappoint; at various times throughout the mandate period, Lebanese Sunnis, Druze, Shi'a and Christian personalities made contact with the Jewish Agency to explore possibilities for mutual satisfying endeavours. Lebanon was, by reputation, a nation of merchants and businessmen and Lebanese of all political and religious stripes approached the Jewish community in Palestine with an interest in tapping into the wealth and international influence Jews allegedly held. One early Sunni interlocutor was none other than Riad al-Sulh, future drafter of the National Pact, who only later came to the conviction that Christian–Muslim cooperation was the way to preserve Lebanon's interests. Relations with the Lebanese Druze were enhanced by introductions from Palestinian Druze, who were enjoying generally positive relations with the Jews in Palestine.[4] It was not necessarily obvious at the time that Lebanon's sectarian divides would work against Zionist interests and not on their behalf.

The most enthusiastic Lebanese suitors were clearly the nationalist Maronites, however. Not unaware of the fractious nature of Lebanese society and even of the divisions within the Maronite community, the Jewish Agency responded warmly to friendly Maronite overtures nonetheless. This willingness to entertain Maronite visitors and visions reflected in part the absolute rejection the Zionist project in Palestine was receiving from virtually all corners of the Arab world. Although Agency representatives were received more or less hospitably in many Arab political, editorial and financial circles, even the most polite of conversations generally ended with Arab admonishments that Zionists would do well to abandon their goals for independent Jewish statehood and settle for the status of a protected minority in Arab Palestine. It is no wonder then that Zionist agents in the field reported with excitement the Zionist sympathies of the Maronite upper crust and their proposals for joint Maronite–Zionist ventures in finance, public relations, politics and diplomacy. A small number of ultranationalist Maronites and Zionists became convinced that the two westward-looking minorities, similarly beset by large numbers of Muslims resisting their claims, shared a 'natural harmony of interests.' Individuals in both communities suggested a 'minority alliance', with other potential partners including the Druze, Shi'a, Copts and Kurds. Sceptical majorities in both camps argued, however, that even together the minorities still constituted a minority in the overwhelmingly Sunni Muslim Middle East, and that regional stability required that the

Zionists and Christians reach accommodations with the Muslim majorities in their respective countries.

Like the Jewish Agency, Israel considered the minority alliance theory intermittently for decades, without ever producing a definitive policy. The strongest argument in its favour was that 'beggars can't be choosers.' Israel's political isolation demanded that it befriend any and all willing allies, who often emerged from among the region's minorities and especially among the Maronites, which made Lebanon a particularly promising neighbour. The tendency of Maronite contacts to profess their friendship privately while adopting a more anti-Zionist position in public was enough to give the decision makers in the Jewish Agency pause, however, as was increasing Zionist familiarity with the frequently shifting alliances among Lebanon's competing factions. The Jewish Agency, thus, received each new Maronite proposal with interest and occasionally acted upon some of them, but never expended the necessary commitment to actually test the relationship or predicated Zionist policy upon it. Nevertheless, significant circles in the Zionist/Israeli foreign policy establishment clung to the notion that authentic Lebanon was Christian Lebanon, which was in turn supportive of Zionist aspirations in Palestine, believing that this sympathetic Lebanese bent was but temporarily inhibited by pan-Arab, pan-Islamic or pro-Palestinian Arab forces. It followed that once these forces either petered out, or were otherwise neutralized, Lebanon would be free to express its natural affinity for a Jewish neighbour. These Zionists mistakenly thought they were allowing for Lebanon's political weakness with the oft-heard adage that Lebanon could never be the first Arab country to make peace with a Jewish state, but that it would surely be the second.

Israel and Lebanon finally met as sovereign states on the battlefield during the first Arab–Israeli War in 1948. Lebanon's army of some 3,000 troops was too small to pose a serious threat to the Israel Defence Forces (IDF), but Israeli strategists worried about the northern border insofar as it might provide a gateway into Israel for the more formidable Syrian armed forces, or for the Arab Liberation Army under the command of Fawzi al-Qawuqji. The first week of the war saw only limited clashes between Lebanese and Israeli troops in the Galilee. Shortly thereafter Lebanon's armed forces captured two Israeli border settlements, but did not advance further, suggesting that it had no designs on Israeli territory. In fact, Israel believed that Lebanon's real objective was to stem the flight of Palestinian Arab refugees into that country, an exodus which Lebanon believed Israel was purposely provoking. In late October 1948 the Israeli army recovered the two Jewish settlements and pursued the Lebanese troops back across the border, capturing 14 Lebanese villages in the process.[5]

In March 1949 Lebanon became the second of the four Arab combatants to sign an armistice agreement with Israel, after Egypt. The negotiations proceeded without rancour, and instead of meeting in a neutral third country, as had Israel and Egypt, delegates took turns crossing the border for hospitable meetings which alternated between Ras al-Nakoura and Rosh Hanikra, on the Lebanese and Israeli sides of the border, respectively. Negotiations bogged down only when Israel attempted to link its withdrawal from the 14 Lebanese villages to a Syrian withdrawal from Israeli territory. Once Israel dropped the Syrian-linkage demand, the Israeli–Lebanese armistice was easily concluded. In its wake the Israel-Lebanon Mixed Armistice Commission (ILMAC) met regularly, operating efficiently to arrange for the return of livestock and teenagers who strayed across the border and sailors who had drifted off course; facilitating the removal of landmines from each other's territory; and coordinating activity to stop cross-border smuggling and thievery. Unlike the other MACs, which met sporadically and broke off in the mid-1950s, the ILMAC operated regularly until the eve of the 1967 war and gave Israel and Lebanon an official conduit through which to communicate.

The post-1948 period found Lebanon still divided on the most basic question of national identity, and the mandate era tradition of Lebanese groups seeking outside help in their conflicts with one another carried over into the post-independence period. Arabists argued for nurturing Lebanon's commonalities with the other Arab countries. The Arab Nationalist Movement included Palestinians among its leadership and focused on coordinating a united effort by the Arab states to recover Palestine. Druze leader Kamal Jumblatt's Progressive Socialist Party advocated for a socialist system, with the goal of achieving internal Lebanese unity. The Syrian Socialist Nationalist Party, a holdover from the 1930s, continued to call for the recreation of 'Greater Syria' including Syria, Lebanon, Palestine, Jordan and Iraq, and looked to Damascus for guidance and support. Egyptian President Gamal Abd al-Nasser's challenge to the West in the 1950s inspired and funded the growth of Sunni Nasserite groups in Lebanon, fueling the fears of Lebanon's Christians. Ultranationalist Maronites continued to agitate for a separate Christian, western, Lebanese orientation, surreptitiously angling for Israeli backing.

With only armistice agreements and no peace treaties on any border, Israel was still open to hearing its furtive friends out. Shortly after Israel achieved independence in 1948, former president Emile Edde and Archbishop Mubarak separately contacted their old friends in the new Israeli foreign ministry, seeking Israeli assistance in schemes for overthrowing the al-Khoury government and returning ultranationalist Maronites to power; shortly thereafter representatives of the Phalange (*al-Kataeb*), a Maronite party with a paramilitary wing which had not been a pre-state Zionist ally, also approached Israel, seeking assistance in the context of the 1951 Lebanese elections. But despite a flurry of meetings and correspondence, Edde and Mubarak received only kindly words and the Phalange came away with only a small, ineffectual amount of money.[6] Having judged the likelihood of any of these actors successfully taking power to be almost nil, Israel was sympathetic to, but unswayed by appeals to a common cultural bond between it and Lebanon's Christians. By the time of Israel's independence, writes Itamar Rabinovich, the Foreign Ministry had come to understand that:

[M]ost Maronites had accepted the post-1943 pluralistic Lebanese system and that Israel, too, ought to accept it as an established fact . . . This, indeed, was done for the next twenty years, during which Israel's relations with Lebanon were a marginal aspect of its Middle Eastern policies.[7]

One can, however, discern vestiges of the minority alliance concept in Israeli Prime Minister David Ben-Gurion's 'policy of the periphery', developed during that first decade of Israeli independence. The premise was that Israel could escape its isolation by allying with other non-Arab or non-Sunni countries and communities on the periphery of the Arab–Israel conflict region, such as Turkey, Iran, Cyprus, Ethiopia and the Sudan. Like the minority alliance plan, this policy assumed that the Sunni Arab majority would not quickly reconcile with Israel, and that Israel should look to other minorities for allies. Had an independent Christian Lebanon ever come into being, it would have been a natural part of the periphery.

There is scholarly and partisan disagreement over the extent to which Ben-Gurion and others actually attempted to make the minority alliance concept operational. At the center of the debate are several diary entries by Ben-Gurion in 1937 and 1948 and a 1954 exchange of letters between a (temporarily) retired Ben-Gurion and Prime Minister Sharett, in which they explicitly argued the pros and cons of a foreign policy based on cooperation with regional minorities such as the Maronites. As early as 1937 David Ben-Gurion had spoken of an alliance between the future Christian and Jewish states. Three times in his 1948 war diaries he recorded his belief that the emergence of a strong Christian mini-state in Lebanon allied with Israel would be a positive outcome of the war for which Israel should strive.[8] He repeated this idea in his correspondence with Sharett in 1954, but Sharett warned that the Maronites had neither the power nor the desire to establish a truncated Christian Lebanon, and that Israeli interference would lead only to disaster.[9] The idea lay dormant until Ben-Gurion joined Sharett's cabinet as Minister of Defence and raised it again. In his diary Sharett noted that Chief-of-Staff Moshe Dayan shared Ben-Gurion's interest in a treaty between Israel and a newly reconstituted (with Israeli help) Christian Lebanon. Twice Sharett recorded a proposal by Dayan that Israel 'buy' a Lebanese officer who would declare himself the Maronites' savior and call upon the Israelis to help him establish a Christian regime, in full alliance with Israel.[10] Sharett sidetracked his more aggressive colleagues with a promise to set up a commission to study the issue, relegating the Maronite–Israel question to a dusty back corner of Israeli foreign policy. Familiarity with the personalities of Ben-Gurion and Sharett and the relationship between the two men suggests that had Ben-Gurion been set on pursuing the Maronite option, he would not have been so easily put off. And although Maronites continued to contact Israel for possible assistance in times of political crisis in Lebanon, Israel charted a careful course of infrequent and limited compliance only.

A major test of Israel's intentions towards the Maronites arose in 1958. At that time Lebanese President Camille Chamoun was coming under harsh criticism from his Muslim constituency and Nasser's legions for his unabashedly pro-Western stance. Adopting many positions hostile to Nasser's pan-Arab programme,[11] Chamoun deepened the Muslim–Christian divide. The two sides, respectively, expressed excitement and fear at Nasser's creation of the United Arab Republic, a union between Egypt and Syria, in February 1958. In July 1958 an Arab nationalist coup brought down the pro-Western Iraqi government, exacerbating an existing conflict in Lebanon between those supporting the West and the status quo and Arab nationalists demanding a more demographically representative government, with policies more aligned with those of the other Arab countries. As expected, some Maronite envoys made contact with Israeli officials, asking for weapons, money and other assistance in holding off the Muslim challenge to Maronite privilege. Israel certainly preferred that the Chamounists prevail; with their advocate, Ben-Gurion, having regained the premiership from Sharett in 1955, it would seem that this was the opportunity to openly commit Israeli resources and troops to the Maronite cause which the prime minister had long desired. But Ben-Gurion opted for 'immense pragmatism'.[12] Israel's contributions to Lebanon's 1958 national crisis were a pledge to guard the Israeli–Lebanese border region against Syrian saboteurs, which allowed General Fuad Chehab to call back Lebanese forces from the border (although he would refuse to commit them to battle on Chamoun's behalf); an intelligence gathering mission in Beirut's harbour conducted by Israeli special forces; and the transfer of a small amount of weapons.[13] The 1958 crisis ended with insignificant Israeli input when Chamoun called in the United States Marines to impose order and then resigned. The more neutral and widely respected Chehab, founder and commander of the Lebanese army, succeeded him in the presidency. Chehab's administration restored the delicate status quo, and Israel's relatively hands-off approach to Lebanon, for a little longer.

Within ten years, however, circumstances developed in Lebanon with dire consequences for Israeli–Lebanese relations. Lebanon's perpetual weakness and its citizens' penchant for calling in outside help made it particularly vulnerable to the machination of third parties.[14] The penetration of Lebanon by two outside actors, the Palestine Liberation Organization and the Syrians, figured heavily in the negative course of Israeli–Lebanese relations in the 1960s and 1970s.

Enter the PLO

The PLO arrived uninvited, as had the Palestinians. The 1948–49 Arab–Israeli war had made Lebanon the reluctant home to some 100,000 Palestinian refugees. Concerned that the largely Sunni refugee community would upset the uneasy sectarian balance on which Lebanon's stability depended, successive Lebanese governments enacted highly restrictive laws designed to prevent the absorption of Palestinians into Lebanese society. For years Lebanon kept the lid on its Palestinian problem by isolating most of the refugees in squalid refugee camps, marginalizing them within the few towns where they lived by denying them the right to own property or work in a myriad of professions, and practising social, economic and civil discrimination against them. Unpopular among the Christians, the Sunni middle class, and the poor Shi'a peasants in the south, many Palestinian refugees were expelled by the government from the immediate border region to areas north, thereby reducing the number of infiltrations across the border into Israel, whose wrath Lebanon was anxious to avoid.[15] For most of the 1950s and early 1960s, vigorous policing by both Israel and Lebanon kept the border between them largely quiet.

But the arrival of Yasir Arafat and his small *Fatah* guerrilla movement in Lebanon set in motion a series of events which resulted in an increasing level of hostility between Lebanon and Israel. In the aftermath of the 1967 Arab–Israeli war, and riding high after the strong PLO showing against Israeli forces in the Battle of Karameh, Jordan, in March 1968, Arafat merged *Fatah* with the newly reinvigorated Palestine Liberation Organization and assumed leadership of both, setting up headquarters in Beirut. An umbrella organization loosely encompassing multiple Palestinian groups of different political ideologies, but united in promoting armed resistance against Israel, the PLO found an eager audience for its message of revolutionary freedom fighting and Palestinian empowerment among the refugees. In a series of clashes between the guerrilla groups and the Lebanese security agencies, the PLO took over the administration of the refugee camps. There they organized the refugees, created an internal infrastructure, and worked with the United Nations Relief and Works Agency (UNRWA) to facilitate the provision of emergency aid and health care for Palestinian refugees, and to increase opportunities for education and employment among the Palestinians stagnating in Lebanon. The PLO fostered various educational, professional and political institutions, despite Lebanese obstructionism. Thanks to PLO attention the long suffering refugees developed 'an enhanced Palestinian national and cultural identity',[16] while the PLO earned the loyalty of the refugee constituency, now numbering some 300,000, among them a large pool of eager recruits looking to join the PLO guerrillas.

But along with its good works and social services, the PLO was also creating a state within a state. The rank and file rapidly took over southern Lebanon, where PLO fighters ran roughshod over Lebanese Shi'a and Christian villagers, set up military training camps, and launched cross border terrorist attacks into northern Israel. Israel responded with its policy of 'disproportionate retaliation', designed to punish the host nation and compel it to rein in anti-Israel activity emanating from its territory. On a local level, Israel hoped that its severe reprisals for each PLO attack would encourage the indigenous population to reject the Palestinian intruders operating among them. But the feeble central government in Beirut proved unable to control

Palestinians operating in the south, the Lebanese army responded inconsistently – sometimes clashing with the *fedayeen* (one who sacrifices himself) and sometimes facilitating their operations – and the unarmed civilians were in no position to challenge the armed guerrillas. Israel, thus, took matters into its own hands. In December of 1968 Israel signalled an escalation in its willingness to make Lebanon a battlefield in the context of its fight with the PLO. Two days after an Israeli civilian plane at the Athens International Airport was attacked by the Lebanon-based Popular Front for the Liberation of Palestine (PFLP), Israeli helicopter gunships raided Beirut's International Airport, destroying 14 commercial aircraft belonging to Lebanon's Middle East Airways along with other Lebanese aircraft. Outraged, Lebanon was incapable of acting against the PLO or responding to even this spectacular a projection of Israeli military might, right in the heart of the Republic. The government resorted to lodging a complaint against Israel with the UN Security Council and initiating the process of calling up reserve forces; in January 1969 the government stepped down the state of alert with no palpable effect on either of the foreign parties duelling so destructively on Lebanese turf.

Of course Lebanese public opinion was of different minds regarding what the country's proper response should be to the PLO activity which was provoking Israel's wrath. Suggestions ran the gamut from calls on the far right for expelling the PLO and Palestinians from the country to demands from the far left for rallying to the Palestinians' side and celebrating the PLO's willingness to attack the Israeli foe. Many Muslims had resented Lebanon's refusal to participate in the 1967 war, ostensibly fought to recover Palestine (to which they hoped Lebanon's Palestinian refugees would return). Arabist in orientation, they supported any group willing to challenge Israel. But many Christians resented the increasingly brash behaviour of the armed commandos in Lebanon and the army's reluctance to vigorously confront them. When rising tensions among the Lebanese factions threatened to bring the Lebanese house of cards crashing down, external Arab parties intervened to mediate a resolution among them and the PLO. Brokered by President Nasser, the November 1969 'Cairo Agreement' between PLO leader Yasir Arafat and the government of Lebanese President Charles Helou was designed to forestall confrontations between the Lebanese army and Palestinian guerrillas by regulating Palestinian activity in Lebanon. Incredibly, however, this 'regulation' worked to the advantage of the PLO commandos, who won validation of their right to pursue armed struggle against Israel and a free hand in conducting military operations from within designated spots along the Israel–Lebanon border. In surrendering control over sovereign Lebanese territory to the PLO, Lebanon guaranteed itself a role as an active front in the Palestinian–Israeli conflict and the target for continued Israeli military operations.

In 1970 the Palestinian hold over southern Lebanon was reinforced with an influx of PLO fighters and their families fleeing Jordan, where another

Palestinian state-within-a-state and a guerrilla challenge to the Jordanian regime had provoked 'Black September', an all-out Jordanian assault on the Palestinian resistance organizations. Overwhelmingly Sunni, the new Palestinian arrivals worried Lebanese Christians who were fearful of being subsumed in a rapidly growing Muslim majority; concerned prosperous Sunnis that the delicate sectarian balance which had rewarded them for years was in jeopardy; angered Shi'a in the south now dominated by the guerrilla groups, and promised an increase in Israeli military attention to Lebanon. Indeed, southern Lebanon's southernmost regions, now dubbed *Fatahland* because of the predominance there of Yasir Arafat's *Fatah* organization, became a primary theatre of operations in the Arab–Israeli conflict. For the next decade southern Lebanon served as a training and staging ground for PLO forces, the launch site for periodic Katyusha rocket attacks into the Israeli Galilee, and the jumping-off point for terrorist strikes against civilian targets in northern Israel. A deadly cycle of strikes and counterstrikes alternated across the Israeli–Lebanese border, with Lebanon powerless to extract itself from the crossfire. Chasing one another around the globe, Israel responded to the massacre of its athletes in the 1972 Munich Olympics by the PLO group 'Black September' with another operation in the heart of Beirut. In April 1973, Israeli commandos (led by future Israeli Prime Minister Ehud Barak, disguised as a woman) infiltrated the Lebanese capital from the sea, travelled to the homes of three PLO leaders and assassinated each of them before successfully escaping.

Entrenched in Lebanon, the PLO lost some of its focus on recovering Palestine and became embroiled in the power plays and conflicts increasingly roiling relations among the Lebanese factions. Leading Maronite families (the Gemayels, Chamouns and Franjiehs) raised their own militias, dedicated to preserving the status quo with its institutionalized Christian supremacy; together they formed the Lebanese Front. The rival National Front was a loose alliance of Sunni Muslim groups, Druze, leftist Christians and Palestinian forces. Key among the disputes between them was the position of the PLO and the presence of so many Palestinians in Lebanon. Firefights increasingly broke out between the Maronite militias and PLO elements and on 13 April 1975, the Maronite Phalange charged the PLO with complicity in a failed assassination attempt against Pierre Gemayel, founder of the Phalange. Within hours of the attempted hit, Phalangists held up a bus in Beirut and murdered the 27 Palestinians they found among the passengers. After months of rising tensions and reciprocal episodes of bloodshed, the events of 13 April ignited the tinderbox that was Lebanon. With its citizens continuing to self-identify with their clans or religious communities and lacking a common 'Lebanese' identity, Lebanon dissolved into a web of warring sects, each with its own militia, all seeking outside backing in their fights with one another. The Lebanese army originally professed neutrality, but finally dissolved as troops defected to return home to fight with their local militias. As if the horrors of war in general were not enough, the battling Lebanese injected a quintessentially Lebanese sectarian element when one faction or another threw up roadblocks, halted innocent motorists, and shot those with the 'wrong' affiliation on their identity cards. Israel closely tracked the PLO's role as a principal actor in the Lebanese civil war, hoping to see the organization weakened or perhaps even destroyed. Instead, however, the fighting drew in another outside force of even greater concern to Israel.

Syria's interests in Lebanon date to what Damascus considered France's artificial division between them in 1920. Syria never recognized the legitimacy of that partition, and acted to retain influence, indirectly or directly, within its smaller neighbor. But unlike the Palestinians, the Syrians entered Lebanon by invitation. Surprisingly, it was a cry for help from the government of President Suleiman Franjieh, who feared that the predominantly-Muslim National Front and its Palestinian allies were poised to triumph over the Christian Lebanese Front defending the status quo. Anxious to halt the war before the Christians were driven from power, Franjieh called on the regime in Damascus to intervene and impose a ceasefire. President Hafez al-Assad had made Syria a champion and generous backer of the Palestinian and Arab nationalist causes, but responded positively to Franjieh's call nonetheless. Syria was more interested in preserving the Lebanese status quo (weak and responsive to Damascus) than in seeing a newly independent and radical Lebanon dominated by the National Front and the PLO emerge on its border. When Syrian troops moved into Lebanon in April 1976, Druze leader Jumblatt and PLO chief Arafat demanded that the Arab states restrain Syria. At hastily called Arab summits in Riyadh and Cairo, nations not ready to sign Lebanon over to complete Syrian domination raised an 'Arab Deterrent Force' (ADF) to intercede in the Lebanese war and restore balance among Christians, Muslims, Druze and Palestinians. The first units of the ADF entered Lebanon several weeks later in April 1976 and successfully quelled the bloodletting for a while. Within several months, however, the few non-Syrian troops were withdrawn, and the ADF became a largely Syrian affair focused on keeping the uneasy calm and facilitating a Lebanese political arrangement responsive to Syrian interests.

The 1976 intervention of the Syrian army rang alarm bells in Israel; as in 1948, the defence establishment perceived Lebanon as a threat insofar as the Syrians might make it another invasion route or encourage cross-border PLO operations. Along with keeping the PLO and Syria away from the border, Israel also preferred that southern Lebanon remain available should the IDF need to use it to outflank the Syrians in a new war.[17] Watchful and wary as Syria initially defanged the Muslim-Palestinian forces (Syria would switch sides in 1978 and help the Muslims and Palestinians against the Christians), Israel's strategic concerns grew along with the number of Syrian forces in Lebanon. The prospects of a Syrian take-over of Lebanon or the establishment of a radical Lebanese government hostile to Israel were equally unpalatable for Israel. Israel had relied on its 'deterrence posture' to warn Syria away from activity in Lebanon near the Israeli border, but as Syrian involvement in

Lebanon deepened, Israel and Syria exchanged communication via the United States and arrived at an unwritten 'red line' agreement. The red line, roughly consistent with the course of the Litani River some 40 km north of the Israeli–Lebanese border, was a boundary below which Syrian troops and proxies would not venture and beyond which Israeli troops and clients would not cross. Designed to prevent Syrian–Israeli clashes in Lebanon, this agreement, indirectly negotiated and scrupulously observed, successfully precluded a conflict between Syrian and Israeli forces at that time.[18] The presence of so many Syrian troops in Lebanon, however, and Syria's fluctuating support for elements hostile to Israel, meant that in terms of Israeli–Lebanese relations, Lebanon and Israel each saw the other as a danger to its own well-being.

Syria and Israel may have restrained themselves from armed combat with one another, but not so the various Lebanese groups, who soon resumed open hostilities. Cautiously satisfied that Syria was confining its interests to Lebanon north of the Litani, Israel sought advantage in its sphere of influence to the south. In 1976 a mutinous Greek Catholic army major backed by the Maronite Chamoun family, Sa'ad Haddad, declared southern Lebanon 'Free Lebanon' and put together a band of local Christians and Shi'a dedicated to keeping the PLO out of the immediate border region. Breaking tradition by openly declaring common cause with Israel, Haddad asked for support and his Free Lebanon Army (later the South Lebanon Army) received weapons, materiel, training and financing from the government of Yitzhak Rabin. Members of more powerful Maronite militias based in northern Lebanon and dominated by the Gemayel and Chamoun families also made contact with Israel. They too received significant arms, training and money, although their Israeli contacts were concerned by their lack of professionalism and coordination and appalled at the brutal internecine conflicts among them.[19] While this policy was a departure from providing the very modest aid Maronite supplicants had occasionally received in decades past, Rabin still tried to move cautiously, aiming to help the Christians help themselves while keeping the IDF out of the fray.

But the frequency with which Haddad's forces called on the IDF for backup support began to draw Israel more deeply into the Lebanese fray than Rabin wanted; the IDF first used artillery shelling on behalf of its partners in southern Lebanon in November 1976.[20] Also in 1976 the Rabin government began a public relations campaign of sorts by opening the 'Good Fence' at the Israeli town of Metula on the Israeli–Lebanese border. There south Lebanese inhabitants of all faiths could come for food, shelter, sanctuary and medical attention; some Lebanese were also allowed to find work along the Israeli side of the border. Touted as a strictly humanitarian response to the suffering of south Lebanese civilians, the 'Good Fence' was also designed to win Lebanese hearts and minds, as well as to enhance Israeli intelligence about events in Lebanon and serve as a conduit across the border. Although, on the face of it, stepped-up Israeli support for Haddad's southern Lebanon forces and the

Maronite militias may look like the consummation of a courtship 50 years in the making between Israel and Lebanon's Christians, national security interests were actually driving Israeli policy.

Conclusion

Mandate memories may have perpetrated a sense of familiarity and even friendship with the Maronites, but Israel was largely unmoved to action by the biblical and cultural arguments for a Jewish–Christian alliance. Successive Israeli governments after 1948 did entertain Maronite advances as they did covert contacts from other, generally more important movements and leaders from elsewhere in the Arab world. The literature on Israel's clandestine Arab partnerships in neighboring countries is extensive and demonstrates that Israel was motivated by its pariah status to forge undercover relationships with movements and governments throughout the Middle East, most of them Sunni and Arab, in an attempt to influence events in a region formally closed to it.[21]

Lebanon's fragmented confessional system repeatedly sent Maronite emissaries on secretive missions to plead for Israeli backing in one or another election or crisis, knowing its political isolation made Israel inclined towards listening to their proposals. But the ineffective outcome of mandate era cooperative experiments restrained Israel from committing serious resources or predicating foreign policy on a Maronite–Israeli partnership; even the 1958 opportunity garnered but modest Israeli support. Appreciative of pro-Zionist proclivities among some Lebanese Christians, Israel nonetheless refrained from seriously interfering in Lebanon's domestic disputes until it perceived the emergence of a new national security threat emanating from there in the late 1960s. From 1948 to 1968, a quiet Israeli–Lebanese border made for relatively benign relations between the two countries.

It was the presence and anti-Israeli activity of the PLO in Lebanon which provoked a more sustained Israeli interest in its northern neighbor, escalating throughout the 1960s and early 1970s into serious Israeli aggression against Lebanon. The outbreak of the civil war in 1975 and Syria's deepening involvement in Lebanon raised the ante for Israeli concerns about its northern border. Increasing Israeli receptivity to Christian appeals for aid after 1975 reflected not affection or cultural bonding with the Christians as Christians but rather a tactical appreciation for their shared opposition to PLO and Syrian dominance in Lebanon.

There has been no census in Lebanon since 1932; hard evidence of the steep decline in the Christian population is too politically sensitive. But in the years since then, the Muslim portion of the population had clearly outstripped the Christian, while the Shi'a had overtaken the Sunni. As their numbers declined, the Christians' residual political power became increasingly disproportionate; to the Muslims it became increasingly galling. Christian fears that the presence in Lebanon of hundreds of thousands of Palestinian refugees, overwhelmingly Sunni, would rip the delicate fabric of Christian—Muslim coexistence in Lebanon proved prescient, although it took the arrival of the PLO and its fighters to unravel the fragile Lebanese skein, resulting in the outbreak of the civil war. Lebanon's weakness and the central government's inability to control its population and territory made Lebanon particularly vulnerable to third-party interference: by the PLO, by Syria and by Israel. Between 1968 and 1978 the presence and activity of the PLO and Syria in Lebanon provoked a new and more menacing Israeli policy towards that country.

The civil war brought all three historical elements together – warring Lebanese looking to outsiders for help; Israel, the pariah, tempted by opportunities to partner with Lebanon's Christians but reluctant to submit wholly to their entreaties; and weak Lebanon's domination by third parties hostile to Israel and demanding Israeli attention. The result was the deterioration of Israeli–Lebanese relations from the benign to the malign between 1948 and 1978. In March 1978, amplification of these elements, combined with an aggressive new Israeli leadership, would take Israeli–Lebanese relations in even more negative directions.

3 From the Litani to Beirut – Israel's invasions of Lebanon, 1978–85

Causes and consequences

Asher Kaufman

Introduction

How can one understand the Israeli invasion of Lebanon on 6 June 1982? Was it the final expression of a longstanding Jewish-Israeli policy vis-à-vis the neighbour to the north which began in the early twentieth century when some Zionists were contemplating a minority alliance with Lebanese Christians? Was it an inevitable move, given legitimate Israeli security concerns due to the threats posed by the Palestinian armed struggle coming from Lebanon since the late 1960s? Or was it a deviation, a drastic shift from previously held policies and views that not only fundamentally altered the dynamics between Israel and Lebanon, but also reconfigured the internal dynamics inside these two states?

Given the magnitude of the 1982 invasion of Lebanon and its far-reaching consequences, scholars have long attempted to explain it but have, all in all, drastically differed in their analysis. One author argued that the invasion can only be understood through the prism of Israeli attempts to constantly meddle with the internal affairs of its Arab neighbours as part of its intrusive and interventionist regional policies. Hence, the invasion on June 1982 was simply a manifestation, albeit an extreme one, of this approach.[1] Another author argued that given Israel's 'security dilemmas' it had no choice but to invade Lebanon in 1982.[2] The invasion was, thus, a result of a snowball effect which started in the late 1960s and reached its natural conclusion with the decision to invade Lebanon, first in 1978 and when this limited operation failed to achieve its goals came the next and inevitable step in 1982.

Other scholars, however, have argued the exact opposite. One contended that the 1982 invasion 'resulted primarily not from a gradual exhaustion of less drastic means for addressing the problem [of security] but rather from a fundamental redefinition of the problem presented to Israel by the Lebanese scene'.[3] Thus, Israel invaded Lebanon not because it exhausted all other options from the late 1960s to the early 1980s but rather because of a new strategic design that Israeli Minister of Defence, Ariel Sharon, tried to implement through the invasion. Yet another scholar argued that the only way one can understand the 1982 invasion of Lebanon is by seeing it as an aberration, a drastic departure from formerly held Israeli policies and actions towards Lebanon. By no means, he maintained, could it be considered a manifestation of the so-called 'minority alliance', a concept that never took an operative turn towards Lebanon until after 1976.[4]

This chapter takes the latter two interpretations as its underlying premise, arguing that the 1982 invasion of Lebanon can only be regarded as a watershed event in the history of the Arab–Israeli conflict in general and Israel and Lebanon in particular. Its roots can at best be traced to 1976 and even then no inevitable process had characterized the events that led to the 1982 invasion.

The chapter is divided into four sections. The first section discusses Israeli–Lebanese dynamics from roughly the beginning of the Palestinian armed struggle originating from Lebanon in the late 1960s until the 'Litani' Operation in 1978. The second section examines the road to the 1982 war by looking at three particular events that contributed to Israel's decision to invade Lebanon. Section three provides an overview of the invasion and its short-term results. The fourth section discusses the rise of Hizbollah, the 1985 withdrawal and the establishment of the Israeli self-proclaimed security belt. The article concludes with a discussion on some of the short- and long-term consequences of the first Lebanon war.

The road to the 'Litani' Operation

After the expulsion of the Palestinian organizations from Jordan in the years 1970 and 1971, Lebanon became the prime territorial base for their armed struggle against Israel. Using the weakness of the Lebanese state and enjoying support from left-leaning Arab nationalist circles in Lebanon, the Palestinians slowly created and controlled a state within a state in Lebanon. Large parts of south Lebanon as well as the Palestinian refugee camps throughout the country became, effectively, exterritorial enclaves under the control of the PLO. This process was further exacerbated following the eruption of the civil war in April 1975 where the PLO participated as arguably the most heavily armed militia, at least during the first few years of fighting.[5] Thus, from 1975 until the Israeli invasion of Lebanon in 1982, Palestinian guerrillas were engaged in two interconnected military fronts, one inside the Lebanese civil war and the other vis-à-vis Israel.

Israel had been engaged in low intensity warfare against Palestinian guerrillas in Lebanon since 1968. Only three years earlier, the Palestinians officially launched their armed struggle against Israel, and by 1968 their guerrilla organizations were already a dominant force in Jordan and Lebanon. In Lebanon, Israeli cross-border raids, which attempted to wipe out the Palestinian armed presence there, used two methods to achieve this objective. First, the Israeli military confronted Palestinian fighters in their launching bases, primarily in south Lebanon – *Fatahland*, as this region came to be called – in order to gain a decisive military victory over them. Second, Israel attempted to exert pressure on the Lebanese government so that it would expel the Palestinian organizations from the country, as had occurred in Jordan. To generate this pressure, the Israel Defence Forces (IDF) targeted Lebanese national facilities, such as the airport in Beirut, and caused mass migration of mainly Shi'a inhabitants from the south to Beirut, with the conviction that this human crisis would eventually pressure the Lebanese government and would lead, in turn, to the termination of the Palestinian armed presence in the country.

The eruption of the civil war in April 1975 only exacerbated this dynamic between Israel, Palestinian guerrillas, the Lebanese state and the population in south Lebanon. Concern that the Palestinians and their Lebanese allies would win over Lebanon, dominated discussions among policymakers within Israel who feared that such an eventuality could turn Lebanon into an active confrontation state against their country. The fact that 1974 and 1975 were marked by a sharp increase in Palestinian terror attacks against Israeli targets only heightened these fears.[6]

Additionally, as of early 1976 Syria became deeply involved in the Lebanese civil war. In May of that year, the Syrian military entered the country, attempting to put an end to the fighting, restore stability and impose a *pax Syriana* over Lebanon. Hafez al-Assad had then been in control of Syria for six years, bringing stability to the country and positioning Damascus as an important and leading axis in inter-Arab politics. Lebanon, therefore, became a test case for Syria's regional ambitions. This raised concern in Israel that the Syrian front in the north would be extended to include not only the Golan Heights but also Lebanon. After all, the 1973 war was still a very fresh and painful memory in Israel and the concern over Syria's schemes was genuine. Eventually, after indirect negotiations between Syria and Israel, through the mediating services of the United States, a system of red lines was established where Syria agreed not to use its air force and navy in Lebanon, and not to extend its military activities south of the Beirut–Damascus road to the region that Israel regarded as vital to its security interests. Interestingly, this was roughly the area that Israel occupied in its June 1982 invasion of Lebanon. The 'red lines' agreement lasted until April 1981 but, to be sure, the Syrian presence in Lebanon until 1982 and beyond continued to preoccupy the minds of Israeli decision makers who, on the one hand, regarded it as a potential threat to Israeli national security and, on the other hand, reconciled with it so long as Syria reined in the Palestinian organizations in the country.

First contacts between Israeli officials and Lebanese Christians occurred within a few months after the eruption of the civil war in two different regions and contexts. In south Lebanon, local Maronites from near the Israeli–Lebanese boundary approached Israeli officials and asked for military and humanitarian assistance, following the disintegration of Lebanese state authority in the south of the country.[7] At the same time, Maronite leaders, most notably from the Sham'un and Gemayel families, made first contacts with Israeli officials and reluctantly asked for military assistance in their war effort. Behind this half-hearted appeal was the realization that the balance of power in the civil war was tilting against the pro status-quo, anti-Palestinian, camp. Syria, which entered Lebanon in order to assist Christian militias against the Palestinian guerrillas that had threatened the status quo in Lebanon, changed its orientation by the summer of 1977 and began siding with the latter camp. In order to tip the balance of power over the pro-status quo camp, some Lebanese Christians approached Israel seeking assistance and hoping to exploit to their advantage its war against the Palestinians in Lebanon.

The first two years of Israeli aid to its Christian allies in Lebanon were marked by cautious involvement limited primarily to arms supplies. Prime Minister Yitzhak Rabin was concerned that over-involvement could entangle Israel in Lebanon and he, therefore, made efforts to limit this assistance, defining it as 'helping the Christians to help themselves.' Nevertheless, despite this cautious approach, it is important to note that this was the first time that Jewish and Christian-Lebanese cooperation took an operative turn. Since the emergence of the Zionist movement in Palestine, Jewish leaders regarded Lebanon and its Christian population as a possible ally in a region that is predominantly Arab Muslim. Some thought that Jews and Christians could and should cooperate in a 'minority alliance' against the dominant Arab Muslim population that rejected both the existence of a Jewish state in Palestine as well as a Christian, western oriented state in Lebanon.

These ideas, however, did not bear fruit until the late 1970s. On the Christian-Lebanese side it was always apparent that cooperation with the Jewish state was counterproductive to their political survival in the region. Furthermore, from the early 1940s Christian political elites sought integration in the Arab world rather than isolation from it. On the Jewish-Israeli side, mainstream politicians never made genuine efforts to translate the 'minority alliance' into an operative political strategy towards Lebanon. After all, until the late 1960s Lebanon remained largely out of the violent orbit of the Arab–Israeli conflict and did not pose much of a challenge to Israel. It follows that, as far as Israel was concerned, there was no need to stir up matters in Lebanon.

By the time the Likud party won national elections in May 1977, Israel was already assisting Christians in Lebanon in a variety of ways. In south Lebanon it was providing military, organizational and financial support for two predominantly Christian enclaves that would later become the nucleus of Israel's security belt. The 'Good Fence' in Metula provided access for south Lebanon's residents who sought medical assistance and jobs in Israel. In the Christian port town of Junieh, north of Beirut, ships landed, loaded with military equipment in support of the Christian militias that participated in the civil war in the central and northern sections of Lebanon. It was the rise of Likud to power, however, that brought an expansion of Israeli involvement in Lebanon. The new prime minister of Israel, Menahem Begin, brought with him to office not only a more conservative and belligerent approach towards the Arab–Israeli conflict, but also a new tendency to place this conflict in a Jewish historical narrative of persecution and Jewish counter-triumph. Consequently, he also viewed Christians in Lebanon in light of this historical perspective and equated their political plight with persecution by their Muslim neighbours. Accordingly, he believed that Israel held a moral obligation to assist them in their war in Lebanon.[8]

Additionally, the beginning of the Israeli–Egyptian peace talks in November 1977 and the categorical exclusion of the Palestinian leadership from these negotiations pushed the PLO to respond to this challenge by increasing its military confrontation against Israel. On 11 March 1978, Palestinian combatants coming from the Lebanese coast town of Dammur landed on the Tel-Aviv–Haifa coastal road, hijacked a public bus and began a trip of terror that culminated in the death of 37 civilians and left a further 78 wounded. This terrorist operation posed the first major challenge for the new government with regard to Lebanon and the Palestinian armed organizations in this country. The government responded by launching a military campaign that aimed at destroying the Palestinian military infrastructure in south Lebanon (despite the fact that this was not where the Palestinian combatants came from) in a geographical belt that covered approximately 40 km in length and 10 km in width, bordered in the south by the international boundary and in the north by the Litani River. For the first time since 1948 the full force of the IDF was used and Lebanese territory was occupied in a direct breach of that country's sovereignty. Nevertheless, it needs to be emphasized that the 'Litani' Operation still remained within the realm of normative Israeli reactions to the Palestinian armed presence in Lebanon. Geographically, the operation focused on the region that has always concerned Israel and did not exceed it. Furthermore, the objectives of the operation were tactical and limited in their political scope and did not include the ambitious aspirations for regional change that would characterize the 1982 invasion.

The 'Litani' Operation did not succeed in achieving its prime objective. During the operation PLO combatants withdrew north of the Litani River and largely avoided confrontations with the Israeli military. It became clear to Israeli decision makers that if they wished to wipe out Palestinian armed organizations by military force, a limited operation would not succeed in achieving this end. Furthermore, in response to a Lebanese protest to the United Nations (UN) against the Israeli invasion, the Security Council passed Resolution 425, thus, internationalizing the conflict. The resolution called upon Israel to withdraw from south Lebanon and established the United Nations Interim Force in Lebanon (UNIFIL) with the mandate to 'confirm the withdrawal of Israeli forces from southern Lebanon, restore international peace and security and assist the Government of Lebanon in ensuring the return of its effective authority in the area withdrawn by Israel'. From that moment on, UN deployed units became a permanent feature in the landscape of south Lebanon, often criticized by both Israel and Lebanon for 'not doing enough' to meet their mandate. Nevertheless, the two states have consistently endorsed the extension of UNIFIL's mandate, demonstrating that both regarded the UN presence in south Lebanon as important for their interests.

The withdrawal to the international border of Lebanon could not have been confirmed because no formal demarcation procedure was carried out by the UN and the Lebanese state could not have regained its sovereignty over the region because, as part of the civil war dynamics, it lost its authority over much of its national territory, south Lebanon included. In 2000, with the Israeli withdrawal from south Lebanon, the UN would try to complete Resolution 425 and address these two issues – the demarcation of the boundary and the extension of Lebanese sovereignty over the area from which Israel had withdrawn – with only partial success.

In any case, Israel withdrew its forces from the occupied strip of south Lebanon and handed over most of its positions to the predominantly Christian militia, which was headed by Major Sa'ad Haddad, and supported by Israel since late 1976. This exposed the extent of Israeli involvement in this region. In fact, by that time Haddad's militia had become a full-fledged client of Israel, supported by military equipment and training and fully financed by Jerusalem. From 1978 on, members of Haddad's militia were not only on Israel's payroll but they and their family members gained access to job opportunities and other welfare and economic facilities inside Israel. This created a strong link of economic dependence of this community particularly during the years of the Lebanese civil war, where Israel became their economic source of support. Additionally, Israeli officers and military and civilian advisors of the south Lebanese militia became a permanent feature in south Lebanon, making the international boundary between the two states hollow.

The slippery slope to the 1982 invasion

In retrospect, it is possible to single out three events that took place between April and July 1981 that set the final stage for the Israeli invasion of Lebanon in June 1982. The two years that passed from the 'Litani' Operation until April 1981 were marked by increasing tension and frequent border skirmishes between Israel and Palestinian guerrilla organizations. During these two years, Bashir Gemayel consolidated his power as the undisputed leader of most Maronite factions by assuming control of the Lebanese Forces and positioning himself as one of the most important warlords of the civil war. His ties with Israel were further strengthened and he became the most important Christian-Lebanese leader with whom Israel had contacts and to whom it provided military aid. Seeking to drag Israel into a full-fledged military involvement in Lebanon and assist in getting rid of the Syrian and PLO presence in the country, Gemayel managed in April 1981 to entice the Israeli government to support him in a Lebanese Forces–Syrian military confrontation in the town of Zahle. This crisis, known as the 'missile crisis' where Israel gunned down two Syrian helicopters and in response Syria advanced anti-aircraft missiles into the Lebanese Beqaa, terminated the Syrian–Israeli 'red lines' understanding and put the two states on the brink of a military clash that was only mitigated following American mediation efforts.[9]

Second, from May through July 1981 the Israeli–Lebanese boundary was enflamed again in the most severe Israeli–Palestinian confrontation since the 'Litani' Operation. Twelve days in July were particularly violent, where Israel heavily bombed PLO headquarters in Beirut and in response Palestinian units managed to fire rockets at the entire northern region of Israel, paralyzing civilian life while the IDF was unable to bring a complete halt to the attacks. Also here, the fighting ceased as a result of American mediation efforts that were concluded in a first ever negotiated ceasefire agreement between the PLO and Israel. The Israeli government was displeased by the agreements with Syria and the PLO. There was hardly any question that as far as Israeli decision makers were concerned, it was only a matter of time before the next round of confrontations would take place.

The third significant event that took place in the summer of 1981 was the June national elections in Israel in which Menachem Begin's Likud party won again. This time, however, the human makeup of the new government was substantially different from Begin's first cabinet, which had been manned by more cautious and pragmatic figures. The two most important persons who were responsible for taking Begin's government further to the right were Yitzhak Shamir as Minister of Foreign Affairs and Ariel Sharon as Minister of Defence. Together with the IDF chief of staff, Rafael Eitan, who even earlier had been eager to transform Israeli policy towards the PLO in Lebanon to a more aggressive stance, the country was now led by a group of politicians and military men who were much more prone than previously to an invasion of Lebanon. It needs to be emphasized, however, that these civil and military leaders did not operate in a political and ideological vacuum. Since 1976, within the Israeli security apparatus, particularly among *Mossad* (Israeli Secret Services) agents who had been involved in strengthening the Maronite–Israel cooperation, there had been a growing tendency to support increasing involvement in Lebanon. After all, in Israel of 1981 the notion of accommodating the Palestinian national aspirations and establishing a Palestinian state in the West Bank and Gaza was almost sacrilegious. The other alternative, supported by most Jewish politicians and accepted by the majority of the Jewish public was to strike the Palestinian national movement whose centre of operations was at that time still in Lebanon.

In any case, Sharon's new position as Minister of Defence was arguably the most important determinant in setting off the snowball that would lead to the June 1982 invasion of Lebanon. Sharon brought to his position a new strategic design for Israel in the Middle East, viewing it as a regional superpower that needed to assert and demonstrate its strength. Consequently, he believed that the Palestinian guerrilla organizations in Lebanon could be defeated militarily and that this should lead to a general disintegration of the Palestinian national movement, what the Israeli sociologist Baruch Kimmerling called Palestinian politicide.[10] Sharon also believed that in correspondence with

Israeli regional aspirations it needed to bring an end to the Syrian presence in Lebanon and to guarantee the establishment of a pro-Israeli government in this country.

Plans to execute this ambitious strategy began to materialize in the IDF under the code name *Oranim* (Pines) Plan.[11] Two *Oranim* plans were prepared, one small and one large. Small *Oranim* stipulated essentially a repetition of similar goals as in the 'Litani' Operation, i.e., an occupation of a narrow strip of land in south Lebanon, possibly wider than occupied in 1978, but with the limited goal of targeting Palestinian combatants in this occupied region. Large *Oranim* stipulated the occupation of large parts of Lebanon all the way to the Beirut–Damascus road, with the purpose of achieving the following three objectives: wiping out the Palestinian military presence in Lebanon, driving the Syrian military out of Lebanon and facilitating the establishment of a pro-Israeli government in the country.

Begin and Sharon brought the large *Oranim* plan for governmental approval as early as December 1981 but were surprised to find that the majority of their colleagues did not approve of the plan, fearing that the IDF would not be able to carry out this plan on the operational level. Some of the critique focused precisely on Sharon's ambitious regional plans, particularly with regards to Syria and to the occupation of Beirut and the installation of a pro-Israeli government there. Interestingly, we know from soldiers' testimonies that as of late 1981, the IDF began conducting operational manoeuvres, including in Lebanon itself, in preparation for a mass invasion of Lebanon, based on the large *Oranim* plan.[12] Sharon gave orders to prepare the military for such an undertaking while at the same time trying to obtain governmental approval for the invasion. Sharon attempted on several other occasions to obtain cabinet approval for large *Oranim* but ultimately failed on similar grounds. No doubt both Begin and Sharon were waiting for the right opportunity to execute this ambitious and grandiose plan. It was only a question of time.

The 1982 invasion

An assassination attempt on the Israeli ambassador to Britain, Shlomo Argov, on 4 June 1982, turned into the excuse that Sharon and Begin had long been waiting for. In response, Israeli warplanes attacked Palestinian positions in Lebanon and in less than 24 hours the Israeli–Lebanese border was in flames, for the first time since the July 1981 ceasefire agreement between the PLO and Israel. Although the Abu Nidal Palestinian splinter group was behind the assassination attempt and the PLO was quick to disclaim any responsibility, Israel targeted PLO positions in order to provoke the organization to respond, which in turn would provide it with a pretext to launch a military assault against the Palestinian organization in Lebanon.

On the evening of 5 June, the government of Israel held a special session and voted for a military operation in Lebanon with the declared aim 'to place all the civilian population of the Galilee beyond the range of the terrorists' fire from Lebanon, where they, their bases and their headquarters are concentrated'. In the same statement the operation was given the Orwellian name 'Peace for Galilee'.[13] It was stated that the Israeli forces were not to attack the Syrian military unless it initiated an attack against the IDF. The government statement concluded with the declaration that 'the state of Israel continues to aspire to sign a peace accord with independent Lebanon, while maintaining its territorial integrity'.[14] Based on subsequent military and governmental communiqués it was also assured that the IDF would not occupy any Lebanese land beyond a roughly 40 km cut-off line from the international Israeli–Lebanese boundary. Thus, the cabinet members voted for a limited incursion reminiscent of the 'Litani' Operation of 1978 and with narrow strategic goals.

However, within a few days from the beginning of the invasion it became crystal clear that there were other objectives behind the decision to invade Lebanon. By 8 June the IDF was actively engaged in an offensive against Syrian forces deployed in Lebanon and by 13 June Israeli forces arrived in the outskirts of Beirut, connected with units of the Christian Phalange and began an almost two-month siege of Beirut. Thus, Sharon's three covert goals were exposed: wiping out the Palestinian military presence in Lebanon and destabilizing the Palestinian national movement, forcing the evacuation of Syrian forces from Lebanon and installing a pro-Israeli government in the country.

The chronicles of Sharon's deception and manipulation have been told and re-told numerous times, and will not be repeated in detail here.[15] In essence, Sharon manipulated the Knesset, the government and probably also Prime Minister Begin himself and gained approvals for military moves in Lebanon that exceeded the declared goals of the invasion. Thus, what began as a limited military operation that won the overwhelming support of most Jewish politicians and Jewish public opinion intentionally and incrementally evolved to become the big *Oranim* plan. Once Sharon was forced to stop the advance of the IDF because of government criticism, growing public disapproval and international pressure, he used 'crawling' tactics, which eventually brought Israeli forces to the Beirut–Damascus highway. Soldiers' testimonies from that time period recount a complete disconnect between their combat experience in Lebanon and news that they heard from Israel about supposed ceasefires and lulls in fighting.[16]

The invasion of Lebanon was the largest military campaign conducted by Israel since the 1973 war. An estimated 80,000–100,000 soldiers were directly engaged in the invasion. An all-out assault from ground, air and sea preceded the advance of IDF soldiers.[17] This style of warfare was part of an overt tactic aimed at minimizing Israeli casualties, even at the expense of massive Lebanese and Palestinian civilian casualties. Indeed, on the way to Beirut, the IDF either occupied or besieged major urban centres, engaging in massive shelling of Palestinian guerrillas whose positions were often located in densely populated refugee camps and in and around Lebanese towns and villages.

During the two-month siege of West Beirut similar tactics were employed. Large sections of the city with its 300,000 civilians were indiscriminately bombed and electricity, water and food supply were frequently cut off in order to force the PLO leadership to succumb to local pressure and agree to evacuate the city. The figures of Lebanese and Palestinian casualties testify to the extent of devastation caused by the invasion. By the end of August Lebanese police statistics showed a total of 17,825 dead and 30,203 wounded.[18] By November the police reported on a total of 19,085 fatalities, 84 per cent of them civilians.[19] Reports of property damage also reflect the extent of destruction as a result of the Israeli assault. For example, a June 1982 UN account reported that Israeli forces destroyed 35 per cent of the houses in the Bourj el-Shemali refugee camp, 50 per cent in El-Buss, 70 per cent in Rashidiyeh, and 100 per cent in Ein Hilwe; also in the Shatila camp, over 90 per cent of the homes were destroyed or badly damaged, while all structures in the Bourj el Barajneh camp were entirely destroyed. Add to these figures the estimated 800,000 civilians who were internally displaced as a result of the Israeli incursion and one gets a grim picture of the June–August 1982 invasion of Lebanon and its effect on the civilian population in the country.

Although Bashir Gemayel, Israel's most important ally and the linchpin for the success of the entire scheme, got exactly what he wanted from the Israeli invasion, he did not measure up to Sharon's expectations. Aware of local sensitivities in Lebanon with regards to cooperation with Israel, and understanding the limits of his own military capabilities, he refused to engage his forces with PLO combatants in Beirut. Furthermore, he brushed aside Israeli demands to sign a peace deal with Lebanon, understanding that this could be death for any attempt by him to form coalitions with other political forces at the end of the war. Despite these obstacles, by August it seemed that most of Sharon's objectives had been achieved. On 27 August Gemayel was elected president of Lebanon, literally under the protection of Israeli tanks; and on 1 September, after a two-month bloody siege of West Beirut and following international mediation, the PLO concluded its evacuation from Beirut. By then Syrian forces were also out of the Lebanese capital, deployed in the Beqaa region, away from Israeli-controlled areas. Yet, on 15 September, the Phalange headquarters in Beirut were blown up by a Lebanese emissary of Syria, killing Gemayel and scores of his supporters. The next day Christian Phalange forces entered the Palestinian refugee camps of Sabra and Shatila and for three consecutive days massacred hundreds of undefended Palestinian civilians.[20] From here it was only downhill for Israel in its Lebanese adventure.

Sharon's scheme began to tumble like an edifice of cards following the assassination of Gemayel and the subsequent massacre at Sabra and Shatila. Disapproval of the war in Israel, which had already dominated public discourse as early as the beginning of July, and that even crept into the army ranks, now reached unparalleled heights. If at first, criticism focused on 'morality *of* war', or on the actual decision to go to war, viewing it as Israel's first war of choice, then following the massacre at Sabra and Shatila criticism shifted to issues related to 'morality *in* war', or the actual conduct of the IDF in the war.[21] The mass and unparalleled public pressure forced the government to order the establishment of an independent commission of inquiry to investigate the massacre.

The Commission of Inquiry into the Events at the Refugee Camps in Beirut (the Kahan Commission) submitted its report in February 1983 and concluded that direct responsibility for the massacre rested with the Christian Phalanges, while indirect responsibility lay with a few Israeli leading politicians and military officers, for being negligent in performing their duties. Ariel Sharon was found to bear personal responsibility 'for having disregarded the prospect of acts of revenge and bloodshed by the Phalangists against the population of the refugee camps and for having failed to take this danger into consideration'.

Consequently he was forced to resign from his office as Minister of Defence. The commission also strongly reproved Rafael Eitan and other senior military officers. As for the Prime Minister, the Commission concluded that Menachem Begin was not directly involved in the affair but still held some overall responsibility. It nevertheless did not recommend his resignation. Seven months later, Begin resigned from office and from the public eye in general explaining his decision with the famous statement 'I cannot take it any longer'.[22]

Although the Kahan Commission did not investigate the war as a whole and its reprimanding recommendations were limited to the Sabra and Shatila massacre, there was no question that the entire war was on trial. In fact, following its recommendations the architects of the invasion were all put out of office and the new leadership could have taken the opportunity to get Israel out of Lebanon earlier rather than later. This, however, did not take place, since the Israeli government, still prisoner of Sharon's pretentious scheme, continued to insist that a withdrawal from Lebanon be conditioned with a signing of an Israeli–Lebanese peace treaty. In May 1983, a treaty was eventually signed with Amin Gemayel, the new president of Lebanon, brother of the slain Bashir, but it was not worth the paper on which it was written. Israel, by then, was looking for a fast way to get out of Lebanon and began to redeploy its forces in a gradual receding line of withdrawal. Syria, on its part, reestablished its power in the territories that were vacated by Israel and continued to meddle in the areas that were still under Israeli control, further undermining Israeli authority in the country.

In the Syrian–Israeli deterrence dynamics, Israel had very little leverage to use. With no domestic support for the extension of the war and with growing frustration over what was called in Israel 'sinking in the Lebanese swamp', the Israeli government could not really threaten Syria with another military confrontation. Hence, while Israel was steadily losing ground in Lebanon, Syria was consistently gaining the ground lost by Israel.[23] In March 1984, a year after the signing of the Israeli–Lebanese peace treaty, Amin Gemayel announced its abrogation, thus, recognizing the supremacy of Syria in Lebanon and Israel's moribund strength.

Hizbollah, the 'final' withdrawal and the establishment of the security zone

The fact that the Shi'as of Lebanon have so far been hardly mentioned in this chapter is deliberate. This absence from the narrative reflects their absence from the radar screens of Israeli policymakers from 1975 to 1983. Although Shi'as were the population that suffered by far the most from Israeli raids and incursions into Lebanon from the late 1960s, by the early 1980s they were already a growing political and military force that could not and should not have been ignored. Israeli officials who orchestrated the contacts with Maronite leaders in Lebanon simply overlooked them. With the benefit of hindsight, of course, this was one of the gravest mistakes of Israel during its invasion of Lebanon and its lengthy aftermath.

The rise of Hizbollah in Lebanon is dealt with elsewhere in this volume, but it is sufficient to note here that if revolutionary Iran was the ideological mother of Hizbollah and Syria was the instrumental father, then the Israeli invasion of Lebanon could be considered to be the midwife that brought the Shi'a organization to life. Indeed, the invasion mobilized Shi'a sympathizers of the Islamic revolution in Iran who had already established their cells and networks in Lebanon prior to June 1982, particularly in the Beqaa region. With Iranian ideological, financial and military assistance and guidance Hizbollah emerged into a full fledged organization that took advantage of the weakness of Palestinians in Beirut and of the Israeli gradual withdrawal from Lebanon.

It slowly but surely established its presence in the Lebanese capital and in south Lebanon, a region that had been traditionally the stronghold of Amal, the other Shi'a movement led since 1980 by Nabih Berri.[24] By early 1983, Israel was already engaged in guerrilla warfare against the Shi'a organization with very little information and knowledge about its new fervent adversary that emerged in Lebanon. From that moment on, the overwhelming majority of Israeli casualties in Lebanon were a result of Hizbollah's determined guerrilla warfare – fuelled by religious fervour and sustained by politically empowered Lebanese Shi'as – in an attempt to drive Israel out of Lebanon. Thus, what began as an invasion to get rid of the Palestinian armed presence in Lebanon took an unexpected turn by becoming a guerrilla war that had little to do with the initial reasons for the invasion and which radically transformed Israeli–Lebanese dynamics.

It took Israel exactly three years from the day of the invasion to finally 'withdraw' from Lebanon. The July 1984 national elections in Israel resulted in a tie between the Likud bloc and the Ma'arakh (Labour-led alignment of parties in Israel). By then, the Israeli death toll from the war exceeded 600.

Financially, the occupation of large parts of Lebanon constituted a major burden on the then dysfunctional Israeli economy. There seemed to be a consensus that the war had reached its natural conclusion and that it was time to withdraw from Lebanon. Indeed, the national unity government that was formed following the elections voted in January 1985 to pull the IDF out of Lebanon in three stages.

The third stage, where according to the government decision 'the IDF will deploy along the Israeli–Lebanese international border while maintaining a zone in southern Lebanon where local forces (SLA) [South Lebanon Army] will operate with IDF backing',[25] was completed on 10 June, 1985, when the government officially declared the end of Israeli presence in Lebanon. Thus, in fact, the government voted for two contradictory acts – complete withdrawal on the one hand, and maintenance of the security zone guarded by the South Lebanese Army and supported by Israel, on the other. Israel was the only player who believed the withdrawal to be complete; Hizbollah and the rest of Lebanon did not.

Conclusion

The 1982 invasion of Lebanon and its lengthy aftermath was not a result of an implementation of an ill-conceived and simplistic 'minority alliance' policy, nor was it a natural outcome of Israeli confrontation against Palestinian terror coming out of Lebanon since the late 1960s, a sort of a last resort after all other options had been exhausted. Rather, it was an aberration from previously held policies vis-à-vis Lebanon that emanated from a particular ideological worldview of a few politicians and military officials who sought to use Israel's unmatched military superiority in the Middle East in order to realize their hegemonic aspirations in the region. If until 1980 Israeli incursions into Lebanon were mostly limited to the south of the country and focused primarily on combating Palestinians, then the invasion of 1982 used the Palestinians as a pretext for attaining much more ambitious goals.

The Lebanon war, as it became popularly known in Israel, was the first non-consensual war that gave birth to the largest anti-war movement in the history of the country. N. S. Eisenstadt, the renowned Israeli sociologist, wrote that the war transformed Israeli society, weakened its civility, increased its divisiveness, created a breakdown of many normative restraints in public behaviour and weakened the feeling of shame which led to violence and growing intolerance.[26] Only by looking at Israel 'before and after' the 1982 invasion can one comprehend the extent of this war's aberration.

The invasion also transformed Lebanese society and the course of the civil war. With the Palestinians largely out of the 'game' and Hizbollah entering the war and fighting on two fronts – against Israel and against its Lebanese rivals – the civil war now reached unparalleled heights of violence and mayhem. Gone were the pro and anti-status quo camps that characterized, at least in part, the Lebanese civil war. The invasion may have eliminated the

Palestinian threat for Israel, but it introduced a new challenge, in the image of Hizbollah, which was more organized, more ideologically committed and better financed. Moreover, Hizbollah successfully used its war against Israel as leverage for improving its lot inside Lebanon. Thus, the anti-Israeli guerrilla war also became a tool for Shi'a empowerment within the Lebanese domestic arena. Given Shi'a dislike of the Palestinians in Lebanon until 1982 and arguably beyond, and Shi'a initial support for Israel during the first days of the invasion, it is quite remarkable to consider the transformation that this community has gone through in its attitude towards the Jewish state.

The only 'achievement' of the invasion – wiping out Palestinian terror from Lebanon– also proved to be questionable, becoming a double-edged sword for Israel. The idea that it was possible to eradicate Palestinian nationalism by force proved to be entirely fallacious. True, the Palestinians lost their important base in Lebanon, but the centre of their national movement simply moved to a 'new' location. Many reasons account for the eruption of the Palestinian *Intifada* in December 1987. But, it is evident that the weakness of the 'outside', as a result of the 1982 invasion, facilitated – among other things – the rise of the 'inside' as the locus of the Palestinian national struggle. From that moment on, the West Bank and the Gaza Strip became the territorial focus of the Palestinian struggle against Israel, in complete contrast to what Ariel Sharon hoped to achieve following the invasion of Lebanon.

While it is somewhat possible to understand the motivation behind the creation of a security zone in south Lebanon from 1976 to 1982, it is difficult to comprehend why it was maintained and even expanded from 1985 until May 2000. After all, the Palestinian organizations did pose a threat to Israel and as of 1975 Lebanon became a 'free for all' country. Israel, therefore, considered the region roughly 40 km north of its border with Lebanon as vital for its security interests and until the invasion of 1982 focused its energy in this region. But as of 1985, the Palestinians in Lebanon no longer posed a serious threat to Israel. Instead, the threat was now coming from Hizbollah combatants whose objectives were entirely different than those of the Palestinians. While the latter sought to liberate Palestine and used Lebanon as their launching base, the former aimed at liberating south Lebanon from Israeli occupation.[27]

To be sure, Hizbollah also wished Israel would disappear from the face of the earth and that Arab Palestine would be established in its stead, but its struggle against Israel in Lebanon was focused and limited in scope – getting Israel out. The Lebanon war could have reached its conclusion then, in 1985, but instead it dragged on for 15 more years, further empowering Hizbollah, facilitating in part the Syrian return to and occupation of Lebanon and continuing the erosion of Israel's moral and military standing in the region.

4   The emergence of Hizbollah and the beginnings of resistance, 1982–85

Hussain Sirriyeh

Introduction

A certain enigma surrounds the objectives and policies of Hizbollah within Lebanon and in the region, even regarding its global reach. It has been hard for the Lebanese authorities and for a larger number of critical Lebanese citizens to deal with it, both as a militia and as a political party. Israel has also been encountering difficulties in handling Hizbollah as a non-state actor that is challenging Israeli policies in Lebanon and the region. The situation has been complicated by the fact that this non-state actor has intimate links with two radical states in the region, Iran and Syria, and has been gaining popular support among the Arab/Muslim public, in view of its resilient confrontation with Israel and the United States. However, although these difficulties have been more apparent since the Israeli withdrawal from South Lebanon in May 2000 and Israel's inability to eliminate or crush Hizbollah as an organisation in the war of summer 2006, there was already evidence pointing to the above difficulties right from the time Hizbollah emerged on the Lebanese scene.

This chapter will attempt to throw light on the origins and emergence of Hizbollah as a Lebanese militia and an armed organisation, devoting itself to resisting the Israeli occupation of Lebanese territory, and flexing its muscles to achieve wider aims in the region. It examines the elements in the operational environment, both within and outside Lebanon, that led to the rise of Hizbollah, assesses the evolution of its internal structure, investigates its domestic, regional and world views and appraises its policy programme until the Israeli substantial withdrawal from Lebanon in the spring of 1985.

The rise of Hizbollah in the Lebanese and regional contexts

Although the Arabic encyclopaedia of Hizbollah traces the origins of the party to the political environment of the late 1950s and early 1960s, with the agitation for independence in the Middle East as well as worldwide,[1] the societal background for its emergence may go back to the early 1970s, with the gradual escalation of Palestinian military activity against Israel and the drastic effects these activities had on the Shi'a of South Lebanon. A large number of this community was forced to emigrate from the South to the slums of Beirut. It will be hard to disentangle the regional from the Lebanese domestic developments that led to the emergence of Shi'a political organisations. On the domestic level, the Shi'a community began to be mobilised due to economic and political reasons. Although the process of modernisation had been a major factor underlying this mobilisation, the active consciousness of the community was not necessarily the 'outcome' of this process, as Augustus Norton has maintained,[2] but rather the result of further developments that took place on the domestic Lebanese scene as well as in the region. On the Lebanese level, two important developments affected the Shi'a. One of these was the increasing economic deprivation, especially with the continuing Israeli attacks, hence, the growing relevance of the feudal forces (*zu'ama*), which were supposed to look after this community.

The other development was the growing shift in the demographic balance with the expanding size of the Shi'a community (in comparison with other sectarian communities), hence, the growing discontent with the National Pact of 1943. This was accompanied by the perceived failure of the *zu'ama* to represent this community, having themselves benefited from this pact. Although there has been no official census in Lebanon since that of 1932, unofficial figures by the early 1970s gave the Muslims of Lebanon a majority over the Christians, indicating that the Shi'a community was now the largest in numbers.[3] The awareness of the Shi'a was enhanced by the rise of the personality of Imam Musa Al-Sadr, his forming in 1974 of the Movement of the Deprived and, in 1975, of its militia, Amal (*Afwaj Al-Muqawamah Al-Lubnaniyyah* – Lebanese Resistance Detachments). Three other developments facilitated the further mobilisation and radicalisation of the Shi'a: the disappearance of Imam Al-Sadr on 31 August 1978 while on a visit to Libya, the Israeli invasion of Lebanon in March 1978 (and in 1982) and the successful establishment of the Islamic Republic in Iran in February 1979.[4] The disappearance of Imam Al-Sadr revived the Shi'a belief about the Hidden Twelfth Imam and helped to elevate Imam Al-Sadr to a high level in Shi'a perception. Norton quotes a member of the Amal Movement that Imam Al-Sadr's disappearance was 'the single most important thing' that happened to the Movement.[5] As for the Israeli invasion of Lebanon, it led to further pressure on the Shi'a of South Lebanon to emigrate, especially with the consequent formation of the Army of South Lebanon, under the leadership of Sa'ad Haddad, which was monitoring security there. The establishment of the Islamic Republic of Iran emboldened the Shi'a and enhanced their political and psychological strength in Lebanon.

These historical events interacted with the theological dimension, which also helped to facilitate the rise of Hizbollah. Official Hizbollah sources refer to three theologians whose thought left an impact on the younger clerics who were decisive in the eventual formation of Hizbollah. The first was Imam Musa Al-Sadr, who was instrumental in persuading Lebanese authorities to establish the Higher Shi'a Islamic Council, which he then headed and which was entrusted with looking after the interests of the Shi'a community. Another senior cleric was Ayatollah Muhammad Mahdi Shams Al-Din, who was Deputy Head and later Head of the above council until he died in 2001. The third important cleric has been Ayatollah Muhammad Hussein Fadlallah, who has been more closely linked with Hizbollah.[6] They studied in the seminaries in Najaf, Iraq, under the clerical guidance of Mohsin Al-Hakim, Abu Al-Qasim Al-Khoi and Muhammad Baqir Al-Sadr. The former two died naturally in 1970 and 1992 respectively, whereas Baqir Al-Sadr was sentenced to death by the Iraqi Ba'thist authorities in April 1980. The most controversial figure among the three clerics in Lebanon is Ayatollah Fadlallah. He is said to have been the 'spiritual guide', the 'actual leader', the 'reference jurist' or the source of 'intellectual inspiration' for Hizbollah.[7] Whatever the truth, it would be safer to assume that, although Fadlallah's opinion and *fatwas* may be acceptable to Hizbollah, he may not be functionally connected with the party.

Connected with the above theological perspective is the argument advanced in an influential work on Hizbollah by Joseph Elie Alagha. He stressed that the origins of Hizbollah go back to 1978 when Abbas Al-Mussawi, the former teacher of the present Secretary-General of Hizbollah, Hassan Nasrallah, travelled from Najaf to Ba'albek in Lebanon and established *Hawzat Al-Imam Al-Muntazar* (Seminary of the Expected Imam) and began his *da'wah* (call) there.[8] The historical and theological perspectives intersect with the organisational axis in explaining the formation of Hizbollah. The organisational component consists of at least five elements: two at the domestic level and three other regional factors. One of the regional elements was the Israeli invasion of Lebanon in June 1982, reaching and occupying part of the capital, Beirut. The Israeli invasion signalled the failure of the Lebanese state to provide a range of political goods for its citizens, including security and the freedom to participate in the political process.[9]

This led to the emergence of several strands of resistance led by the Amal Movement, some Islamic committees, a branch of the Al-Da'wah Party (which since 1968 had been operating clandestinely in Iraq), the Lebanese Union of Muslim Students and a number of independents. Islamic Amal, under the leadership of Hussein Musawi, was created as a result of splitting from the main Amal Movement in order to fill the vacuum left by state failure. The reason for the split was that the mother Amal leader, Nabih Berri, agreed to participate in the National Salvation Committee formed by the former Lebanese President, Elias Sarkis, which included the leader of the Lebanese Forces, Bashir Gemayal.[10] It is not clear from the sources how the radical elements in these resistance forces coalesced together and became cadres in Hizbollah because at that time (1982) Hizbollah had not yet declared itself to be publicly formed.

But in order to close the gaps regarding the formation of Hizbollah two more steps were needed at the regional level: gaining Iranian approval, and hence support, and securing Syria's agreement because of its proximity and involvement in Lebanon. Hizbollah sources vaguely mention that nine of the senior personalities (three representing the Association of Clerics in the Beqaa, three from the Islamic Committees and three from Islamic Amal) prepared a working paper regarding the formation of an Islamic party abiding by the Guardianship of the Jurisconsult (*Wilayat al-Faqih*). The paper was presented to Ayatollah Khomeini at the time and, as the Jurisconsult approved it, it became a 'legitimate' document. This was followed by the dissolution of the existing organisations in order to form the party that was eventually called Hizbollah.[11] What was left was the need to obtain Syria's agreement. Ronen Bergman, an Israeli journalist specialising in matters of intelligence asserted that the successful Israeli strike against the Syrian air force (downing about a hundred Syrian planes and destroying all the Syrian Soviet-made anti-aircraft missiles in June 1982) had done damage to the Syrian President Hafez Al-Assad's 'ego'.

This led Al-Assad to agree to the despatch of some 3,000 Iranian Revolutionary Guards (which were later reduced to 500) to Lebanon and the establishment of a guerrilla organisation there to strike at the Israeli military. However, as Syria was concerned to limit, but not to eliminate, the Iranian presence in Lebanon, it put restrictions on the Revolutionary Guards there.[12] If Syria could succeed in controlling the Iranian influence and the activities of Hizbollah, it could also use this organisation as a card in its negotiation with Israel for a political settlement. Hence the formation of Hizbollah came as a result of the intertwining of historical, theological and organisational elements at the internal and external levels.

The internal structure of Hizbollah

Although Hizbollah was probably formed in June 1982, it announced its organisation publicly on 16 February 1985, in an Open Letter addressed to the *mustafadin* (Downtrodden).[13] Although the choice of the name Hizbollah was based on the Qur'anic verses (*Surah* 5, verse 56 and *Surah* 58, verse 22), one writer questions the validity of this reading of the Qur'an by stating that Hizbollah as referred to in the Qur'an meant the followers or soldiers of God and not an organisational structure of a party.[14] Little is known about the internal dynamics or workings of the party, but we know that it has had four public leaders, the last three of whom have been Secretary-Generals of the party (Ibrahim Amin Al-Sayyed, Subhi Al-Tufayli, Abbas Musawi and Hassan Nasrallah). The leaders are elected by a Consultative Council that consisted of twelve, nine or seven members at different times. It has five councils (the Holy War, Political, Executive, Parliamentary and Judicial Councils), each headed by a member of the Consultative Council.[15] Hizbollah's founders were concerned not to create a party in the traditional sense of the term and wanted also to recruit as many supporters as possible. There was also debate among the founding leaders as to whether to call the new organisation Hizbollah or *Ummat* Hizbollah (The Community of the

Party of God). They then settled on the term Hizbollah in order to adhere to the Qur'anic verse. However, in order to recruit a multitude of supporters, the party established a network of institutions in the three areas of Shi'a concentration (the Beqaa, the southern suburbs of Beirut and South Lebanon). These included religious schools, social services, including free medical services, media services in the fields of print journalism, radio and TV, educational institutions, female institutions, scouts and even offered institutional help in the fields of agriculture and construction.[16]

This was an attempt to close the gap where the Lebanese state failed to provide for the (mainly Shi'a) community. As Lara Deeb notes, to call somebody a 'Hizbollah supporter' is 'a vague phrase' as there are official party members, fighters, resistance elements, volunteers for the social services, recipients of aid from Hizbollah organisations, voters for the party and sympathisers with Hizbollah Resistance. In her view, the best way to envisage the relationship among various ideologies, positions and activities is to conceive of 'imperfectly overlapping circles and ideas that are constantly shifting'.[17]

Hizbollah's domestic, regional and world views

A general illustration of Hizbollah's views was initially provided in the Open Letter that was officially announced on 16 February 1985. The party's major aim in Lebanon was to expel the Israelis from the country. The party was also determined to drive out the Americans and the French who came to Lebanon in 1982 as part of the Multi-National Force. The letter also expressed Hizbollah's preference for the establishment of an Islamic rule (Islamic state) in Lebanon. However, the Encyclopaedia of Hizbollah explained later that, although Hizbollah still adhered to the idea of an Islamic state as the best vision, it remains a free optional choice. On the practical level the party needs to prepare the proper grounding in Lebanon for the establishment of such a state, citing the Qur'anic verse (*Surah* 2, verse 256) that there is no compulsion in religion. It has also been maintained that it was Ayatollah Fadlallah who stood behind the idea of the 'Lebanonization of Hizbollah' by adopting a new approach to the Lebanese political system based on cooperation rather than an abolition of the system. This was why the Hizbollah leaders were publicly non-committal about the establishment of an Islamic state in Lebanon.[18]

This means that the multi-sectarian nature of the Lebanese state does not permit the establishment of an Islamic state and that such an idea would not be imposed on Lebanese society. The major preoccupation of Hizbollah was to expel the Israelis while leaving it to the Lebanese people to choose the system of rule that they would like. This indicates the adoption by Hizbollah of a flexible and pragmatic position with regard to the domestic Lebanese scene, which was later exemplified (in 1992) in the party's participation in the Lebanese parliamentary elections as it became integrated into the Lebanese political system. This pragmatism was also illustrated in their openness towards the Maronite community, although the Open Letter states that the Phalange Party was considered a local enemy of Hizbollah. On the regional level, the main commitment of the party was to accept the Guardianship of the Jurisconsult as reflected in the policy of the Islamic Republic of Iran. The Iranian supreme religious leader is considered by Hizbollah as its ultimate authority. The party receives financial, military and political support from Iran, although Hizbollah tends to couch its terminology in Pan-Islamic terms, and essentially advocates a Shi'a perspective, both in its interpretation of the Islamic texts and its political outlook.[19] It is even conditional on the party members to accept the Guardianship of the Jurisconsult before they are being considered for party membership. Although Syria plays an important role as conduit of Iranian support for Hizbollah, it is not mentioned in the Open Letter. A major component of Hizbollah's regional view is the perception of Israel as the basic enemy along with the United States and, at that time, France. The Open Letter conceives of the liberation of the Lebanese territory as a prelude to 'Israel's final obliteration from existence and the liberation of venerable Jerusalem from the talons of occupation'.[20] This would imply that, even if the remaining territory of Lebanon were to be freed (Shebaa Farms) from Israel, Hizbollah would continue its confrontation with Israel until Jerusalem (or Palestine) is liberated. Hence Hizbollah's regional mission is connected with the fate of the Arab–Israeli conflict, not just the Israeli presence on Lebanese territory.

On the global level, the Open Letter indicates that the US, which is also called 'the world arrogance', is regarded as being behind 'all our catastrophes' and conceives an alliance between the US, Zionism and the Phalangist forces in Lebanon.[21] In fact, Hizbollah perceives the world as divided between oppressed and oppressors, the latter being 'the countries of the arrogant world', especially the US and, at that time, the USSR, which compete for influence in the Third World. Hizbollah adheres to the slogan of the Islamic Republic of Iran: 'neither East nor West', even putting both superpowers on the same level.[22] However, the US is considered as Islam's main enemy. There can be no compromise or mediation. Even the United Nations helps to serve the interests of the superpowers.[23]

In fact, Hizbollah's domestic, regional and global views intersect in blaming the Lebanese government for adopting a compromise policy and in criticising the reconciliatory policies of the defeatist Arab regimes (Jordan, Egypt, Arafat's PLO and Ba'thist Iraq) towards Israel and in perceiving an alliance between the US and Israel. Hizbollah considers the resort to violence in the name of *jihad* as the only way to combat these enemies.

Hizbollah's policy programme, 1982–85

The policy programme of Hizbollah proceeded at the levels of Lebanon, the region and expressing hostility towards Washington in particular. On the local level it demonstrated a remarkable flexibility and adjustment to the system, not only by adopting a non-committal position regarding the establishment of an Islamic state in Lebanon, but also by adopting a more benign approach towards other Lebanese confessions. This position was implicit in the Open Letter issued by Hizbollah on 16 February 1985 and in the explanation given later by its leaders, who emphasised the 'specificities' (*khususiyyat*) of the country and the resort to political methods that were deemed suitable.[24] The position of adjustment was reflected in the participation of the party in the parliamentary elections of 1992 and the subsequent dialogue with the Christian parties. Also on the Lebanese level, tension emerged between the Shi'a community and Palestinians because of the impact of the Israeli attacks on South Lebanon, Hizbollah regarded the eruption of the war of the camps between Amal and the Palestinians in 1985–88 as regrettable. The main cause of that war resided in Arafat's refusal to control the camps and disarm the Palestinian fighters. Eventually Hizbollah and Syria managed to arrive at a settlement of this bitter internecine conflict by limiting the armament in the camps to individual small arms and medium calibre weapons.

The *raison d'être* of Hizbollah remained however resistance against Israel. This resistance was initially led by the Lebanese Resistance (until 1986), before being usurped by the Islamic Resistance. Hizbollah had already succeeded in foiling the 17 May 1983 provisional agreement between the Lebanese government and Israel which would have ended the state of war between both sides and which, in the view of Hizbollah leaders, would have been to Israel's advantage.[25] Even so, Hizbollah displayed an ability to adjust to changing circumstances. While refusing to acknowledge the legitimacy of the Jewish State, it was not beyond condoning indirect understandings with Israel designed to avoid Lebanese and Israeli civilian casualties on both sides.

However, Hizbollah continued to resist the Israeli occupation of South Lebanon after Israel had withdrawn from most of Lebanon by the spring of 1985. In its attempt to lead the military resistance against Israel, Hizbollah had early on resorted to suicide bombings, claiming that they were martyrdom operations that were justified according to its interpretations of Islamic texts. The first successful operation was carried out by Ahmad Qasir against the headquarters of the Israeli military in Tyre, South Lebanon in November 1982. Besides its military resistance, Hizbollah continued to cooperate with Iran and Syria, the two main actors in the region supporting its activities. Hizbollah followed the Iranian line, especially during the Khomeini era when he was the supreme spiritual leader. The ties with Iran continued after Khomeini died. As for Syria, the cooperation between both sides was very much a marriage of convenience in view of Syria's pivotal role in acting as a channel for Iran's financial and military support. It poses the question: should Damascus ever reconcile its interests with Israel, if tensions arise with Tehran over the future role of Hizbollah in any new regional dispensation?

But throughout the 1980s, continued reference was made to the continuing struggle between the 'arrogance of the world' (*mustakbirin*) and the 'downtrodden of the world' (*mustafadin*). Consequently, whatever violent acts came to be associated with the movement, these remained, according to Fadlallah's worldview, defensive acts in the name of Islam and were, thus, to be condoned. As such, the struggle that Hizbollah now engaged upon was seen as inseparable from the wider confrontation between *dar al-harb* (House of War) and *dar al-Islam* (House of Islam). The struggle against Israel was seen as an inevitable catalyst to the destruction of the Jewish State and the liberation of *al-Quds* – the city of Jerusalem – from 'Zionist occupation' and the removal from Lebanon of a confessional order that suppressed the people and served only the interests of Western intervention. Hizbollah also placed strong emphasis upon the creation of an Islamic dispensation in Lebanon, to be achieved in coordination with the wider Islamic community or *umma*. Accordingly, Hizbollah eschewed deliberately the previous symbols of the Lebanese state, adopting instead their own iconography that impressed loyalty to their radical view of Islam upon Lebanon's fragmented political scene.

Hizbollah was elevated to international recognition on the world stage by its association, proved or otherwise, with acts of extreme violence against Western and Israeli targets. Such acts included not only the bombing of the Marine barracks in Beirut, a simultaneous attack on the French peacekeeping troops, the bombing of the United States embassy in East Beirut on 20 September 1984, the skyjacking of an American airliner to Beirut on 14 June 1985, the bombing of the United States and French embassies in Kuwait in December 1985, and the kidnapping, and in some cases murder, of Western hostages in Lebanon between 1984 and 1991. The rationale behind such acts often proved hard to discern, although Western, and in particular American support for Israel was always cited to justify such acts. But it was the campaign of guerrilla war waged by Hizbollah against the Israel Defence Forces (IDF) occupation of south Lebanon between 1982 and 1985, particularly the crude, but effective use of suicide car bombs resulting in the deaths of over 600 Israeli servicemen, that allowed the organisation to exercise increased political power in Lebanon.

Martin Kramer maintained that the resort to suicide attacks and kidnappings of foreigners violate some principles of Islamic laws. It was this latter method that came to define Hizbollah in the Western imagination throughout the 1980s. As the Iran–Iraq War erupted in September 1980 and as Iran was in need of arms and spare parts for its military equipment purchased previously by the Shah from the West, the kidnapping of hostages was used to exert pressure upon Washington to sell such equipment. This episode became known as the Iran Contra Affair or hostage-for-arms deal after it was disclosed that the proceeds from the sale of arms and spare parts – using Israel as a conduit – had been funnelled to support the Nicaraguan Contras in their struggle to overthrow the left-wing government of Daniel Ortega in direct contravention of laws passed by the United States Congress.[26]

The extension of Hizbollah operations outside the region, in particular its involvement in the attacks against Israeli and Argentine Jewish targets in

Buenos Aires, in 1994, the 1995 Khobar Towers bombing in Saudi Arabia and Hizbollah's alleged involvement in other intelligence operations in Germany and Cyprus, led one writer to argue that given its global reach, Hizbollah should, as a designated terrorist organisation, be included as a target as part of the 'War on Terror'.[27] While it is sufficient to note that the evidence linking Hizbollah to these events remains contested, its leaders have come to realise that involvement in such activities beyond the region threatens to inflict more harm than any good that could potentially accrue to the movement.[28] This did not mean however that Hizbollah remained averse to securing financial donations from abroad, particularly from expatriate Lebanese Shi'a in West Africa and South America, though it should be noted that the movement remained dependent upon the financial and material largesse of Tehran to support its military and social activities both inside and outside Lebanon.

Conclusion

This chapter has argued that on the level of internal politics, Hizbollah regarded itself as a legitimate actor in the Lebanese political scene, despite the fact that it remained reliant upon external support, most notably from Iran. Alagha argues however that from the mid-1990s two shifts occurred in Hizbollah's approach: one was its drift away from total obedience to the Guardianship of the Jurisconsult after Khomeini's death; the second that the party had acquired more Lebanese authenticity and became more autonomous in decision making.[29] However, Hizbollah has had a Shi'a bent right from the start and, as Hizbollah sources indicate, the commitment to the Guardianship of the Jurisconsult is still emphasised despite the death of Khomeini and his replacement by Ali Khaminei. Hizbollah sources also stressed that, notwithstanding its receiving military and financial support from Iran, the party is Lebanese in its leadership, cadres, the area of operations, the territory it has been defending and where its cadres have attained martyrdom and it is not an Iranian party.[30] Nonetheless, Hizbollah throughout the 1980s remained in thrall to Iranian policies throughout the region and abroad and continued to serve Iranian interests across the Middle East and beyond. Hizbollah has demonstrated a pragmatic approach, both in Lebanon and across the region, and was able to adapt itself to changing circumstances in Lebanon during the 1990s, most notably in establishing a dialogue with Maronite elements in Lebanon and toning down its previous commitment to the establishment of an Islamic state. It has also illustrated its readiness to enter into indirect agreements with Israel regarding the targeting of military personnel, and the return of some captives and the bodies of combatants held by both sides.

By the 1990s, therefore, the evidence suggests that there had been an incremental change in the orientation of Hizbollah away from overt radical fundamentalism towards practical accommodation with the Lebanese political scene. To be sure, spokespersons for the movement continued to indulge in the rhetoric of confrontation, particularly with regard to Israel. But Hizbollah, while refusing to define its position following any future Israeli withdrawal from Lebanon, remained careful to lay the foundations for its survival as a political movement. This included recognition of the prevailing political order in Lebanon – a redefined confessionalism – and an acceptance by the movement to work within this dispensation. It was the extent to which this accommodation with the confessional system was strategic, rather than just tactical which would come to define the future of the Party of God in Lebanon.

5   Hizbollah – from terror to resistance

Towards a national defence strategy

Daniel Sobelman

Introduction

This chapter surveys the development, stage by stage, of the conflict between Israel and Hizbollah, from the movement's inception in the early 1980s through today. Hizbollah's military profile will be addressed in its twin aspects – primarily as a guerrilla force in 'resistance' against Israel's presence across southern Lebanon, but also as an agent of acts of violence falling within the definition of terrorism.

While Hizbollah was waging a campaign of attrition against the Israel Defence Forces (IDF) and the South Lebanon Army (SLA) in the Security Zone, a modus operandi began to emerge in which the organisation gradually established a balance of deterrence by imposing 'rules of the game' in its face-off with a far superior state actor. In a course parallel to its military undertakings, Hizbollah also sought deeper integration into the national framework. In time it forged its way into the political rubric and parliamentary institutions of the state. Although the balance of deterrence twice broke down during the 1990s, on the whole it proved sustainable and useful for both parties. Hizbollah managed to impose 'rules' on Israel which exposed IDF and SLA soldiers to attacks only within the Security Zone. On the other hand, these 'rules' of mutual containment also posed significant restraints for Hizbollah. A further consequence was the inevitable toning down, though not the abandonment, of its maximalist ideology calling for the annihilation of Israel, thus, slowly accommodating the rhetoric of realpolitik.[1]

12 July 2006: a crucial underestimation and 33 days of war

On 7 July 2006, five days before Hizbollah's cross-border abduction which triggered the Second Lebanon War, the Beirut daily *Al-Mustaqbal* featured an article which in retrospect rings clairvoyant. Three weeks earlier an Israeli soldier, Gilad Shalit, was abducted by Palestinian militants near Israel's southern border and taken hostage into Gaza. Israel, in the words of the Lebanese journalist, had since then been in a state of 'craziness', conveying threatening messages to Damascus and Hizbollah lest they be tempted to carrying out a similar provocation. 'What passed in previous incidents will no longer pass today', commented Nasir al-Assad, adding that 'it is not an exaggeration to say that Lebanon is directly vulnerable to dangers'. He went on to observe that whereas in past years the United States might have subdued Israel, such restraints could no longer be counted upon, 'It should be unnecessary to state that opening a front in southern Lebanon – whatever the circumstances – will expose Lebanon to "Israeli madness"; neither will it benefit the Palestinians'.[2]

Nasir al-Assad's article appeared at the height of the 'national dialogue' which brought all the major political factions in Lebanon to the round table in what seemed like a promising endeavour to resolve by consensus Lebanon's outstanding issues, the most contentious of which was the future role of Hizbollah's military wing. On 29 June 2006 the factions convened for their ninth session. Sa'ad-al-Din al-Hariri – the son of the former Prime Minister Rafiq al-Hariri, who was assassinated in February 2005 – was the foremost spokesman of the anti-Syrian bloc, as well as the owner of the *Al-Mustaqbal* daily. He was quoted the very morning after that round of discussions, warning that Israel was in a 'crazy' frame of mind and therefore 'it is of paramount importance to assure the success of the tourist season'.[3]

And the interest of Lebanon, as al-Assad's article made pointedly clear, was above all 'to avoid "volunteering" military operations that could this time around exact of Lebanon a very heavy price'. Quite bluntly al-Assad stated that:

> Indeed the next days and even the next hours may present a great challenge to the country and the Lebanese people. The real challenge at hand is how to place the national interest at the very top of our priorities in light of the looming dangers.[4]

On the very same day of al-Assad's article, al-Hariri held a discreet late-night meeting with Hizbollah Secretary General Hassan Nasrallah.[5] It is entirely reasonable to assume that al-Hariri, who was flying out that same night to China, sought to dissuade Nasrallah against any escapades vis-à-vis Israel: indeed, following the war it was disclosed that al-Hariri had 'personally' warned Nasrallah against provocations.[6]

The tenth round of the 'national dialogue', scheduled for 25 July, never convened. On 12 July Hizbollah units penetrated Israel over the western sector of the border and ambushed an IDF patrol. They abducted two soldiers, brought them back into Lebanon and sent rockets into Israeli settlements. Israel's decision not to react this time in a circumscribed and proportionate manner led to a 33-day war, fuelling a deep ongoing political and inter-ethnic rift within Lebanon itself, which was as serious and dangerous as any since the civil war.

Miscalculating Israel's response

Two weeks after the ceasefire went into effect, Nasrallah was exceptionally forthcoming by admitting that had his organisation estimated that 'there was the probability of even one per cent' that the kidnapping would result in war, the attack would 'absolutely in no way' have been carried out.[7] If this is so, how then *did* Hizbollah assess Israel's response? After the war, Nasrallah confided that Hizbollah had been braced for 'a severe but limited' Israeli retaliation, explaining that 'we expected their action in Lebanon to be along the same lines as they displayed in Gaza, possibly somewhat greater'.[8]

Hussein Haj Hassan, a Hizbollah member of parliament, later admitted that:

> [W]e estimated that after the abduction operation we would experience a day or two in which one or two villages would be destroyed, and that would be all. This would be followed by some negotiation for a prisoner exchange. These are after all the rules of the game, so to speak.[9]

Hussein Khalil, an advisor to Nasrallah, was quoted as having said to Prime Minister Fouad Siniora, hours after the abduction that 'the situation will calm down within 24 to 48 hours'.[10]

Hizbollah's critical misreading of Israel's presumed retaliation had been overly reliant on its close monitoring and otherwise sound analysis of Israel's habitual conduct along its northern border since the IDF pullback from South Lebanon in May 2000. During these six years Hizbollah managed to create an effective deterrent capacity. Its July 2006 misjudgement was a reflection of its understanding of those same unwritten 'rules of the game' which routinely had kept Israel at arm's length. In the opening days of the war, one of the most oft-repeated expressions in the Israeli media referred to 'changing the rules of the game'. Israel was apparently determined to inflict mortal damage to Hizbollah's build-up just over its northern border. 'Your government wished to change the rules of the game? So be it, let the rules of the game change', declared Nasrallah on the second day of the war.[11]

1982: a time of beginnings

It is customary to speak of the June 1982 Lebanon War as *the* formative year for Hizbollah, in an *ad hoc* reaction to the Israeli invasion. It would be more exact to view that year as the beginning of a process that by early 1985 saw the official founding of Hizbollah. The first days of what in Israel is now referred to as 'the first Lebanon war', following Israel's invasion of Lebanon on 5 June 1982, saw a lively movement of delegations along the Iran–Syria–Lebanon axis. Just one day after the invasion, Iran, although pre-occupied with its war with Iraq, hastily dispatched a senior-ranking military mission to Damascus to offer assistance to the Syrians, Lebanese and

Palestinians. Syria, which had in late 1979 declined a previous offer to send Iranian units to Lebanon, now welcomed Tehran's offer in light of Israel's invasion, which was viewed as a strategic threat to Syria's national security. Thus, an almost immediate consequence of the Israeli invasion was a Syrian–Iranian military pact. At the time, these developments received minor attention in the Lebanese press. The Beirut daily *Al-Safir*, for example, made a brief mention at the bottom of one of its inner pages of the return of a delegation of the Amal Movement from Damascus, where it had met with Iranian representatives. Amal was then the foremost Shi'a organisation in Lebanon. Iran, eyeing the Israeli invasion as an opportunity to establish its own foothold in Lebanon, hoped to do so via Amal.

On 15 June, a very brief item in *Al-Safir* could be found at the bottom of page 8, noting the arrival in Damascus of 400 Iranian volunteers from the ranks of the Revolutionary Guard who were awaiting passage into Lebanon to take part in the battles.[12] This newly emerging reality soon led to a split within Amal over a proposal by Lebanon's President Sarkis calling for the formation of 'a national salvation authority' to confront the Israeli invasion. Nabih Berri, the head of Amal, believing this to be a springboard for promoting the interests of the Shi'as in Lebanon, was willing to align himself with the president's plan. However, his more radical deputy Hussein al-Mussawi broke with him and Amal, forming, along with others, 'Amal al-Islami', a more devoutly Islamic movement with a pro-Iranian orientation.[13]

At the same time, smaller militia units enjoying varying degrees of Iranian patronage began to emerge. It is in this climate, and against this backdrop, that the origins of Hizbollah are to be traced. While it is almost certain that even minus the Israeli invasion Iran would have been seeking ways to channel its attention to the Lebanese arena, Israel's Operation 'Peace for the Galilee' provided the trigger for Tehran's involvement.[14] Yitzhak Rabin, then Minister of Defence, admitted later that the manner in which the Shi'a population came to confront Israel:

> [W]as one of the surprises of Operation Peace for Galilee. It was as if the Shiite genie had escaped from the bottle in an unexpected way. The most neglected and marginalised ethnic group in Lebanon suddenly seized the opportunity to stand up and claim its proper place within Lebanese society, serving its communal self-interests by waging a terror campaign of its own against the IDF.[15]

The 1980s: showcase terrorism and kidnappings

Throughout its history Lebanon has been a playing field for power struggles between several major actors and outside interests. During the 1980s, participants in these power moves included Iran, Syria, France, the United States, the USSR, Israel, Iraq and Libya. Even before both Israel's invasion and the formation of Hizbollah, Lebanon had become a convenient setting in which

Western targets were attacked, settling scores between regional actors, including Iraq, Iran and France.[16] It was widely thought that the background of these attacks lay in the assistance extended by Paris to Iraq in its war with Iran.[17]

The final collapse of any semblance of Lebanese central authority came in the wake of Israel's invasion, with the ensuing atmosphere of chaos and near-total breakdown of security. In general, this remained characteristic of Lebanon until the end of the civil war in 1989 and the consolidation of Syrian hegemony over Lebanon. Despite this raging civil disorder, certain elements managed to advance their own agendas, taking full advantage of the eclipse of an effective central government. One such determined interest group was Iran together with Hizbollah, which had set their sights on the expunging of all foreign forces then on Lebanese soil: Israel, the United States and France.

The very first suicide attack officially claimed by Hizbollah was by Ahmad Qasir, a 19-year-old Shi'a who on 11 November 1982 drove an explosive-laden truck straight into the Israeli army headquarters in the southern city of Tyre, killing 76 Israeli personnel and 15 detainees.[18] In April 1983 a suicide bomber demolished the US embassy. In October, twin suicide attacks were carried out simultaneously against the Multinational Forces which had landed only a few months earlier with the mission of restoring stability to the country. Two powerful blasts claimed the lives of 241 American servicemen, along with 58 French soldiers who, as part of the Multinational Force sent to Beirut had been tasked with overseeing the evacuation of PLO forces from the Lebanese capital.

Hizbollah confronts the Israeli occupation of South Lebanon

In the quarter-century since the organisation came into being, Hizbollah has steadily adapted its tactics to the changing exigencies in which it found itself. Its focal conflict with Israel was particularly affected by the powerful regional players, Israel and Syria, which necessitated constant organisational adjustment.

The invasion of Lebanon had brought the IDF within artillery range of the Syrian capital. From its perspective, and in no small measure as a lesson from Israel's deep 1982 incursion, Damascus concluded that Lebanon itself constituted strategic territorial depth. In the words of Faruq al-Shara, today Vice President of Syria, 'we are not interested in controlling Lebanon. We are anxious that others might want to take control of Lebanon and impose their will on Syria. This is the real Syrian-Lebanese fear'.[19] Hizbollah, for its part, concurred with this line of thought. According to Naim Qassem:

> As we can see from the map, Lebanon either sides with Israel or with Syria. It cannot remain outside the sphere of influence of both of them. Thus, it is preferable for Lebanon to be with Syria rather than with Israel.[20]

By late 1989, Lebanon at long last enjoyed a period of stability, with a reconstituted central government in Beirut, albeit a government largely subject to Damascus. The Taif Agreement brokered by Saudi Arabia ended the civil war. This was accompanied by the disbanding of the various militias and armed factions that had been active during the civil war. Hizbollah, however, remained the only organisation which was never disarmed, agreeing instead to turn its entire military activity to the Security Zone, where Israel and the SLA had redeployed after Israel had pulled back from most Lebanese territory in 1985.

The stabilising of the internal arena, together with Hizbollah's commitment to redirecting its armed struggle to the Israeli occupying forces, gave rise to two parallel processes. Within the domestic political sphere, Hizbollah had initiated a process which was described by several independent observers as 'Lebanonisation', but which Hizbollah itself referred to as *Infitah*, that is, 'opening up'. Amal Saad-Ghorayeb has suggested that this was an expression of the organisation's recognition that its original aspirations – embraced publicly in its first party manifesto early in 1985 – aiming to transform Lebanon into an Islamic Republic had been 'unrealistic'.[21] The unmistakable benchmark in Hizbollah's 'Lebanonisation', was its decision to formally enter the political arena and participate in the 1992 parliamentary elections.

Meanwhile, Hizbollah continued perfecting its combat skills through training and field experience. Its guerrilla operations exhibited an increasing professionalism which was reflected in the mounting numbers of Israeli troops killed in South Lebanon. Ahmad Nizar Hamzeh collated statistics on the number of military actions conducted by Hizbollah during the 1990s. He found that Hizbollah had carried out 1,030 operations in the first half of that decade, whereas between the years 1996 until Israel's withdrawal in May 2000, the Shi'a militia had raised the number of its attacks to 4,928.[22] During the second half of the decade Israel's annual combat losses in South Lebanon were between 20 and 25, although in 1999 the figure dropped to 12 soldiers and one civilian.[23]

But beyond this, the more interesting and significant development was Hizbollah's success, beginning in the early 1990s, in gradually establishing a balance of deterrence vis-à-vis Israel. The rules of the game which co-evolved between the sides defined the nature and the scope of the confrontation, containing and restraining the intensity of the conflict. Perhaps most pivotal of all the rules of the game was the guiding principle calling for the exclusion of targeting civilians on both sides of the border. Moreover, by the end of the 1990s Hizbollah could bask in yet another important gain in the internal Lebanese context. The ascension to office of President Emile Lahoud at the end of 1998, alongside Prime Minister Salim al-Huss, ushered in an unprecedented warming of the Lebanese state-establishment towards Hizbollah.

This trend gained added momentum following Israel's withdrawal from South Lebanon. The growing embrace of Hizbollah by the state apparatus became so close that in 2002 the IDF intelligence began relating to the northern front as 'The Northern Set' underscoring the tightly integrated coordination between the army commands of Syria and Lebanon with Hizbollah.[24] Michel Suleiman, then Army Chief-of-Staff and today President of Lebanon, reflected that since Lebanon's army was unequally matched to effectively engage Israel's military, it is, thus, Hizbollah which becomes Lebanon's 'smart weapon. . . . and fills the vacuum' left by the weakness of the army.[25]

The 1990s: two defining military campaigns

Throughout the past two decades of conflict, the term 'equations' has become central to Hizbollah's military discourse. One of the first of the 'equations' which the organisation succeeded in imposing upon Israel was the firing of Katyusha rockets in reaction to Israeli operations that resulted either in casualties or in damage to civilian infrastructure. Hizbollah's rocket arsenal made its 'equation debut' in February 1992, shooting Katyushas into Israel in retaliation for the assassination of Nasrallah's predecessor, Abbas al-Mussawi. In his book Qassem explains that after the assassination of Al-Mussawi, Hizbollah introduced the 'new equation' whereby the organisation 'limits the deployment [of Katyushas] to incidents in which its citizens, villages and towns or civilian infrastructure are exposed to Israeli aggression'.[26] Speaking at a ceremony marking the tenth anniversary of Al-Mussawi's death, Nasrallah remarked that 'we have created a balance of fear by means of the Katyusha, which military science likens to a water pistol'.[27]

In retrospect, the two major breakdowns of the 'rules' during the 1990s – Operation 'Accountability' in July 1993, and Operation 'Grapes of Wrath' in April 1996 – might be considered a smaller-scale preview performance of the Second Lebanon War. Both campaigns – which were serious deviations from the 'routine' of the daily, but contained, skirmishing – were initiated by Israel in response to a series of Hizbollah successes on the ground, and the growing feeling that 'something needed to be done' to restrain Hizbollah. Looking back, the outcomes of both campaigns cannot be assessed as advantageous in the long term for Israel: in fact quite the opposite. Although Lebanon sustained considerable damage in these campaigns, it was Hizbollah which preserved its right 'to say the last word' by continuing its Katyusha assaults until the ceasefire literally came into effect – thus enabling it to argue that the organisation could withstand the offensive.

Operation 'Accountability', 25–31 July 1993

Israel launched this campaign, its largest since 1982, following the loss of seven soldiers in clashes with Hizbollah.[28] The Israeli thrust was designed to pressure the civilian population in its path into evacuating the wider theatre of battle and flee northward. This would force the government in Beirut to exert its own pressure on Hizbollah. The rural population throughout southern Lebanon did indeed escape northward, flooding the Beirut environs in their hundreds of thousands; but, nevertheless, Hizbollah maintained its barrage of rockets on northern Israel for all seven days. Gradually, Israel began to narrow its attainable objectives, which Nasrallah was eager to point out:

> From the elimination of *Hezbollah* and the Islamic resistance to the disarmament of *Hezbollah*, then to freezing the operations of the resistance – which implies a recognition of the resistance's right to keep its arms, but in return for freezing its operations. Then, finally came [the proposal] preventing the Katyusha rockets from targeting Israeli civilians in the settlements in northern Israel.[29]

Operation 'Accountability' ended with a set of verbally worked out 'understandings' agreed to by Israel, Syria and Lebanon through the mediation of the United States. According to these Hizbollah was to cease firing rockets in exchange for Israel halting its operation, with both sides committed to excluding civilian targets from future conflict. But as Nasrallah saw it, the end result helped it to regulate the 'rules of the game', further equalising the equation between itself and Israel.

> The rules of the game used to be that we got bombarded while the settlements remained safe . . . but the resistance imposed a new formula through the Katyusha. Thus, we say that we are committed to a new rule, one which was established by us.[30]

Two weeks later, after the ceasefire, on 19 August 1993, seven Israeli soldiers were killed in a clash with Hizbollah. Israel's response was now limited to military targets. This was viewed with satisfaction by Hizbollah as confirmation of the viability of the rules. Over the next three years the organisation was to exploit these 'understandings' to intensify the frequency of its military actions.

A close examination of all the Katyusha firings, as reported in the Israeli press from Operation 'Accountability' through to April 1996, shows that Hizbollah carefully abided by the rules of the game which 'permitted' it to launch rocket attacks on northern Israeli settlements when there had been antecedent attacks involving Lebanese civilians. In one instance, the Shi'a organisation tried to 'stretch' the rules by firing rockets in reaction to the destruction of some abandoned houses in Beit Yahoun village, which Israel claimed were being used by Hizbollah. Judging by its actions, as well as statements by its leaders and commanders, it is fair to say that Israel recognised the status of the rules of the game. In certain situations, the IDF issued early warnings instructing civilians in the north to seek precautionary shelter as soon as there were first reports of Lebanese civilian casualties from IDF or SLA fire – even before Hizbollah threatened to respond in kind.

Thus, Israel felt itself hamstrung in its freedom of movement: Hizbollah was able to operate under the cover of civilian populations, which limited Israel's range of response so as to avoid putting Lebanese villagers at risk, and by inference, Israeli civilians as well. In July 1994 Prime Minister Rabin conceded that Israel was facing 'difficulties' in exercising its right to return fire to sources originating outside the Security Zone.[31] Between 1995 and 1996 Israel approached the United States several times in an attempt to reach revised understandings with Hizbollah. On 22 March 1996 Ze'ev Schiff, senior military commentator for the Israeli daily newspaper *Ha'aretz*, reported that the United States was in fact trying to expand the post-Operation 'Accountability' understandings 'to include not only the exclusion of civilian settlements from conflict, but also to prohibit other fighting methods in the Security Zone'.

Hizbollah exploited quite well, and in Israel's view quite cynically, the very 'difficulty' with which Rabin had been concerned. For its part, Hizbollah had been scrupulous in following the informal rules of the game – firing rockets in retaliation for Lebanese casualties. For example, in October 1994, 15 Katyushas were fired into northern Israel in reply to the killing of seven Lebanese villagers by Israeli fire. In another instance Hizbollah targeted the Galilee following the deaths of two Lebanese citizens.

On this occasion – and ahead of the retaliation – Nasrallah urged the Israelis to 'remain in your shelters today, tomorrow and the next day . . . our patience has run out, since what has happened is a violation of the July understandings, and this aggression has been repeating itself since the beginning of the year'.[32] Alongside its improving strategic parity, Hizbollah's tactical abilities were also constantly on the rise. An IDF officer who had served on the northern front during the years 1995 to 1996 recalls that in 1995 each entry into the Security Zone proceeded according to a '2–6 Protocol', that is, two vehicles with six soldiers. The following year this procedure was upgraded to include three armoured vehicles fitted with equipment-systems for neutralising roadside explosive devices. 'The manner in which I left Lebanon in 1996 was totally different from the fashion when I first entered', the officer reflected.[33]

Indeed, a colonel serving with *Agaf Modi'in* (AMAN – IDF Military Intelligence) was cited in late 1995 as revealing that during the outgoing year Hizbollah had planted 90 roadside explosive devices across the Security Zone, an increase of 50 per cent of such devices over the previous year.[34] This constant growth curve of Hizbollah's military operations in South Lebanon was to continue up until Israel's withdrawal in 2000. However, Israel's patience would soon give out. On 8 April 1996, the IDF instructed the population throughout northern Israel to enter their shelters, following an item on Hizbollah's radio 'Nur' reporting the death of an 11-year-old child in an explosion in the village of Bar'ashit. Despite an Israeli denial that its forces had been operating in that village, a barrage of Katyushas ensued, described as the most intensive of all in the preceding three months. The commander of

Israel's Northern Division, Major General Amiram Levine, declared in response that Hizbollah 'had crossed the red line', and Deputy Minister of Defence Ori Or added 'that the rules of the game have changed'.[35] The next day Israel launched the 'Grapes of Wrath' campaign.

Operation 'Grapes of Wrath', 11–27 April 1996

In contrast to the previous major campaign, Operation 'Grapes of Wrath' was initiated while Israel's attention was already preoccupied with the approaching national prime ministerial elections and with salvaging the peace process in both the Syrian and Palestinian tracks. Israel opened its military offensive following a series of Hizbollah rocket attacks into Israel in retaliation for the deaths of Lebanese citizens. Israel, desperate to revise the rules of the game, attacked Hizbollah's stronghold in southern Beirut at the very outset of the campaign – and for the first time since 1982. However, as was the case in Operation 'Accountability' and a decade later in the Second Lebanon War, here too the measure of Israel's success was inexorably to be linked to its ability to halt the Katyusha barrages. Public statements by Israeli officers were explicit about this linkage.

And the rockets did indeed continue to rain down on the northern settlements throughout the entire campaign up to the ceasefire. Once again we observe the inevitable gap between Israeli declarations of intent issued at the campaign's outset, in contrast to the facts on the ground at its conclusion. For example, Ehud Barak, then Israel's Foreign Minister, was quoted on day one of the campaign, saying: 'Lebanon must exert its sovereignty and bring about the disarmament of Hizbollah'. Other officials suggested that if Hizbollah were to respond to the offensive underway this would lead Israel to seriously escalate its pressure on Lebanon's government until Beirut would plead for Syria to intervene and restrain Hizbollah. A senior IDF officer was cited as saying: 'Let Hizbollah understand that the IDF will no longer tolerate firing on [the northern city of] Kiryat Shmonah'.[36]

Only five days before the campaign's end, Israeli Prime Minister Shimon Peres was unwavering 'that the government will not be satisfied with any results other than those set forth for operation Grapes of Wrath, and by no means will we agree to return to the status quo ante bellum in South Lebanon'.[37] However, developments on the battlefield had a dynamic all of their own. Especially when on 18 April 1996 IDF artillery shells landed inside a UN compound at Kfar Qana, killing 106 Lebanese civilians.

The Israeli campaign was brought to an end, accompanied this time by a series of written – although unsigned – understandings mediated by the United States between Israel, Syria, and Lebanon. In essence this was the first time that the military confrontation between Israel and Hizbollah was explicitly regulated through written understandings. Accordingly, '[a]rmed groups in Lebanon will not carry out attacks of Katyusha rockets or by any kind of weapon into Israel' and 'Israel and those cooperating with it will not fire any kind of weapon at civilians or civilian targets in Lebanon'. The under-standing further stipulated, that '[w]ithout violating this understanding, nothing herein shall preclude any party from exercising the right of self-defense'.[38]

A framework committee with representatives of Israel, Lebanon, the United States, Syria, and France was established to monitor violations of the understandings reached. Hizbollah regarded the manner in which Israel's campaign was concluded as an unprecedented gain. This view was summed up in the press conference convened by Nasrallah at the end of hostilities: 'Israel', he reminded his listeners, 'had set out to destroy our infrastructure, dissolve our movement, and stop the launching of our Katyushas'.[39] From Nasrallah's perspective, the operation was nothing but a more aggressive ver-sion of Operation 'Accountability', a campaign of initially overreaching Israeli declarations, ending more or less with the same 'rules of the game'.[40]

Even more advantageous than the technical and tactical benefits arising from the 'understandings', Hizbollah felt that its status was becoming con-firmed by international recognition – including by Israel – as a legitimate actor. In the years to come, senior IDF officers, in contrast, vehemently criti-cised the understandings, calling them 'a calamity' for tying the hands of the army. In summing up the campaign, Gen. Moshe Ya'alon, head of *AMAN*, reported that in the 16 days of fighting Hizbollah had fired a total of 790 rockets into Israel and the Security Zone. In his words, these were launched under civilian cover – Hizbollah not being averse, and indeed preferring, to fire either from the proximity of UN camps or from within hospitals, mosques and school grounds.[41]

Two defining showcase bombings in Argentina

In the 1990s Hizbollah extended the 'rules of the game' to a distant arena. Although the organisation has never confirmed its global reach, Hizbollah was deeply implicated in two strategic attacks in Argentina – both revenge operations in direct response to specific events in Lebanon that were of strate-gic importance to Hizbollah. The foremost of these was the assassination of its former Secretary General, Abbas al-Mussawi. On 16 February 1992, Al-Mussawi was assassinated, along with his wife and son, by an IDF Apache gunship that opened fire at his car. Qassem wrote that 'in response to the assassination attack the Islamic resistance fired several Katyusha rockets for the very first time' at northern Israel.[42] However, on 17 March, precisely a month and a day after the assassination, a suicide bomber devastated the Israeli Embassy in Buenos Aires, killing 29 and wounding scores of others.

A second strategic attack on 18 July 1994, destroyed the Jewish Community Centre (AMIA) building in Buenos Aires, leaving 85 dead and hundreds wounded. This explosion came just six weeks after 50 Hizbollah cadets were killed in an Israeli air strike in Lebanon. Israel's intelligence serv-ice conducted an inquiry lasting over eight years into these events, and was able to describe in detail how both attacks were carried out by Hizbollah with the guidance and logistical support of Iran. Ibrahim Hussein Birru was a Hizbollah operative who arrived in Argentina a few days ahead of the 1994 attack. A few hours before the explosion, he placed a 'farewell' phone call to his family in Lebanon, during which (according to Israel's investigation) he assured his family that he was soon 'to be reunited' with his brother, who in 1989 had detonated a car bomb targeting Israeli soldiers in South Lebanon.[43]

The two attacks, conducted outside of the familiar 'natural' arena, hardened the balance of terror against Israel. Hizbollah had no need at all to claim official credit, since its deeds were more than enough to deter Israel from further eliminating leading Hizbollah figures. Israeli officials later confirmed this as well, albeit mainly in closed conversations. Thus, the periodic decision to refrain from going after high-value Hizbollah targets derived not from an absence of intelligence, but from the risk of retaliations à la Buenos Aires. It seems likely that Hizbollah had also planned a strategic attack in retribution for Israel's 'Grapes of Wrath' offensive. At the outbreak of the campaign, Nasrallah referred to Israel's out-of-the ordinary bombing of southern Beirut, which he understood to be an attempt 'to place Beirut and its suburbs into an equation that aims to bring security to Kiryat Shmonah', adding:

> I want to be very clear: the response to today's attack of Beirut's suburb will not take place in northern Palestine. What happened today in Beirut's southern suburb has nothing to do with Kiryat Shmonah or with north Palestine. The reply will come elsewhere, at any other place.[44]

The day after Nasrallah's statement, on 12 April 1996, a powerful explosion occurred at the Hotel Lawrence in East Jerusalem. A Lebanese citizen, Hussein Miqdad, who had entered Israel a few days earlier with a false British passport, was critically wounded while constructing an explosive device which he had managed to smuggle into the country. Miqdad was returned to Lebanon at the request of Hizbollah as part of a prisoner exchange in June 1998. The balance of terror reigned for more than a decade – to be precise, until February 2008, when Israel was accused of the assassination in Damascus of Hizbollah mastermind Imad Mugniyeh. This too was an action which Israel had avoided over many years, not for a lack of actionable intelligence, but rather out of concern for the possible repercussions.

In the wake of this assassination, Hizbollah promised to avenge Mugniyeh's death outside the customary boundaries of the conflict. At the funeral, Nasrallah stated,

> The Zionists murdered Hajj Imad beyond the natural borders of the struggle . . . the conflict between us and them has always remained on the soil of Lebanon . . . you have now crossed the line. If it is an open war you want, then you shall have an open war.[45]

In the aftermath of the IDF withdrawal from Lebanon

On 24 May 2000, Israel pulled out of South Lebanon after 18 years of IDF presence in the Security Zone, fulfilling a public campaign promise of the then Prime Minister Ehud Barak, who had committed to bring the troops home within one year if elected.

The withdrawal took place against the backdrop of the collapse of the Syrian–Israeli peace talks. This rendered Israel's pullout a unilateral move rather than one linked in some way to a wider framework of agreement. The withdrawal was, thus, not the result of a political understanding with any Lebanese interlocutor, since in the absence of a parallel deal with Syria, Beirut was unwilling and unable to entertain contact or coordination with Israel. Lebanon equally refused to participate in drawing its own international border with Israel. In lieu of such cooperation the UN decided to delineate a dividing line – the Blue Line – relying on earlier maps of Lebanon and Palestine dating from the period of the British and French mandates.

Unsurprisingly, Hizbollah presented Israel's hasty retreat as an unmitigated victory. With the retreat completed, 25 May has been celebrated as an annual national holiday, but Hizbollah found itself facing the most significant challenge in its history. Suddenly the armed organisation had had the rug pulled out from under its core *raison d'être*: its 'resistance' to the Israeli forces in South Lebanon. The first pressing issue for Hizbollah in the new millennium was to recover its own justification. This was quickly accomplished by identifying a contentious patch of land at the eastern end of the Israel–Lebanon border which abuts the Syrian border as well. This area, known as the Shebaa Farms, was determined by the UN to be Syrian, and Israel was, therefore, under no obligation to evacuate it in the context of Security Council Resolution 425, which referred solely to Lebanon.

Lebanon, prodded by Syria, obliged Damascus by proclaiming the Farms an unresolved territorial dispute – thus justifying ongoing 'resistance' activity by Hizbollah, at least within this specific zone. Four months after the withdrawal, on 6 October 2000, Hizbollah renewed its military activity by capturing three Israeli soldiers in the Shebaa Farms. Hizbollah's rationale was that as long as the Lebanese Government continued to regard the area as 'occupied territory', it would fight for its liberation. Thus, Hizbollah renewed its overt military activity against Israel by latching on to the two outstanding issues which could enable it to address public opinion and claim legitimacy for continuing its 'resistance'. One was the demand for Israeli withdrawal from the Shebaa Farms; the second was the demand for the return of dozens of Lebanese citizens being detained in Israel, as well as the bodies of hundreds of Lebanese killed over the years in South Lebanon. At the unofficial level, Hizbollah began channelling significant energies and resources into efforts to assist the Palestinians in the widespread clashes with Israel which began at the end of September 2000.[46]

In the months and years ahead, Hizbollah would support several Palestinian factions by means of arms shipments and training, and also with additional help which included the infiltration of Hizbollah explosives experts into the West Bank. Nevertheless, Hizbollah's continuing military stance against Israel was meeting with far less support and approval than it had been accustomed to in the past. For the first time, its very existence as a paramilitary organisation quite distinct from the state was becoming an issue for animated public debate. Hizbollah aroused considerable anxiety among its opponents who frequently called into question the organisation's fundamental allegiance to national interests, suggesting that its true priorities overlapped more with the interests of its Syrian and Iranian patrons than with the welfare of Lebanon.

Hizbollah's military operations in the six years between the Israeli withdrawal in 2000 and the outbreak of the Second Lebanon War in 2006 may be separated into two periods. The first, from the Israeli withdrawal to the end of 2002, saw Hizbollah regularly initiate attacks on the Shebaa Farms every few weeks. These resulted in the exchange of limited blows and on two occasions also Israeli attacks against Syrian military targets in Lebanon. In late March 2002, Hizbollah launched two weeks of daily shelling along the Shebaa Farms in response to Defensive Shield, the IDF operation that dealt a lethal blow to Palestinian militant organisations in the West Bank. In April 2002, the organisation announced it would respect the Blue Line with the exception of the Shebaa Farms and that Hizbollah would refrain from targeting Israeli citizens if Israel were to refrain from targeting Lebanese civilians too. Hizbollah sources had said that in spite of the organisation's reservations concerning the Blue Line, 'Hizbollah and the resistance would not touch the Blue Line'.[47]

During the second period, from late 2002 to the outbreak of the war in July of 2006, Hizbollah tailored its military and political activity to regional strategic changes that included several geo-strategic 'tremors': starting with the overthrowing of the Iraqi regime in 2003; continuing with the assassination of former Lebanese Prime Minister Rafiq al-Hariri in February 2005 and culminating with the subsequent withdrawal of Syrian forces from Lebanon in May that year, when nearly three decades of absolute Syrian hegemony over Lebanon came to an end. Each one of these events forced Hizbollah to recalculate its moves.

Generally, Hizbollah advanced its process of *Intifah*, opening up to the Lebanese political arena the more the US accelerated preparations for its invasion of Iraq. From October 2002 onward, hardly a day went by without the Lebanese press reporting meetings held by Hizbollah leaders with all Lebanese political factors, including those opposing the Syrian presence. Prior to this, press coverage of Hizbollah had been dedicated nearly exclusively to its military activity against Israel. Parallel to the increase in political involvement, Hizbollah's military activity gradually decreased to the point where months would go by at a time without disruption of the calm along the

Israel–Lebanon border. Hizbollah described its modus operandi at the time as consisting of periodic 'reminder operations' in the Shebaa Farms,[48] retaliations for Israeli violations of Lebanese sovereignty and mostly as deterring Israel from attacking Lebanon.

In 1999, the last year of Israel's presence in South Lebanon, Hizbollah carried out no less than 1,528 military operations throughout South Lebanon.[49] But in all the six years that separated Israel's withdrawal and the outbreak of the 2006 war, Hizbollah initiated no more than a few dozen such operations. The Syrian withdrawal from Lebanon following its being accused of assassinating Rafiq al-Hariri was a defining event in Lebanon. So long as Damascus enjoyed near-total hegemony over Lebanon, Hizbollah too enjoyed near-untouchable status and the extent of its opponents' criticism had clear limits. Al-Hariri's death and the subsequent Syrian withdrawal from Lebanon created an entirely different political atmosphere in the country. Feeling perhaps on the defensive, Hizbollah entered government for the first time on 19 July 2005 when two of its members accepted ministerial posts in the cabinet.

At the same time, Hizbollah began marketing the organisation's military might as a force indispensable to the defence of Lebanon. In March 2005, Nasrallah explained that Lebanon was in need of a forceful deterrent against Israel. Israel was capable of destroying the Lebanese army 'within three to four hours', he said, therefore, Lebanon should not dismiss the 'resistance'.[50] And for the first time, the organisation had begun suggesting it might be willing to integrate with Lebanon's regular army.[51] During 2005, Hizbollah started advocating the need for a 'national defence strategy' to be reached through dialogue among the various political factions in Lebanon. Hizbollah had proposed a strategy based mostly on cooperation between the organisation and the Lebanese army and utilizing its advantages as a capable guerrilla force poised to confront a classic army.

Hizbollah stretches the rules of the game

Gradual progress as a principle is a key characteristic of Hizbollah's mode of operation, whether vis-à-vis the domestic arena, or the military arena against Israel. Advancing by degrees, Hizbollah has always thoughtfully prepared Lebanese public opinion as well as that of the Israeli adversary, by tailoring its rhetoric as well as by slowly escalating its actions. Typically, the organisation avoids operating 'out of the blue'. For example, in the period before the abduction of three IDF soldiers in October 2000, Nasrallah was careful to incrementally escalate the tone of his public comments concerning Israel.[52]

This pattern repeated itself prior to the 12 July 2006 abduction. In the months leading up to this event, Nasrallah's remarks against Israel grew ever more radical as he declared that the organisation would take action to release Samir al-Quntar, a terrorist serving a life sentence in Israel after infiltrating from Lebanon and killing, among others, an Israeli citizen and his little daughter. Nasrallah left little room for doubt. On 24 April 2006, Hizbollah held an event marking the 28th anniversary of al-Quntar's capture and opened his speech with the declaration that Al-Quntar would be released from jail 'very soon'.[53] Even before, Hizbollah had begun to 'stretch the rules of the game' in late 2005 both directly and by employing indirect, anonymous proxies. On 21 November 2005, Hizbollah attempted an abduction in the Alawite village of Ghajar, which had remained a vulnerable point after Israel's withdrawal from Lebanon.[54] This attempted kidnapping, the first of five, failed.[55] The fifth attempt, which succeeded, sparked the war.

Undoubtedly the attempt at Ghajar marked an unmistakable step up in the daring of Hizbollah, which had also fired rockets and mortars at Israeli communities. For the first time it deployed its advanced anti-tank weapons, which it would later use widely during the war.[56] This unusual escalation caused Israeli authorities to call its northern residents into bomb shelters for the first time since the 2000 withdrawal. But Israel had conveyed the message that there would be no extraordinary reaction against Hizbollah, since the organisation was seeking the escalation of tensions in the region, and as a senior source in Jerusalem said, 'We must not play into the terrorists' hands'.[57] Israel had chosen to contain the incident and, thus, cooperate with the attempts of Lebanese Premier Fouad Siniora to defuse the tension.[58]

Yet another incident occurred in May 2006 clearly illustrating Hizbollah's policy of testing Israel's patience. This was after the commander of the Islamic *Jihad* in Tyre was killed along with his brother by an explosion in his car. About 48 hours later nine rockets were fired into Israel, with at least five of them hitting an IDF base at Mt. Meron. Hizbollah itself refrained from taking responsibility, which had been claimed – and later retracted – by the Islamic *Jihad*.[59] The IDF base would later be the target of further rocket barrages during the July 2006 war. The next time the calm along the border would be violated would be the 12 July abduction operation itself, when Hizbollah pushed the rules of the game to an unprecedented extreme in the border section, entering Israel's sovereign territory and targeting Israeli communities.

Hizbollah following the war in the summer of 2006

Following the 14 August ceasefire, Hizbollah declared a 'divine victory' with far-reaching strategic implications. But the 33 days of war in July and August of 2006 had left the organisation in a position markedly different from how it had emerged from the previous major rounds of violence in 1993 and 1996. Unlike the earlier outbreaks, in 2006 Israel responded with nearly no restrictions, and was even encouraged by certain Arab countries. Despite the arms shipments it continued to receive from Syria during the course of the war, Hizbollah found itself isolated in the campaign as Israel inflicted tremendous damage to the organisation and to Lebanese infrastructure.

The United Nations Security Council Resolution 1701 prohibited the presence of armed organisations south of the Litani River.[60] It facilitated the deployment of Lebanon's army in the south for the first time in two decades, thus, depriving Hizbollah freedom of manoeuvre in its main area of military operations. Indeed, after the war, the Israeli–Lebanese border enjoyed absolute calm – the longest such period of calm in decades. In an interview several weeks after the end of the war, Naim Qassem was asked about the future of the 'resistance' in light of Resolution 1701 and the new reality it imposed on the organisation. Qassem replied that 'we are in a transitional phase', and that Hizbollah was studying the new reality and would adapt itself to the new situation.[61] Two and a half years later, the Shi'a organisation is still coming to terms with its new arena.

Meanwhile, the idea of resolving the question of Hizbollah's arms within a national defence strategy has gained momentum, particularly since the Second Lebanon War, the results of which Hizbollah took to validate its argument that Lebanon must deal with Israel beyond classic military means. During 2008, Hizbollah began urging Lebanon's political forces 'to hasten a decision on the national defense strategy'.[62] More than ever before, the organisation supported improving the capacity of the Lebanese Army to enable it to assume the role that Hizbollah had sought for itself, namely that of defending Lebanon from Israel. For example, Qassem said in May 2008 that:

> [W]e are willing to negotiate over the role of the resistance, its weapons and all related matters within the framework of national dialogue ... we agree to a defence strategy that will make our national army capable of defending Lebanon and preventing Israel from attacking it. Then the [matter of] weapons shall be resolved as part of the defensive strategy.[63]

In September, Nasrallah urged the national unity government to agree to equip the Lebanese Army with 'whatever will enable it to defend Lebanon's sovereignty and every speck of Lebanese soil'.[64] Two months later, he stated that there was 'no disputing that the army holds the key role in defending Lebanon, in any defense strategy, and that we must have a strong army ... the first thing any defensive force must be equipped with is aerial defense and anti-tank weapons. All the world's armies know this'.[65]

Conclusion

By the beginning of 2009 the internal discussion of Lebanon's proposed defensive strategy had been gathering considerable momentum. Michel Aoun, formerly army commander and now Hizbollah's foremost political ally and confidant, drafted a document which outlined the country's domestic and external threats, and suggested ways of confronting them. Positing that 'Lebanon has decided to confront the lurking dangers', Aoun identified 'Israel and its aspirations towards Lebanon' as the primary external threat. In order to deal with this threat, Aoun's document marketed Hizbollah's military capabilities, as demonstrated in the 2006 war, as vital for the deterrence of Israel, and proposed turning Lebanon into 'a resisting society'. Aoun went on to note that:

> [D]eterrence would be founded on two forces: the first is the regular army, whereas the second is the resistance, both of whom would be capable of inflicting losses on the enemy, beyond its ability to sustain. They would do so by adhering to methods of fighting based on small units able to disguise and protect themselves. Such units would not constitute detectable targets for airplanes.[66]

Another fundamental component in Aoun's defensive strategy was 'a modern air defense system', which was also proposed by Nasrallah himself.[67]

On the other side of the political fault line, the Lebanese Forces party – Hizbollah's main rival – was quick to respond with its own detailed defensive strategy. Presenting their draft, the party's leader and long-time Syrian opponent Samir Ja'ja proposed the 'Swiss strategic model' as one which could be emulated by Lebanon – that is, 'adopting a policy of neutrality in foreign policy'. In other words, the remedy for Lebanon's problems lay, according to Ja'ja, in the country's disengagement from the wider Arab–Israeli conflict as well as the concentration of all matters military in the hands of the 'legitimate military forces'.[68] These two divergent approaches are indicative of the ongoing polarity between the pro- and anti-Syrian political camps in Lebanon – differences that reflect a much deeper ideological contest regarding Lebanon's identity within the region.

In the months ahead, the familiar tensions between competing Arab agendas and aspirations, the unrelenting assertion of Iranian influence and those forces opposing it, all contribute to the hegemonic adrenalin driving the region towards a period of dramatic consequence. The future course of Hizbollah will, as always, be affected by issues beyond – and larger than – itself.

6 Israeli counter-insurgency strategy and the quest for security in the Israeli–Lebanese conflict arena

Sergio Catignani

Introduction

This chapter analyses Israel's counter-insurgency (COIN) strategy vis-à-vis the terrorist and guerrilla threats originating in south Lebanon from the late 1970s to 2000. It initially gives a brief overview of Israel's traditional counter-terrorist/counter-insurgency strategy evolved first against the Palestinian Liberation Organisation (PLO) – the period in which Palestinian terrorist and guerrilla activity began to become an important source of threat to Israel's northern border – before exploring in more detail its evolution against the Shi'a Hizbollah's insurgency campaign from the mid-1980s onwards. Whilst touching briefly upon other foreign actors – namely Syria and Iran – as well as the Lebanese ethno-religious cleavages – principally between the Christian and Muslim groups – that have defined Israeli–Lebanese relations, this chapter will focus on how Israel employed its military forces against the threats emanating from southern Lebanon. In doing so, this chapter provides a critical assessment as to the effectiveness of Israel's counter-terrorist and counter-guerrilla strategies in combating anti-Israel groups – most notably Hizbollah during almost three decades of conflict in Lebanon.

Israeli counter-terrorism policy and security measures

Although Israel has dealt with sub-conventional threats to its national security since (and prior to) its establishment in 1948, Israeli deterrence policy has traditionally concentrated on the prevention of full-scale conventional war. This is due to the fact that such warfare could seriously jeopardise not only Israel's basic security, but even its actual existence. In contrast to its deterrent posture vis-à-vis the threat of conventional warfare, Israel's deterrent posture concerning sub-conventional/low-intensity threats has been less clearly devised. David Rodman argues that the 'concept of "massive retaliation" captures best Israel's deterrent posture in the area of unconventional warfare. To deter low-intensity conflict, Jerusalem has consistently promised to retaliate disproportionately against terrorist [and guerrilla] organisations'.[1]

Moreover, since the early 1950s, Israeli counter-terror missions have been characterised by three features. First, they have been chiefly counter-force assaults on terrorist units, bases and critical infrastructure. Second, they have usually inflicted collateral damage given that terrorist bases have been frequently situated in civilian areas. Indeed, whilst Israel has often attempted to circumscribe any collateral damage, it has contended that civilians living close to terrorist infrastructure and who support or endure terrorist operations originating from their area should expect Israeli counter-terror strikes. According to Israeli decision makers, the risk of suffering collateral damage would perhaps reduce the civilian population's desire to provide sanctuary to or collaborate with terrorists. Finally, Israeli counter-terror attacks have generally been conducted in the sovereign territory of a neighbouring Arab state and have been designed to force the target state into withdrawing support for terrorist organisations located within their territory.[2]

By 1967 Israeli counter-terrorist strategy had become firmly entrenched. It was by and large designated as a strategy of retaliation and pre-emption based on deterrence. Counter-terror operations were commonly reactive. Moreover, defensive stratagems were also carried out at quite an early phase of Israel's fight against terror and guerrilla infiltrations. Israel constructed fortified outposts along its borders, positioned minefields all along easily accessible passage routes and buttressed these outposts and minefields with armoured patrols, all in order to stop the Arab terrorist's entrance into Israel. Over the years the Israeli Defence Forces' (IDF) '"perimeter defence system" continually expanded to incorporate such assets as ultra-sophisticated electronic equipment, maritime and airborne reconnaissance, border fences and patrol roads'.[3] This however was to change radically with the election to power of Israel's first Likud coalition government in 1977.

The Likud and the escalation of the Israeli–Lebanese conflict

With the advent in 1977 of the first right-wing government in Israel's history, Israel modified its counter-insurgency/counter-terrorist strategy from a defensive posture of deterrence by reprisal to one of *continuous* offensive and preventive operations. These operations did not remain within the domain of Special Forces units. Increasing numbers, in fact, of regular infantry, armour and artillery units participated in such operations. This change accordingly also led to sporadic large-scale raids by air, sea and land against the growing PLO terrorist and guerrilla infrastructure in south Lebanon, which climaxed in the 1978 Operation 'Litani' invasion and eventually escalated in 1982 into a full-scale three-year war as well as the consequent 18-year occupation of southern Lebanon.

This escalation, as well as the decision to invade Lebanon, was influenced by the fact that Prime Minister Menachem Begin, Defence Minister Ariel

Sharon and the Likud party in general conceived the Israeli–Palestinian conflict in very different terms to previous Israeli left-wing governments. Since
the War of Independence until Likud's 1977 election victory, Israeli governments had consistently underlined the interstate nature of the Arab–Israeli
and, by extension, the Israeli–Palestinian conflict, whilst trying to reduce its
intercommunal aspect. Instead of viewing the Israeli–Palestinian conflict
within the context of a national and interstate dispute, they now perceived the
conflict as an intercommunal and internecine war.

Terrorism (along with other sub-conventional threats) was traditionally
seen as a major security nuisance, rather than as an existential threat to Israel.
These threats, in any case, had to be dealt with determined force, but they did
not warrant the full mobilisation of Israel's economic, political and military
resources as major conventional warfare threats did. Historically-speaking,
Israel *only* initiated a war in the face of an existential threat that came in the
semblance of major conventional warfare. Until Likud came to power, terrorist organisations were generally punished with limited, but not always
proportional, force. With the Likud victory, Israeli security decision makers
began to see the PLO and its violent activities 'for the first time as a strategic
danger and not only as a nuisance terror'.[4]

With Menachem Begin in power and particularly once Ariel Sharon
became Defence Minister in 1981, Israel's traditional security concept
based on a defensive deterrent posture in order to maintain the status quo
was radically changed and fully, if not tragically, operationalised with the
1982 Lebanon War. The modified concept of security that led to the Lebanon
War no longer sought to foil threats to Israel's existence through the use of
defensive means, nor was it based on Israel's self-conception as a *status quo*
state.[5] War was given 'wider scope and transformed into an instrument,
which aided in the realisation of political objectives' that were unrelated to
any notion of deterrence.[6] With Begin and Sharon in power, such political
objectives became increasingly ambitious, particularly in relation to
Lebanon.

Because the Israeli–Palestinian conflict came to be perceived by the Begin
Government in intercommunal dimensions, the use of terrorism by
Palestinian groups came to be seen as not only a physical threat to the state of
Israel, but also as an existential menace against the Jewish community as a
whole. According to Dan Horowitz, viewing the Israeli–Palestinian conflict
in intercommunal terms had obvious military operational implications: 'It
implied a lowering of Israel's threshold of provocation which raises the likelihood of belligerent conflict in the wake of widespread, extended terrorist
activities'.[7] With freedom of movement in the south and with Syrian backing
to its north, Palestinian groups increased their cross-border terrorist activities, which peaked in early 1978. Due to the fact that the Begin government
deemed such attacks increasingly as an existential threat it was only a matter
of time before it would decide to escalate the conflict in order to unleash the
IDF against PLO forces in Lebanon.

Operation 'Litani'

On 11 March 1978, a *Fatah* terrorist unit, employing inflatable rafts, landed ashore in Israel, shot several Israeli beachgoers and hijacked a bus on the Haifa–Tel Aviv highway. In the resulting shootout with Israeli security forces near Tel Aviv, around 35 passengers on the bus as well as nine of the 11 terrorists were killed. On 14 March, Israel sent a 25,000-strong IDF armour/mechanised task force into south Lebanon with the declared intent of flushing terrorists from the border area and of creating a 10 km buffer zone. As with the subsequent invasion of Lebanon in 1982, the IDF did not cease its advance until it had taken most of the territory in Lebanon south of the Litani River. Hence, the name given to the IDF's limited invasion was Operation 'Litani'.

Israel's unwieldy invasion gave the PLO and other Palestinian units enough time to retreat behind Syrian lines and, thus, not much damage was meted out against them. Israel's incursion, which progressed gingerly and behind heavy artillery and air support, furthermore, led to hundreds of Lebanese civilian casualties, extensive collateral damage and over 250,000 refugees.[8] Within days the United Nations Security Council passed two resolutions as a result of Operation 'Litani': 1) Resolution 425 called on Israel to withdraw from all Lebanese territory and; 2) Resolution 426 established the United Nations Interim Force in Lebanon (UNIFIL), a peacekeeping force that was tasked with the job of confirming the withdrawal of Israeli forces from Lebanon, restoring international peace and security and assisting the government of Lebanon in guaranteeing the return of its effective authority in south Lebanon.[9]

None of these goals were achieved, principally due to UNIFIL's inability to fully deploy in south Lebanon as a result of Israel's decision to create a buffer zone there under the control of the Christian-Maronite Free Lebanon Army. UNIFIL was also not able to guarantee the re-establishment of the Lebanese government in south Lebanon because of the fact that the ongoing civil war and continual Syrian manipulation of intra-Lebanese politics left the Lebanese central 'government' even more powerless in its feeble attempts to reassert its authority in the south. Finally, UNIFIL was also incapable of re-establishing peace and security in south Lebanon given that all major and proxy players involved in the cross-border conflict discovered very quickly that UNIFIL's peace-keeping mandate could be easily flouted.

Mounting US and international pressure led Israel to eventually redeploy from south Lebanon, but not on the UN Security Council resolution's terms. As stated earlier, when Israel withdrew from Lebanon it turned over control of the border area to Sa'ad Haddad's Free Lebanon Army. This decision was taken as a result of Israel's lack of confidence in UNIFIL's ability to clamp down on Palestinian terrorist and guerrilla activity. Such activity, despite the deployment of Haddad's Free Lebanon Army in south Lebanon, did not decrease. It actually reached its apex in the summer of 1981, when 33 settlements in northern Israel were bombarded contemporaneously by Russian *Katyusha* missiles for 10 days leading many citizens to flee their homes in the Galilee.[10] Palestinian attacks and Israeli reprisal operations quickly escalated. Consequently, in July 1981 US Ambassador Philip Habib was sent by the Reagan Administration to negotiate a ceasefire between Israel and Lebanon. A ceasefire agreement was reached by the end of the month. Whilst the ceasefire restrictions applied to cross-border operations originating from either country, they did not apply to Palestinian or Lebanese actions taken against Israel's Maronite clients within Lebanon itself or to operations carried out against Israel on other fronts. A second major round of hostilities was bound to happen given that further terrorist attacks would easily goad Israel into retaliating, probably in a disproportionate manner, as would occur the subsequent year.

The 1982 Lebanon War

Growing frustration with the IDF's inability to curb PLO terrorist attacks led the Begin government to consider escalating the conflict in order to mete out a deadly blow to the PLO terrorist infrastructure in Lebanon. Preparations for an Israeli invasion of Lebanon, which were taking place as early as the summer of 1981, were substantial and, hence, difficult to conceal. On several occasions Israeli Prime Minister Begin and other members of his government had to provide reassurances to the Reagan Administration that Israel would not attack Lebanon unless provoked.

By April 1982, the IDF was ready to invade Lebanon. Yet, Israel required a clear provocation in order to initiate such an invasion. As the PLO was virtually abiding by the Habib ceasefire (at least in relation to cross-border attacks until early 1982), Israel had to conjure up such a provocation. Consequently, on 9 May, Israel targeted Palestinian bases in Lebanon. The PLO struck back with artillery fire against Kiryat Shmonah and, thus, the ceasefire quickly collapsed. However, this brief exchange was still deemed insufficient to warrant a full-scale Israeli invasion. The provocation that Sharon and Begin so earnestly sought out came in the guise of a failed assassination attempt on Israeli Ambassador to Britain, Shlomo Argov. Ironically the assassination was conducted by the Abu Nidal terrorist group, a bitter opponent of Yasser Arafat's PLO. Yet, Israel accused the PLO of carrying out the attack and the following day launched large-scale air raids on PLO camps in Lebanon. Three days after the assassination attempt, on 6 June, Israel launched a massive ground invasion that was to seal its calamitous fate and permanence in Lebanon for the subsequent 18 years.

Whilst Israel conducted effective military operations when confronted by Syrian air and ground forces in the Beqaa Valley during the initial phase of its invasion,[11] the cumbersome and slow advance of IDF units, which had to deal with the difficult and jagged terrain, prevented the IDF from capturing and/or killing smaller and lighter PLO units. These were able to disperse amongst the rural terrain or the civilian populated areas. Although the specific operational developments of the Lebanon War go beyond the scope of this chapter, one can concur with Zvi Lanir's overall assessment of the IDF's performance during its major combat operations, which were characterised:

> by an excess of force and overwhelming superiority in firepower. The enemy was to a certain extent outgunned rather than outmanoeuvred, pounded into submission instead of being outflanked, crushed by siege instead of being overwhelmed by a war of movement.[12]

The official aim of Israel's invasion of Lebanon, dubbed Operation 'Peace for Galilee', 'was to remove [Palestinian] terrorists from firing range of the northern border, approximately twenty-five miles'.[13] However, the war's real and much more ambitious goals were the following:

> To strike hard at the PLO militarily and politically and thereby enable dictation of the Israeli autonomy plan on the West Bank, to wipe out the Syrian stronghold in Lebanon [. . .], to change the balance of interethnic power in Lebanon [. . .], and bring about a peace treaty ensuring Israel's hegemonic status in Lebanon.[14]

Instead of just aiming to flush out Palestinian units from south Lebanon up to the Litani River (as had been attempted in the 1978 'Litani' Operation), Defence Minister Ariel Sharon and Prime Minister Menachem Begin saw the Lebanon War as a major opportunity for establishing an Israeli-friendly government in Lebanon that would improve Israel's security in its northern areas, as well as for dismantling completely the PLO's Lebanese political and military infrastructure, which had continued to grow since the early 1970s. By defeating the PLO, Begin and Sharon hoped to eradicate once and for all militant Palestinian nationalist self-determination, thus, allowing their government to impose very limited autonomy arrangements on the Palestinian population residing in the Occupied Territories of the West Bank and Gaza Strip which were deemed as more benign and, thus, more malleable to Israeli diktats regarding its future political status.[15]

In short, by using military force to achieve major political ends Israel had shed the security establishment's traditional conception of what the use of the military instrument could achieve: mainly the maintenance of the status quo through deterrence or through the use of quick and decisive military force the re-establishment of the status quo ante.

The war in Lebanon, which was perceived as a 'war of choice' – as opposed to previous wars of 'no choice' when Israel was required to fight under the perception that its existence was under existential threat – and, thus, entailed a 'preventative campaign' was judged as 'morally and legitimately questionable within the IDF tradition'.[16] The lack of a national consensus regarding the legitimacy of this preventative and discretionary war, as well as the moral dilemmas that IDF units faced when operating in densely populated civilian areas brought about the rise of conscientious objection within the IDF (an heretofore rare phenomenon), demoralisation, instances of dehumanizing behaviour and a general lack of national consensus on how the war should be prosecuted and, more importantly, on how it should be terminated. Already by 1985, senior officers within the IDF were warning Israel's political leadership echelons and Israeli public in general about the detrimental effects that the occupation was having on the moral fibre, but also on the operational readiness of forces operating within Lebanon. Maj.-Gen. Menachem Einan, then chief of the IDF planning branch, had stated that 'the continuous friction with the local population had a "degrading effect" on Israeli soldiers'.[17]

Agitating the *Shi'a* hornet's nest

Ironically, the major Israeli challenge in controlling Lebanon after its 1982 invasion was not actually contending with the remnants of the PLO fighters. Contending with new ethno-religious groups that were endangered more by the Israeli–Christian alliance than by the Palestinians became Israel's main preoccupation instead. During the initial phases of the invasion Israel, for example, faced major challenges in the area of the Chouf Mountains area where it found itself enmeshed in the middle of a struggle between local Muslim and Druze militias. Following Israel's withdrawal to the Awali River in 1983, its main challenge emerged in the form of the newly established Shi'a organisation, Hizbollah (Party of God).[18]

As opposed to the secular Shi'a Amal movement – which by the late 1980s had reduced the intensity of most of its anti-Israel military operations – Hizbollah was founded on the Iranian revolutionary principles of Ayatollah Khomeini. Its primary goals were to expel Israel and other foreign militaries from Lebanon, to protect its communities from ethno-religious reprisals and ultimately bring about Islamic rule in Lebanon. Established in 1983, Hizbollah's military wing, the *al-Muqawama* or 'Islamic Resistance' comprising around 300 core fighters with a reserve of around 5,000 armed sympathisers, began operating against Israeli and allied Christian units with substantial military and economic support from Iran. Henceforth, Iran would become another major foreign power involved in the ongoing Israeli–Lebanese conflict, thus, complicating even further the Israeli–Lebanese strategic equation.

Although initially alarmed at Iran's support for such an Islamic fundamentalist organisation, Syria came to view Hizbollah by the late 1980s as a valid proxy combatant against Israeli strategic aims regarding Lebanon.[19] Syria, in fact, came to increasingly support Hizbollah attacks against Israel, as long as its own strategic interests vis-à-vis Israel and Lebanon were not jeopardised by them. With direct support from Iran and with the passive connivance of Syria, Iran would be able to provide the Islamic Resistance with substantial guerrilla tactics training as well as sophisticated weaponry such as 'BM-21 rocket-launchers and AT-3 guided missiles . . . SAM-7 anti-aircraft [and] . . . Stinger' missiles.[20] By the late 1980s, these and other weapons, such as the lethal roadside explosive devices, would increasingly be used by Hizbollah combat units to conduct ever more elaborate ambush attacks and assaults on IDF and South Lebanon Army (see later) combat patrols and outposts throughout the security zone.

These developments were rather unfortunate for Israel as during the initial stages of its invasion Israel could have potentially won over the Shi'a community. Despite Shi'a–Palestinian enmity since the mid-1970s, Israel had neither identified nor rewarded the Shi'a as possible allies against the PLO, taking continued Shi'a passivity for granted.[21] Whereas the southern Shi'a population had originally greeted the Israeli invasion positively and had reached out for help against the Sunni-dominated PLO, by 1982, the Shi'a had turned against the Israelis, who became increasingly viewed as oppressive occupiers. This view was reinforced by the various actions Israel undertook in order to consolidate its bureaucratic and security hold over the territories under its control, but particularly in the trouble spots of south Lebanon following its redeployment to the security zone in 1985. Israel's inability to co-opt the Shi'a community into fighting the PLO initially and its subsequent inability to adopt a more nuanced counter-terrorist/counter-insurgency approach to the growing Hizbollah threat, in order to nip its activities in the bud, resulted in major missed opportunities that were to prove very costly to Israel in the long run. As Clive Jones noted, 'Israel's approach to the problem of *Hizb'allah* in south Lebanon from 1985 onwards was pre-ordained, with set assumptions regarding the various communities with counter-insurgency methods biased towards offensive operations'.[22] Thus, despite Israel's change and variation in counter-terrorist/counter-insurgency tactics employed against Hizbollah from the mid-1980s onwards, Israel for the most part returned to operate according to its pre-Likud era counter-terrorist/counter-guerrilla strategy of deterrence by massive retaliation, thus, achieving nothing more than the maintenance of the status quo (i.e., continued occupation and the continuation of the Israeli–Lebanese war of attrition), rather than Hizbollah's defeat or the achievement of a comprehensive political settlement with Lebanon.

Soon after their redeployment to south Lebanon the Israelis, in fact, commenced extensive road-building works, the imposition of Hebrew road signs, 'a postal service between the south and Israel, and linked Lebanese telephones near the Israeli border into the Israeli system'.[23] The IDF, with the South Lebanon Army's assistance, also increased the number of (indiscriminate) cordon and sweep operations amongst the various villages and towns scattered around south Lebanon often causing collateral damage, the arrest of innocent civilians, and the theft of personal belongings. The destruction of homes as a punitive measure for those suspected of abetting terrorist-guerrilla fighters, the imposition of long curfews and arbitrary economic blockades and the periodic cut-off of electricity and water provision on local and, increasingly Shi'a, communities could not but alienate and drive them to take up arms against the Israeli occupation.[24] As a reaction to such Israeli measures, Hizbollah initially operated through the use of devastating suicide bombings, which also targeted the growing presence of the multinational peace-keeping contingent in Lebanon.

In November 1982, for example, a Hizbollah suicide bomber targeted an IDF headquarters building in Tyre, killing 75 IDF soldiers. On October 1983, Hizbollah targeted the US and French peace-keeping contingents stationed at Beirut International Airport with two massive suicide bombings leading to the killing of 241 American servicemen (220 Marines, 18 Navy personnel and three Army soldiers) and 58 French paratroopers. This attack eventually led the US to withdraw its forces from Lebanon by February 1984. In 1983, a second Shi'a suicide bomber struck the IDF/*Shin Bet* (Israeli General Security Service) headquarters near Tyre. This attack led to a much stronger Israeli retaliation than had occurred after the November 1982 attack.[25] Within hours of the attack on the Tyre headquarters, the Israeli Air Force (IAF) attacked the areas of Mansouriye and Bhamdoun near the Beirut–Damascus highway that were suspected of hosting Syrian-backed terrorist elements. According to Lebanese reports 69 people were killed and 120 wounded; of these, three were officers and 19 soldiers of the Syrian army.[26] The routine of conducting reprisal, if not punitive, air strikes was to become even more common during Israel's occupation of south Lebanon as shall be seen further on.

The cost of maintaining its forces throughout Lebanon, which increasingly became targets of opportunity for,[27] amongst others, Amal, Hizbollah and the remaining PLO units, led Israel to re-evaluate its deployment in Lebanon and eventually to seek, also as a result of US pressure, a peaceful resolution with the Lebanese government it had helped institute under the leadership of Israel's principal Christian-Maronite ally and president-elect Bashir Gemayel. Negotiations between Israel and Lebanon resulted in a peace treaty on 17 May 1983 between the two states. However, Israel was not able to enjoy the benefits of its initial victory given that Bashir Gemayel was assassinated on 14 September by Syrian intelligence. His brother and successor Amin Gemayel, under Syrian pressure, compelled the Lebanese government to eventually abrogate the treaty. Israel's failure to obtain a peace agreement with Lebanon ended its dream of establishing a new political order in Lebanon whereby a friendly Christian-led government would guarantee the safety of Israel's northern communities.

Thus, the only major achievement Israel could console itself with was its success – following the destructive siege of Beirut during the summer of 1982 – in getting the PLO leadership exiled to Tunis and other Arab capitals, following a US-brokered ceasefire that had come into effect on 18 August. This agreement also led to the deployment of 350 French Paratroopers, 800 US Marines and additional peacekeepers that would supervise the withdrawal of the PLO from Beirut. Despite this limited achievement, the effects of Israel's siege of Beirut, had brought about not only a major humanitarian crisis amongst the local civilian population, but had also begun to raise significant ethical concerns amongst IDF personnel, who could not understand the logic behind such (medieval) methods of warfare.

Armour brigade commander Colonel Eli Geva, for example, refused to fire in his sector in Beirut during the IDF's siege of Beirut given his concern for the potential civilian casualties that would result from such an attack. Following repeated orders and attempts by his senior commanders to convince him to follow orders, Colonel Geva was relieved of his command. Whilst there were no other cases of conscientious objection that occurred at such a high rank, by the end of the war almost 200 IDF personnel were tried and imprisoned for their refusal to serve in Lebanon. More importantly, many reservists following their return from military service in Lebanon began to mobilise and coalesce into protest movements – such as *Yesh Gvul* ('There is a limit' or 'there is a border') – against the Lebanon War and subsequent occupation. Such controversial protests served only to complicate Israel's continued deployment in Lebanon.

They became even more vociferous after the massacre of Palestinian civilians in the refugee camps of Sabra and Shatila on the southern outskirts of Beirut. On 16 September 1982 Christian Phalangist militiamen had entered the camps and in a killing spree lasting for 48 hours murdered over 800 Palestinians ostensibly in retaliation for the assassination of Lebanese President-elect Bashir Gemayel two days previously. Whilst ethnic cleansing and acts of revenge were not new to Lebanon's fractious confessional order, the fact that IDF units guarded the outskirts of the refugee camps during the massacre and indeed, had provided illumination shells to light the camp up at night implicated them directly in the events surrounding the massacre. In turn, Israel faced severe international condemnation for its role in the events surrounding the bloody massacre at Sabra and Shatila, condemnation that only served to fuel the ire of those Israelis who believed that the cost of the war – moral, political and economic – could no longer justify Israel's continued presence in Lebanon.[28]

The south Lebanon 'security zone'

Due to this debacle and the growing costs of the invasion, Israel tried to quickly untangle itself from its imbroglio in Lebanon. Two alternatives were debated by Prime Minister Shimon Peres' national unity government, formed by the Centre-Left Ma'arakh (Labour alignment) and Right-wing Likud parties. The first alternative was a total unilateral withdrawal from Lebanon; the other was the creation of a 'security zone' controlled by the IDF and the South Lebanon Army (SLA), a revamped and renamed version of Haddad's original Free Lebanon Army, which since 1984 had come under the command of Gen. Antoine Lahad. Likud Cabinet ministers Yitzhak Shamir, Moshe Arens and Ariel Sharon believed that only by retaining an Israeli presence in south Lebanon could Israel prevent it from becoming a training ground and launching pad for anti-Israel military activities again. They deemed that an 'an "insulation layer" between Israel and the non-Christian population of Lebanon would deny terrorist groups access to the border and would reduce the threat of artillery fire against targets in Israel'.[29]

Again, Israel's decision to maintain a buffer zone whereby its Christian ally, the South Lebanon Army (SLA) would take care of remaining Palestinian and growing Shi'a terrorist-guerrilla activity was predicated on its belief that both UNIFIL and, more importantly, the Lebanese government were incapable of doing this. Even prior to the 1982 Lebanon invasion Defence Minister Ariel Sharon had set out the rationale for maintaining a cushion in south Lebanon by stating that 'we have to establish a buffer zone in Lebanon as it is clear that the Lebanese government will do nothing to stop terrorism'.[30] The advocates of the 'security zone' got their way and on 14 January 1985 Defence Minister Yitzhak Rabin announced the IDF's redeployment to southern Lebanon, which occurred by June 1985.

Following the establishment of the 'security zone', around 2,500 SLA soldiers, mostly comprising Christian officers, but also many Shi'a recruits, were deployed along a network of hilltop compounds running parallel to the Israeli border. These compounds contained platoon to company-sized units supplied with, amongst other things, machine guns, heavy mortars and ground surveillance equipment. This network of SLA outposts were, furthermore, supported by 1,000 IDF soldiers who could call upon IDF artillery fire and air support from units stationed just across the border when needed. Although the SLA was tasked with guarding the security zone it quickly became apparent that the IDF would have to carry out the more challenging operations such as ambush patrols vis-à-vis the increasingly more effective Hizbollah guerrilla units.[31] Whilst Israel was intent on targeting Hizbollah in order to wear down its military capabilities, it also tried to intimidate the local population into impeding its support of its activities through the threat of punitive measures. IDF retaliatory strikes that could cause collateral damage were seen, rather erroneously, as a way of deterring the local population from harbouring Hizbollah fighters. According to then government coordinator for activities in Lebanon Uri Lubrani, 'They [i.e. Hizbollah] are not winning [the] hearts and minds of local people by exposing them to [Israeli] retaliatory attacks'.[32] Such measures together with Hizbollah's 'hearts and minds' strategy, though, had the opposite effect in that a growing portion of the Lebanese population began to sympathise with its anti-occupation activities. IDF/SLA retaliatory attacks, in fact, galvanised rather than deterred the local Shi'a population.

With the help of Iranian funding Hizbollah could provide through its *Jihad al-Bina* ('Holy Struggle for Reconstruction') extensive social services (e.g. medical care, primary and secondary education and cultural activities) and public utilities (e.g. sewage services, gas and electricity provision, etc.), which the Lebanese central government was unable to provide.[33] Families bereaved by the conflict (including those related to Hizbollah fighters) received pensions.[34] The provision of such services, the ability to quickly reconstruct what the IDF and SLA would destroy through their military operations, and Hizbollah's radio, *Al Manar* TV (and eventually internet) propaganda machine played a crucial part in winning the hearts and minds of the local Shi'a population. In other words, the more the IDF and SLA sought out to punish Hizbollah and its supporters and the more collateral damage and civilian casualties were instigated, the greater support Hizbollah received from the population due to its reconstruction, aid and welfare activities and ability to air the perceived injustices and real damage suffered by the Lebanese at the hands of Israel and its allies.[35]

Besides providing support on the ground, the Shi'a population began to express its support for Hizbollah also through the ballot box. In 1992 Hizbollah, in fact, participated in Lebanon's first parliamentary elections following the end of the Lebanon civil war. By participating in subsequent elections and Lebanese politics in general, Hizbollah was able to further legitimise its nationalist credentials, thus, insuring it against any attempts by other parties to interfere with its military activities. Hizbollah's participation in politics also enabled it to work for a larger redistribution of national resources for the relatively poor Shi'a community. This, as a consequence, reinforced its popularity amongst its Shi'a constituency.[36]

It was hoped that the security zone would improve the security of the northern communities in Israel. Between 1985 and 1992 skirmishes between the IDF/SLA and Hizbollah or Amal forces were rather limited in number and circumscribed mostly to the security zone. For the most part, it did enhance the security of Israel's northern communities during most periods, except when Hizbollah would target northern Israel with heavy rocket barrages usually in retaliation to prior IDF or SLA military operations, which had directly resulted in Lebanese civilian casualties. This was the case in particular during Israel's 1993 'Accountability' and 1996 'Grapes of Wrath' Operations, as we shall see.

Yet, the cost of maintaining the security zone was relatively high in economic, political and military terms.[37] Israel, in fact, had not envisaged remaining for so long in south Lebanon, but redeploying from the area did necessitate certain preconditions which Syria, Iran and their proxy armies were not willing to fulfil. Syria, in fact, acted as the main spoiler against Israel's plans to leave Lebanon on favourable security terms: in sum, the attainment of a peace agreement with Lebanon and the demilitarisation of south Lebanon. As the actor with the most influence over Lebanese politics, since its 1976 intervention and as the main guarantor of peace following the signing of the 1989 Taif Agreement that ended the Lebanon civil war, Syria could easily manipulate Lebanon into frustrating any Israeli attempts at resolving the Israeli–Lebanese conflict. This was effectively done by allowing Hizbollah, which was the only post-civil war militia in Lebanon to overtly maintain arms, to continue its insurgency campaign against Israeli and SLA units.[38]

Given the fact that Israel possessed the strategically valuable Golan Heights captured from Syria during the 1967 Six Day War, Damascus was unwilling to allow Lebanon to make peace with Israel without having first met Syrian demands. For security reasons, Israel wanted to hold onto at least some of the area permanently. Syria, understandably, wanted all of the Golan Heights back. Accordingly, both Syria and Lebanon insisted on a comprehensive resolution with Israel that would result in the return of the Golan to Syria and the withdrawal of Israeli troops from southern Lebanon. Because the main power brokers could not reach a compromise – even during the 1990s peace process interlude – in their supposedly intractable positions, Israel felt that it had no other option, but to remain in south Lebanon in order to guarantee the security of its northern communities.[39] And yet, the more Israel remained in Lebanon the more it paradoxically created the conditions for greater conflict and, ultimately, its insecurity. This time the source of such insecurity came in the guise of the (much deadlier) Shi'a fundamentalist terrorist and guerrilla organisation, Hizbollah. Its capacity to adapt to Israeli counter-measures and its ability to challenge the IDF's military primacy through asymmetric warfare tactics forced Israel to update on an ongoing basis its own counter-terrorist/counter-insurgency approach.

Israeli counter-insurgency in the 1990s

By the early 1990s Israel had developed, in fact, an intricate counter-terrorist/counter-insurgency strategy based on both active and passive defence measures. According to Shmuel Gordon, Israel's counter-guerrilla strategy and operational doctrine in Lebanon consisted of five interrelated elements: 1) passive defence; 2) active defence; 3) offensive operations; 4) deterrence; and 5) negotiation and diplomatic efforts.[40]

'Passive defence' consisted of defensive measures employed to protect Israeli civilians from *Katyusha* and other rocket and heavy mortar attacks. These comprised of advanced fortifications embedded in the security zone- and high-tech security fences with electronic sensor capabilities on the border as well as of hospitals, psychiatric care and civilian services within the target areas in northern Israel. The core of Israel's passive defence measures was the high-tech security fence, which contained various early warning and detection systems in order to block any terrorist/guerrilla infiltration into Israel proper. 'Active defence' consisted of limited operations such as infantry and Special Forces patrols and ambushes, which aimed to 'search and destroy' Hizbollah units within the security zone before they could carry out attacks on Israel or against units stationed within the zone itself. Finally, 'offensive operations' were those operations that entailed IDF units infiltrating areas beyond the security zone and into Hizbollah safe havens. This aspect of Israel's counter-guerrilla strategy was aimed at giving the IDF the operational initiative in order to hopefully put Hizbollah on the defensive. The IAF was often at the heart of such offensive operations given that they usually included air sorties targeting Hizbollah infrastructure, training camps as well as the targeted assassination of important Hizbollah leaders.

Although the main aim of these operations was that of improving Israel's deterrent posture vis-à-vis Israel's state and sub-state enemies involved in the Lebanon quagmire, Israel's retaliatory operations increasingly lost their deterrent effect. Already by the mid-1980s some Israeli officials had come to realise that terrorism originating from Lebanon could not be stopped altogether through the use of the military alone. Then Defence Minister Yitzhak Rabin stated in January 1987 that,

> This is a prolonged war against terrorism from Lebanon. . . . We tried once in 1982 (with the invasion) to bring an end to it by one large action. We didn't succeed. There is no one way to cope with border terrorism . . . as long as there will be no central government that will be in control of all of Lebanon's territory. We have to devise a policy to cope with it. Not to eliminate it. It is impossible to eliminate.[41]

This became especially the case as Hizbollah's operations became more effective and deadly during the 1990s given its ability to adapt to Israeli measures designed to improve the safety of its and the SLA's units in south Lebanon. For example, when the IDF employed a fixed line of SLA defensive outposts, Hizbollah began frontal attacks. When the outposts were reinforced, Hizbollah began employing mortar and missile barrages. By the mid-1990s Hizbollah attacks on IDF/SLA outposts had become very elaborate combined tactical assaults. A typical Hizbollah attack would consist of two squads of around four guerrillas each. The first squad would attack an IDF/SLA outpost at close range with light and heavy machine gunfire, rocket-propelled grenades and advanced anti-tank missiles. The second squad would be located around 5 km away and provide 81 mm or 120 mm mortar fire support. Such attacks would last only a few minutes prior to the guerrillas escaping the area as IDF artillery or helicopter units struck suspected exfiltration routes.[42] When IDF tactics changed to a more mobile force, Hizbollah responded by adopting lethal ambushes as well as roadside bombs.

Guerrilla operations aimed at IDF and SLA units from 1985 were mostly carried out by Hizbollah, which between June 1985 and early 2000, was able to inflict at least 20 deaths per year on the IDF.[43] Accordingly, the IDF's operations became increasingly focused on force-protection measures and, thus, more cautious. Force protection often entailed relying increasingly on stand-off weapons systems such as artillery and air force units. IDF artillery barrages and air bombardments in turn resulted in collateral damage and civilian casualties. Such incidences incited rather than deterred Hizbollah from engaging Israeli units, and often, into retaliating by targeting Israel's northern communities through rocket attacks.

However, with no real political option at hand, Israel was left to 'cope' with Lebanese-based guerrilla and terrorist activity by increasing its military fight against Hizbollah. Attempts to decapitate the leaders of Hizbollah and Amal were also carried out as they were seen as a deterrent measure against further military activity. And yet, with the IDF helicopter missile attacks that killed Hizbollah leader Abbas al-Mussawi, his wife and five-year-old son in February 1992 – they were returning from a memorial rally for another former Hizbollah leader, Sheikh Ragheb Harb, who had been killed eight years before by the IDF – Hizbollah insurgent actions notably escalated. Not only did Hizbollah augment its attacks on IDF/SLA units in south Lebanon, but it also renewed the shelling of Israeli towns in northern Israel. The wave of rockets during the week following Mussawi's assassination was the heaviest and most prolonged against northern Israel since the invasion of Lebanon in June 1982.[44]

Hizbollah also resorted to international terrorist activities. For example, Hizbollah targeted, allegedly with the help of Iranian intelligence, the Israeli embassy in Buenos Aires in March 1992, causing 30 deaths and 253 casualties. It was an attack widely viewed as retaliation for Israel's targeted killing of Sheikh Abbas al-Mussawi a month earlier.[45] Such escalation on all fronts was also due in part to the fact that Mussawi was replaced by an even more radical and pro-Iranian successor, Sheikh Sayyed Hassan Nasrallah. The conditions for escalation had been set. Hizbollah attacks almost trebled between 1992 and 1993 from 63 to 158 incidences.[46] It was only a matter of time before Israel would resort to another major retaliatory campaign in order to try to restore its flagging deterrent posture vis-à-vis Hizbollah.

Operation 'Accountability'

Israel's major retaliatory strike, dubbed Operation 'Accountability' and launched between 25 and 31 July 1993, was instigated as a result of two major attacks on Israeli targets. On 28 June 1993, Hizbollah's *Katyusha* rockets caused civilian casualties in the town of Kiryat Shmonah, and in July, attacks in the south Lebanon Security Zone by Ahmad Jabril's Popular Front for the Liberation of Palestine – General Council Command (PFLP-GC) and Hizbollah killed nine IDF soldiers. Prime Minister Rabin, thus, decided that the IDF needed to carry out a major retaliatory strike in order to discourage further attacks on Israeli targets. Fears of suffering considerable casualties with a ground forces incursion, led the IDF to conduct the operation solely through the use of artillery and air strikes.

The operation's main aim was to obliterate Hizbollah command and training centres, rocket launching positions as well as the homes of Hizbollah commanders. Israel also sought to target Lebanese civilian population areas (including south Beirut) in order to disrupt civilian life and encourage an internal refugee crisis. By carrying out such punitive strikes, Israel hoped to discourage the local population from continuing its support of Hizbollah as well as to pressure the Lebanese government into cracking down on Hizbollah political activities and into disarming its military wing. The IDF bombarded over 30 Shi'a villages, which caused 147 civilian fatalities and the mass evacuation of over 350,000 people towards Beirut.[47] Operation 'Accountability', however, failed outright to achieve any of Israel's stated aims and in effect led the Lebanese government and the population to rally around Hizbollah. It also strengthened Hizbollah's determination to keep on fighting the Israeli occupation. Hizbollah, in fact, retaliated in kind with *Katyusha* rocket barrages, which led to the death of two and the injury of 13 Israeli civilians from Kiryat Shmonah.[48]

As a result of this mutually destructive campaign, Hizbollah and Israel came to a mutual understanding on how to prosecute future combat without involving their respective civilian communities. In negotiations carried out with American and Syrian intermediation, Israel agreed to refrain from future shelling of Shi'a villages in south Lebanon in return for Hizbollah assurances not to fire rockets against northern Israel. Hizbollah's success in limiting Israel's future retaliatory attacks to strictly military targets could be seen as a major achievement for the party. Despite using the cover of local populated areas, Hizbollah managed to present itself as sensitive to the civilian population of Lebanon in a way that contrasted sharply with the often dictatorial behaviour of the PLO when it operated from south Lebanon during the 1970s. Hizbollah, furthermore, was able to use the destruction that Israel had wrought on south Lebanon to its advantage. According to Lebanese newspapers the day after the ceasefire, Hizbollah had begun to repair 'more than 1,000 homes, while 475 had been fully repaired and returned to their owners'.[49]

Clearly, the informal understandings that civilian targets within south Lebanon and north Israel were to be avoided did not mean that other Israeli targets were fair game. The Israeli–Hizbollah understandings did nothing, in fact, to prohibit Hizbollah from targeting IDF/SLA forces within the security zone. This was rather ironic given that attacks on IDF forces in south Lebanon were the primary reason for initiating Operation 'Accountability' in the first place. More crucially, the immediate effect of providing Shi'a (or any other Lebanese) villages immunity from Israeli retaliation was that Hizbollah was able to enlarge and deepen its operational, logistic and intelligence network amongst the civilian population centres dotted throughout south Lebanon. The IDF's job of targeting Hizbollah units and infrastructure consequently became even more difficult given that the cost of supporting Hizbollah activities became almost negligible for the local Lebanese population. Consequently, Hizbollah could operate within populated areas with relative impunity and greater effectiveness. Less than three weeks after the end of Operation 'Accountability', an Islamic Resistance ambush killed nine Israelis within the security zone. Hizbollah attacks, moreover, increased from 187 in 1994 to nearly 350 the following year.[50] Israel did not shy away from retaliating, albeit in a much more constrained manner until Operation 'Grapes of Wrath' in 1996.

Such operational constraints were seen by many in Israel as debilitating the IDF's capacity to employ its forces to their full potential. They were seen as further endangering IDF units that not only had to resort increasingly to pas-sive-defensive measures – thus, making them an even easier target for Hizbollah attacks – but also as weakening the IDF's deterrent posture that could not rely anymore on severe retaliatory attacks following successful Hizbollah operations. Ariel Sharon, for example, argued that:

> The IDF Northern Command forces . . . possess immense power. But they cannot use it, not even in a controlled way. They are bound by the [1993] agreement with Hizbollah which prevents activity in civilian areas. These areas serve the terrorists as launching bases, lookout posts, plan-ning centers. And they provide housing and a haven after their deadly attacks.[51]

The perception within IDF (and SLA) units that they had become 'sitting ducks' subject to the whims of diplomatic and political expediency was bound to have a detrimental effect on the units deployed in south Lebanon. On 30 October 1994, for example, Hizbollah fighters were able to assail an Israeli stronghold in broad daylight, plant their organisation's flag at its entrance and film the whole operation in which IDF units either barely returned fire or shrunk from the attack by taking cover. The soldiers' passiv-ity was attributed to the growing demoralisation of IDF units serving in Lebanon. According to a leading psychologist, under increasing lethal Hizbollah attacks and with the perception of the IDF's withdrawal from Lebanon as imminent, many IDF personnel felt they did not want to be the last soldiers to fall in a war that was about to end given the developments of the post-1992 Madrid Conference and 1993 Oslo Accord peace processes.[52]

Operation 'Grapes of Wrath'

Frustrated with Hizbollah's successful attacks on IDF/SLA units in south Lebanon and with the increasingly lethal Hamas (*Harakat al-Muqawamat al-Islamiyya* – Islamic Resistance Movement) and Islamic *Jihad* suicide terror campaign within Israel, the new Premier, Shimon Peres was determined to portray to his domestic audience that he was serious about Israel's security despite Israel's growing disillusionment with the Oslo peace process. Peres' opportunity to punish Hizbollah for its increasing success came in the spring of 1996.

During March 1996, attacks carried out both by Hizbollah and Amal, resulted in the death of six IDF soldiers, including one officer. The Israeli retaliation came on 30 March in the guise of a large artillery strike on the vil-lage of Yatar, which was suspected of harbouring Hizbollah operatives. The IDF bombardment brought about the death of two civilians. Consequently, Hizbollah replied in kind with *Katyusha* strikes in northern Israel. As the tit-for-tat exchange escalated, the Israeli government decided to sanction an IDF operation, dubbed 'Grapes of Wrath'. The goal of the operation was yet again, to stop Hizbollah's highly disruptive rocket attacks into northern Israel as well as to erode growing popular support for Hizbollah amongst the Lebanese population. The first goal would be achieved by targeting Hizbollah rocket teams and command centres, whilst the second goal would be achieved by pounding Lebanon's civilian infrastructure in order to force the Rafiq Hariri government and the population into turning against Hizbollah.

The opposite, in fact, occurred. During 'Grapes of Wrath', the IDF fired over 20,000 shells from land, sea and air, the Israel Air Force alone conducting 16,000 sorties and attacking 410 targets. Accordingly, 154 Lebanese civilians were killed and another 351 were injured during the campaign.[53] Only 50 Hizbollah fighters were killed during the 16-day operation at a cost of over NIS400 million. Notwithstanding the ferocity of Israel's campaign Hizbollah was still able to fire almost 700 *Katyusha* rockets into the north Galilee region damaging over 1,500 civilian structures.[54] Of the total 639 *Katyusha* rockets fired into Israeli territory during Operation 'Grapes of Wrath', around 28 per cent (81 rockets) were launched on 14 April; the day after an Israeli helicopter gunship attack was carried out on an ambulance in Mansouriye that resulted in the death of six civilians. The day after the attacks in Upper Nabatiyeh (9 civilian deaths) and on the UNIFIL base in Qana (over 100 civilian deaths) on 18 April, Hizbollah fired 90 rockets against Israeli targets.

Thus, instead of deterring Hizbollah *Katyusha* attacks, IDF retaliatory operations actually escalated them.[55] During the campaign, Hizbollah fired an unparalleled 1,100 rockets into the security zone and northern Galilee in retaliation to Israel's air and artillery campaign in Lebanon. Between 1985 and the beginning of 1995 Hizbollah had *only* fired 450 rockets in total against Israeli targets.[56] Israeli actions had: 1) rallied the Lebanese population around Hizbollah; 2) barely degraded Hizbollah capabilities and had, in fact, caused a steep rise rather than reduction of rocket attacks on northern Israel; 3) strengthened Hizbollah's, and by extension Iran's, entrenchment in south Lebanon by providing it the opportunity to reconstruct whatever Israel had destroyed during the campaign. Hizbollah, in fact, was able to rapidly repair and rebuild over 5,000 Shi'a homes in 82 villages and compensate 2,300 farmers that had suffered the brunt of Israel's furious air and artillery campaign.[57]

A ceasefire agreement, similar to that obtained with the 1993 understandings, was reached on 27 April. Both belligerents re-committed to stop targeting respectively their enemy's civilian populations. This time around a Monitoring Committee, comprised of Syrian, French, American, Israeli and Lebanese representatives, was set up and tasked with supervising the ceasefire agreement's main condition of safeguarding civilians from being targeted in future skirmishes. In both Operations 'Accountability' and 'Grapes of Wrath' the doctrine of taking the conflict to the enemy's territory was instead replaced by the principle of transferring firepower to the enemy's territory. The IDF's focus on force protection led to this new approach, which entailed the employment of advanced technology, mainly in air power and artillery, rather than the employment of regular ground forces to attack elusive Hizbollah targets.[58] In between these major flare-ups, the disposition of IDF and SLA forces in south Lebanon also reflected this growing trend towards 'force protection fetishism'.[59]

Since the mid-1990s, various incidents involving IDF casualties following Hizbollah attacks in south Lebanon led Israeli governments as well as the Israeli public in general to increasingly debate the strategic rationale in maintaining troops in south Lebanon. Although casualty numbers remained substantially constant, Israel's growing sensitivity to casualties and the growing war-weariness that Israeli society was feeling, despite the ongoing peace process, led Israeli policymakers to increasingly debate ways of solving the Lebanon conundrum.

Although IDF and SLA units were becoming more static and more reliant on firepower in order to preserve their forces in the face of increasingly lethal Hizbollah attacks, the IDF did attempt to re-take the operational initiative into its own hands by establishing the *Sayeret Egoz* (*Egoz* Reconnaissance Unit), an elite Special Forces unit attached to the Northern Command's *Golani* Infantry Brigade in 1995. *Egoz* was set up so that the IDF could deploy a unit specialised in anti-guerrilla warfare and exclusively concentrated on fighting within Lebanon. By deploying a special unit proficient in the local terrain and in Hizbollah tactics, the IDF hoped to improve its tactical success vis-à-vis its Shi'a foe.[60] Such success would, hopefully, also increase the morale of IDF units stationed in Lebanon. Some initial successes were, in fact, recorded.

Yet, despite the employment of *Egoz* units particularly in counter-ambush and interdiction operations that were often carried out beyond the security zone, *Egoz* operations had a limited effect on Hizbollah's overall operational capabilities for two main reasons. First, the nature of *Egoz* and its operations pressed Israel into experiencing the same weaknesses that other states have suffered when conducting campaigns of attrition heavily reliant on Special Forces missions: their effect has been restricted given their limited size and the circumscribed nature of their 'surgical' strike missions. In a sense, the IDF understood this in early 1997 when it decided to double the number of IDF troops stationed in south Lebanon from around 1,000 to 2,000.[61]

Second, despite *Egoz*'s greater knowledge of the local terrain they operated in, human intelligence, which is necessary to effectively operate in COIN missions based on actionable intelligence, was rather limited given the IDF's growing difficulty of gathering valid intelligence from the local Lebanese population. Hence, many of *Egoz*'s operations relied on opportunistic targeting given Hizbollah's skilful ability in concealing the details of its operations. One expert on Hizbollah noted that:

> they never surrender the element of surprise. . . . The Israelis can kill their chiefs when they can, but at the operational level these guys are almost

impossible to spot. The Israelis send out ambush teams on infiltration routes, but we've yet to see any sight that the Israelis have known for sure they were coming.[62]

Hizbollah became very effective in targeting, in fact, the IDF's weakest point, mainly its supply convoys and patrol routes leading to IDF outposts scattered throughout south Lebanon. As a result of increasing ambushes and roadside bomb attacks, the IDF reduced the number of deliveries sent to such outposts in order to reduce the chances of being targeted. The IDF also paved alternative, less-exposed paths throughout the security zone. It put up cement walls at vulnerable sites to block anti-tank missile attacks.[63] Despite such measures, IDF units continued to suffer a constant trickle of casualties, which peaked in 1997 when the IDF experienced its worst combat casualty toll since its 1985 redeployment to the security zone, with 39 soldiers killed.[64]

When these measures proved ineffective the IDF adopted even more force protection adjustments in order to reduce the IDF's casualty toll, which was having not only an adverse effect on IDF morale, but also on domestic public support for the maintenance of the security zone. These adjustments involved, amongst other measures, fortifying further IDF/SLA outposts, reducing the number of foot and armoured patrols and the growing use of helicopter transportation for troop rotation deployments and the provision of supplies. Whilst reinforcing such static outposts improved the security of IDF/SLA units when on base, the decrease in patrols and IDF-initiated ambushes gave Hizbollah units even greater liberty to infiltrate and move throughout the security zone unnoticed. This brought about a further succession of roadside bomb attacks. 'Of the 24 Israeli soldiers killed in south Lebanon in 1998, 16 of them were from roadside bomb ambushes'.[65] Whatever the IDF and SLA did, Hizbollah nonetheless could do better. With casualties becoming ever more controversial in Israel, politicians were again seeking desperately to disentangle themselves from south Lebanon.

The road to withdrawal

On 1 March 1998, the day following a mortar attack that resulted in the killing of a further three Israeli soldiers in south Lebanon, Prime Minister Benjamin Netanyahu stated that Israel was ready to abide by UN Security Resolution 425 to withdraw behind Israel's northern border in exchange for security guarantees from the Lebanese government. That was the first occasion in which an Israeli prime minister had publicly acknowledged Resolution 425.[66] The fact that the resolution had been recognised by a hawkish Israeli leader pointed to the fact that Israel was anxious to extricate its forces from Lebanon. The importance of this reversal of policy from Netanyahu was particularly significant. Even after the disastrous *Shayetet* 13 (Flotilla 13 – Naval Special Forces) mission carried out in south Lebanon on 5 September 1997 that resulted in the death of 12 members of the 16-man team due to a Hizbollah ambush, Netanyahu had appeared resolute over the need to maintain the security zone. He declared shortly after the botched mission that, 'South Lebanon is not Vietnam . . . South Lebanon adjoins our northern border and we cannot take the risk of exposing our communities in Galilee to terrorism'.[67]

Yet, such a policy reversal was still based on Netanyahu's plan – dubbed 'Lebanon-First' – to solve the Lebanon conundrum before pursuing a peace agreement with Syria. As stated above, such a policy was bound to fail under Syrian pressure and fail it did. Such a policy reversal was also due to the fact that Netanyahu was facing the prospect of the SLA's collapse in south Lebanon. With growing rumours of Israel's desire to redeploy from Lebanon and due to the constant siege from Hizbollah's attacks,[68] Gen. Antoine Lahad decided to withdraw the 200-strong SLA unit from the mountain of Jezzine in June 1999, in order to reverse '"the slow death" of his increasingly demoralised force'.[69] This initial redeployment was seen as a major victory by Hizbollah and failure on the part of Israel, which found it increasingly difficult to convince its SLA allies that it would remain in Lebanon, and in the worst case scenario, guarantee the safety of former SLA members and collaborators should it redeploy from Lebanon. The vociferous debate on whether or not Israel would withdraw totally from south Lebanon during 1998 and 1999 could only heighten the SLA's growing fear of abandonment.[70]

Finally, with Israeli prime ministerial and parliamentary elections scheduled for May 1999, Netanyahu was set against former IDF Chief of Staff and the Labour candidate for Prime Minister, Ehud Barak. With Barak behind Netanyahu at the polls in early 1999, Barak declared on 1 March that, if elected, he would order the redeployment of the IDF from Lebanon within one year of gaining office, either through a peace agreement with Syria or through unilateral withdrawal. The boost in Barak's ratings following this promise to quit Lebanon led Netanyahu to reverse his prior resistance to any compromise on withdrawal from Lebanon. Notwithstanding this policy *volte-face* by Netanyahu, Barak was elected into power on 17 May 1999. At every public engagement following his victory he continued to advocate for the full withdrawal of the Israeli troops from Lebanon despite open opposition from the IDF General Staff to such a plan.[71] Fears that south Lebanon would become a major source of terrorist instability and the platform for staging operations against Israel's northern communities again were still being voiced by many Israeli hawks. This was due to their belief that the Lebanese government would still be unable to reign in Hizbollah, that Hizbollah would, in fact, continue its *jihad* against Israel until all of Palestine would be liberated – as Sheikh Nasrallah had declared on several occasions – and that unilateral withdrawal would be perceived as an Israeli defeat in the eyes of the Arab world. This would, it was argued, have a debilitating impact upon Israel's deterrent posture in the wider Middle East.

Despite Barak's determination to withdraw the IDF from Lebanon, he did not shy away from using significant force against Hizbollah during the months leading up to the redeployment. Barak, in fact, was still determined to signal to Hizbollah and to the Syrians – with whom Israel was conducting peace negotiations – that Israel would not tolerate continued violence in southern Lebanon and would, more crucially, not allow President Hafez al-Assad to use Hizbollah as a way of extracting further concessions from Israel during ongoing peace negotiations. For example, within the space of 10 days in November 1999 seven IDF soldiers were killed by Hizbollah roadside bomb ambushes. Israel's retaliatory air strike against a Hizbollah-managed radio station on 22 December in the Beqaa Valley resulted in the death of seven Lebanese family members living near the radio station. The Israeli strike, though, did not deter further Hizbollah attacks. Rather, it led Hizbollah to strike back just as harshly. As a result of these civilian deaths and due to the fact that the IAF raid was conducted outside the security zone, Hizbollah retaliated by launching more than 50 Katyusha rockets at Kiryat Shmonah in the Upper Galilee. Hizbollah Secretary-General Hassan Nasrallah, warned Israeli policymakers that, 'no longer can Israel kill civilians and not pay a price'.[72] The price for Israel, by late 1999, however, had become too high and public opinion had shifted significantly in favour of unilateral withdrawal.[73]

Unable to reach any peace agreement with Syria or Lebanon, and unwilling to suffer further IDF casualties and endure the costs of occupation, Barak pressed for unilateral withdrawal. Consequently, plans were being drawn up despite continued resistance from the IDF General Staff.[74] Between 22 and 24 May 2000, during Operation 'Stamina', the IDF redeployed all of its forces and equipment stationed in Lebanon back to Israel.[75] As expected, the SLA simply collapsed over night. Around 6,000 SLA members and their families fled to Israel in order to avoid the expected revenge that many feared would be exacted by Hizbollah fighters. In the event, such fears proved mostly unfounded.[76]

Conclusion

The IDF's established strategy for fighting terrorist/guerrilla threats in Lebanon was based on the operational doctrine of massive retaliation in order to re-establish Israeli deterrence as quickly as possible. However, as argued throughout this chapter, Israeli counter-terrorist and counter-guerrilla strategy did not take into account the peculiarities of Lebanon and its politics. Indeed, rather than deterring terrorist and guerrilla activities originating from Lebanon, one can argue that Israeli operations often served to aggravate the conflict dynamic between Israel and the Hizbollah from the early 1980s until Israel's redeployment from Lebanon in May 2000.

Moreover, between 1983 and 2000 Israel's occupation of Lebanon – and eventually south Lebanon – led it to implement a strategy of attrition despite the fact that Israeli military doctrine has commonly favoured 'short and sharp operations of an annihilatory form'.[77] During its 18-year stay in southern

Lebanon, Israel had wrought considerable disruption, collateral damage and civilian casualties in the area in order to fight often elusive terrorist and guerrilla threats originating from the Lebanese border to its north. During various phases of the Israeli–Lebanese conflict, particularly once Hizbollah entered the strategic picture, Israel was forced to fight a long-drawn-out asymmetric war of attrition in which all of its conventional strengths – manoeuvre warfare, firepower, quick and decisive battlefield decisions – were frustrated by Hizbollah's cunning guerrilla tactics that eventually sapped *all* of the IDF's morale and Israel's determination to continue to employ south Lebanon as a buffer zone for its northern communities. Former spokesperson of the Rabin and Peres governments (1992–96), Uri Dromi, eloquently expressed Israel's frustration at having to fight a war on Hizbollah's terms when he noted that:

> We have fallen in Lebanon into what the framers of our national security doctrine considered their worst nightmare, namely a war of attrition. This kind of war thwarts the IDF of its main assets – mobility and striking power – while exposing the soft underbelly of the Israeli society: its reluctance to suffer casualties in a protracted war.[78]

Since Israel's June 1982 invasion of Lebanon until its full redeployment from Lebanon in May 2000, Israel had suffered almost 1,000 deaths within the ranks of the IDF, huge economic and political costs and most importantly an erosion of the IDF's status within Israeli society given the controversy surrounding the use of the IDF in maintaining the 15-year occupation of the south Lebanon security zone.

Even though Israel extricated itself militarily from Lebanon nine years ago, politically, Israel's quest for peace on its northern border remains elusive, with many of the underlying sources of conflict – mainly the status of the Golan Heights, peace prospects with Syria and Lebanon and the issue of Palestinian self-determination – still unresolved. The 2006 Lebanon war, while unexpected, stands as testament to this continued reality, a reality that Israeli COIN strategy has done much to shape, but never resolve.

7 'A reach greater than the grasp'

Israeli intelligence and the conflict in south Lebanon 1990–2000*

Clive Jones

Introduction

In May 1999, an article by journalist Ronen Bergman appeared in the Israeli daily newspaper *Ha'aretz*. Titled 'Fighting Blind', the article described the atrophy that marked Israel's intelligence effort against Hizbollah in south Lebanon. He noted that:

> The *Shin Bet*, Army Intelligence and the *Mossad* find themselves facing a formidable challenge in Hizbollah, which has honed itself into a toughened, skilled and highly trained organization. Fifty years from now, perhaps, when the most highly classified intelligence files are unsealed, the true extent of Israel's ignorance about what was happening in Lebanon in the 1990s in general, and within *Hizbollah* in particular will become clear.[1]

Just over a year later, the Israel Defence Forces (IDF) withdrew finally from south Lebanon after 18 years of continuous occupation. It was an ignominious withdrawal brought about by the activities of Hizbollah (Party of God), a largely Shi'a Muslim organization founded in 1982. While supported and financed by Damascus and Tehran, it, nonetheless, enjoyed widespread support throughout south Lebanon and could claim with some justification to have developed into a true manifestation of a popular guerrilla organization.[2] Bergman is undoubtedly correct in his assessment that the role played by Israel's intelligence community in this bitter, if limited conflagration, must await the opening of official archives. Nonetheless, enough material exists within the public domain to allow for at least a tentative analysis to be made. A key argument here is that the application of methods employed initially by the IDF in south Lebanon to counter Palestinian insurgents proved woefully inadequate against Hizbollah. Second, and again with direct reference to operations in south Lebanon, the main burden for collation and dissemination of intelligence fell upon the intelligence branch of the IDF – *Agaf Modi'in* or *AMAN*, though *Shin Bet*, Israel's internal security service also carried wide responsibility, albeit through historical default, for recruiting and running human intelligence (HUMINT) assets. Given that *AMAN* remains part of an

organization where culture and military doctrine exist in a symbiotic relationship, intelligence assessments of Hizbollah tended to reflect a mindset
that viewed the organization as a 'terrorist' rather than a 'guerrilla' movement that happened to be inspired by a particular Islamist agenda. Such 'construction' of the 'other' is important because it denied any efficacy to
sustaining a more benign approach toward the local Shi'a population.
Indeed, Israel's innate distrust of the Shi'a of south Lebanon, a distrust born
from a historical preference for an alliance with the Christian Maronites
came increasingly to haunt Israel's attempts to piece together a coherent intelligence picture of events in south Lebanon.[3]

Much has been written regarding the wider regional context of the conflict
that was waged in the *wadis* (dry riverbeds) and hills of south Lebanon. It
defied easy categorization – a small war, a guerrilla war, an anti-terrorist
campaign, or an insurgency being among the multiple epithets pinned to the
conflict. Perhaps it is best referred to as a Low-Intensity Conflict (LIC), a term
that at least avoids the worst excesses of partisan judgement. But whatever
label is used, it is clear that the context and perceptions that informed Israel's
intelligence operations in south Lebanon were found wanting. In turn, such
shortcomings impacted adversely on Israel's attempts to maintain an effective
HUMINT capability in Lebanon that could better understand Hizbollah or
its military wing, *al-Muqawama* (Islamic Resistance). Indeed, so adept did *al-
Muqawama* become at gathering field intelligence among members of Israel's
proxy militia, the South Lebanon Army (SLA), that the IDF was forced
increasingly to rely on technical means and punitive measures in order to contain, rather than defeat Hizbollah in its self-declared security zone in south
Lebanon. If wisdom remains the art of hindsight, there remain profound lessons to be learnt by Israel's intelligence community from its bitter experience
in southern Lebanon.[4]

Israel: strategy and intelligence

The issue of how doctrine shapes military strategy and, thus, determines a
particular course of action has been the focus of much scholarly debate, not
all of it uncritical. As Norvell de Atkine notes with regard to Washington's
involvement in Vietnam, United States strategists erred badly in their belief
that 'pain thresholds' imposed upon the North Vietnamese approximated to
their own and as such, would force Hanoi to accept a peace on Washington's
terms.[5] Such 'mirror image' beliefs, for example, also explain Israel's rationale for the heavy bombardments of south Lebanon in 1993 and 1996 in the
belief that the scale of suffering inflicted would force Damascus and Beirut to
curb the activities of Hizbollah in south Lebanon. In the case of Israel, the
behaviour of military officers is not only determined by a particular perception of their immediate external environment – the constitutive norm – but
also by received wisdom born from military tradition of how an Israeli
officer, for example, is supposed to act in a given situation. In south Lebanon,

such modes of behaviour derived from Israel's military doctrine did much to undermine the collation and effective use of intelligence in countering the operatives of *al-Muqawama*.

Israel's approach to military doctrine and its application in war is a reflection of its particular position within the wider constellation of the Middle East and has been shaped by both the geographic and demographic asymmetries it faces with regard to its Arab neighbours. This has produced, according to Stuart Cohen and Efraim Inbar, a 'dichotomous' approach to dealing with national security. At the strategic level there is the need to avoid protracted or extensive military commitments that are costly both in terms of men and material – the Jewish state cannot inflict total defeat on potential adversaries and, thus, can only hope to maintain the status quo in a crisis situation. This equates to a constitutive norm. At the operational level, however, Israeli military doctrine has characteristically been offensive. Mindful that their country's lack of territorial depth precludes the possibility of absorbing enemy attacks, Israel's policymakers have traditionally regarded the offence as the only viable means of strategic defence. Consequently, they have advocated 'deterrence by [first strike] denial', not 'deterrence by [second strike] punishment'.[6] Given its sensitivity to incurring high casualties, be they civilian or military, offensive operations are coterminous with the normative behaviour of the IDF.

This emphasis upon offensive operations does, however, go beyond the objective constraints set by Israel's geo-political disposition. Offensive operations designed to secure a decision in the shortest possible time has allowed the IDF to fashion its own environment on the battlefield to suit its particular strengths, thus, promoting an *esprit de corps*. As such, offensive operations have become axiomatic to the IDF, regardless of whether such operations are best suited to securing or maintaining the wider political objectives set by the civilian leadership. Israel's approach to counter-insurgency (COIN) operations or Low-Intensity Conflict (LIC) continues to fall within this offensive rubric and reflects the cumulative experience of confronting Palestinian insurgents over a period of some 40 years.[7]

These operations were the product of thinking inherent within an organization that reified the offence, irrespective of whether such an operational approach – developed through successive conventional wars – was best suited to the political and social complexities normally associated with LIC. Given the widespread opprobrium exhibited towards the PLO among Israeli Jews, the sagacity of the IDF's modus operandi against the Palestinians was never subject to any sustained critical debate. Thus, in countering Palestinian insurgents, both in areas adjacent to the Jewish State and further afield, Israel's operational methods came to embrace regime targeting, selected air strikes, widespread artillery bombardments and limited land incursions as well as full-scale invasion.

While its origins lie in the Cold War literature of strategic studies, regime targeting has been a conspicuous element of Israel LIC operations. At its heart lies the belief that the removal of key individuals from an insurgent organization will induce neuralgic atrophy, leading to the structural implosion in all or part of an insurgent organization.[8] The Israeli air attack on the PLO headquarters at Hammam as-Shatt, Tunis, on 1 October 1985 in response to the murder of three Israelis in Cyprus, and the assassination of Khalil Wazir (Abu Jihad) – regarded by Israel as the organizational brain behind the Palestinian *Intifada* – on 16 April 1988 are testament to the efficacy of such thinking among both the political and military elite in Israel.[9]

Conspicuous by its absence, however, remains any true appreciation of the integral role that a 'hearts and mind' campaign should play in combating insurgents.[10] The widespread use of the term 'terrorist' to describe the PLO negated the need for such investment as this struggle, was, at least until 1993, seen primarily in terms of a zero-sum game between two competing national movements. Whereas the Palestinians in Lebanon have been viewed as a transient community whose 'right of return' to Palestine negates the very idea of a Jewish State, the Shi'a remain indigenous to the region, both in historical and ethnic terms. Therefore, short of mass expulsion by Israel they could not be removed from Lebanon on a permanent basis.

The contours of a 'hearts and minds' campaign was only discernable in Israel's approach towards the Christian Maronite community of south Lebanon, and institutionalized under what has come to be known as the 'Good Fence' policy. This allowed residents of south Lebanon access to medical care and employment in Israel proper, as well as the provision of aid in the form of food, water and medical assistance for communities inside the security zone.[11] For the most part however, Maronite Christian communities were the main recipients of Israel's largesse, a situation rooted in the historical and cultural antipathy both parties had shared towards the Palestinians.[12] The most tangible expression of this alliance was seen in the South Lebanon Army (SLA), a militia force established under Israel's tutelage in 1985 and commanded by a coterie of Christian officers under Antoine Lahad.

The historical alliance with the Maronites obscured for Israel the relative decline in the fortunes of this confession in Lebanon. In 1982, just prior to Israel's invasion, it was suggested by some IDF officers with experience of the Byzantine ways of Lebanese politics that Israel make common cause with the relatively moderate Amal movement, at that time the dominant political organization among the Shi'a of south Lebanon. This proposition was rejected out of hand by Israeli military intelligence on the grounds that the loyalty of too many members of Amal remained suspect.[13] The inherent distrust in Israel's approach to the Shi'a community perhaps should have been questioned. Given the approbation heaped upon the IDF by some Shi'a villagers, particularly in the Jebel Amil region in the early stages of the 1982 invasion, Israel let slip a golden opportunity to forge closer links with a community whose relations with the Palestinians in their midst had become particularly tense.[14] In continuing to 'nail its fortunes to the Maronite mast', Israel's political and military leadership ignored the demographic shift in favour of the Lebanese Shi'a, but failed to mitigate the worst excesses of the invasion and occupation of south Lebanon on a people whose politics were already subject to the radicalizing influence of the Iranian revolution.[15] As such, Israel's approach to the problem of Hizbollah in south Lebanon from 1985 onwards was preordained, with set assumptions regarding the various communities and suffused with LIC methods biased culturally towards offensive operations drawn from a long history of combating Palestinian insurgents. The aforementioned impacted adversely upon Israel's ability to cohere an effective intelligence network in south Lebanon, a *sine qua non* if an insurgency is to be dealt with through a proportionate use of force.

The dominance of *AMAN*, led Israel's intelligence requirements to become biased heavily towards short-term field or contact intelligence, rather than part of a wider appreciation of shifts in Lebanon's political and social composition. Conditioned by the operational need to counter 'the terrorist threat', Israeli intelligence failed to appreciate the rise of Hizbollah as a political movement or to discern the finite agenda that lay behind its more atavistic pronouncements. Accordingly, when speaking before the *Knesset* Foreign Affairs and Defence Committee on 17 October 1995, the former head of *AMAN*, Major-General Moshe Ya'alon noted that Hizbollah, backed by Tehran, had embarked upon a two-stage plan. He continued, 'in the first stage, the organization (Hizbollah) wants to push Israel out of southern Lebanon. In the second stage its aim is [the liberation of] Jerusalem'.[16] It was an assessment more significant in delineating the cognitive boundaries of *AMAN*, than providing an accurate forecast of either the intent or capabilities of Hizbollah. Ya'alon's remarks, presenting as they did Hizbollah as a threat to the national security of the Jewish State, appeared incongruous with an organization whose military wing, *al-Muqawama*, was never thought to have numbered more than 500 guerrillas.

The tendency to extrapolate a worst case scenario from the more extreme religious rhetoric of Hizbollah can only provide a partial explanation for the expression of such sentiment. In his treatment of defence intelligence, Michael Herman notes that the proclivity of military intelligence organizations has always been biased towards planning for 'worst case scenarios'. The result has been that all too often, such assessments become self-fulfilling prophecies.[17] This became the norm for *AMAN*. The failure to give adequate warning of the impending Syrian and Egyptian attack that opened the October 1973 war left huge psychological scars, not least because the Agranat Commission, convened in the conflict's aftermath to examine the failure of intelligence to provide early warning, threatened the national hegemony enjoyed by *AMAN* over intelligence collation and evaluation. The result, as noted by Gideon Doron and Reuven Pedatzhur, has been for *AMAN* to issue such broad-based intelligence assessments that they become almost meaningless or, conversely, to portray a worst-case scenario.[18] The fear of failure, therefore, became part of the culture of intelligence assessment and blurred any distinction that could and should be made between basic threats to the security of the state – that is threats to its very existence – and *bitachon shotef*, current security threats, posed by either guerrilla or terrorist organizations that however violent or intractable, do not present an outright existential threat.

This is not to suggest the legacy of 1973 has produced 'irrational' assessments per se. Rather, it is to highlight the extent to which a 'limited rationality', resulting from the correlation of basic threats with current security threats, and 'adaptive rationality', where past experience and historical analogy informed choice, came to provide the boundaries of choice in dealing with Hizbollah.[19] As one intelligence official opined, following Israel's unilateral withdrawal in May 2000:

> It is possible that we made too much of the microscope and too little use of the telescope. We focused on Hizbollah and on tracking down sites where its military operations were based, and we didn't attribute special importance to Lebanon's socio-political structure, which is an important factor in Hizbollah's policy today.[20]

But, as events were to prove, even Israel's use of the 'microscope' exposed fatal flaws in its intelligence war in south Lebanon.

South Lebanon: Israel's intelligence structures

In his critical assessment of the conceptual approach that chained the IDF to the security zone in south Lebanon, Zvi Bar'el noted that the IDF exercised complete control over policymaking in the Lebanese conflict, a situation which 'grossly violated the crucial distinction which must separate the supply of information data from the work of political decision-making'.[21] That the IDF was able to exercise such hegemony lay in no small part in the position occupied by *AMAN* at the apex of Israel's intelligence structure. The director of *AMAN* and the head of its assessment division serve as principal advisors on intelligence matters to the Israeli cabinet through the Chief of Staff and Minister of Defence. It is their annual intelligence assessment presented to the cabinet that carries most weight in terms of broad strategic planning. Coordination of intelligence gathering and assessment between *AMAN*, *Mossad* and *Shin Bet* takes place through the *Varash* (*Va'ad Rashei Sherutim* – the Committee of the Chiefs of the Services). Yet it is acknowledged that the head of *AMAN* remains the 'first among equals'.

The main burden for cultivating HUMINT in south Lebanon was initially the responsibility of *Shin Bet*. Indeed, its involvement dated back to 1982 when, following Israel's land invasion of Lebanon, *Shin Bet* was tasked with gathering intelligence among the Palestinian refugee camps of south Lebanon, an extension of its previous work in the West Bank and Gaza Strip.[22] The methods employed were often harsh and included beatings, blackmail, sensory deprivation, solitary confinement and on occasion, selected assassination. While configured to deal with any recrudescence of Palestinian resistance, such methods came to be applied to the Shi'a, much to the discomfort of some members of *AMAN* and indeed one former *Shin Bet* officer. Gideon Ezra, later to become a Likud Knesset member, noted that the Shi'a were seen as guilty by association and treated accordingly, the *Shin Bet* ignoring the view that whatever ties the Shi'a may have had with Palestinian groups were often formed under extreme duress.[23]

Attempts to ameliorate the tension between *Shin Bet* and *AMAN* to provide greater intelligence cooperation led, in 1985, to the establishment of *Aleph-Vav-Samekh*, a Hebrew acronym for 'Intelligence gathering and subversion'. Moshe Arens, then serving as Israel's Defence Minister saw the new body as crucial to preventing bureaucratic rivalries from degrading the 'counter-terrorist' effort in south Lebanon. Leadership of *Aleph-Vav-Samekh* was placed in the hands of Haim Boro, a *Shin Bet* officer, but such executive authority did little to assuage the often petty turf wars that continued to characterize relations between *AMAN* and *Shin Bet*. Reflecting on what was clearly a forced marriage of convenience Boro noted that the different organizational principles of the two services remained incompatible. In particular, Boro highlighted the propensity of *AMAN* towards immediate and urgent action, a characteristic he felt to be inimical to the patient collation and interpretation of intelligence. As such, different organizational cultures undermined a productive intelligence effort. By 1987, at precisely the time when Hizbollah was on the rise politically in south Lebanon, the moribund coordinating body was disbanded.[24]

The legacy of this bureaucratic rivalry proved disastrous, resulting in piecemeal information, rather than a coherent, ongoing, intelligence assessment emerging. In turn, both *AMAN* and *Shin Bet* established their own intelligence structures within the SLA as a means to compensate for the atrophy in intelligence cooperation. In 1989, the SLA established its own military intelligence arm, *Mangenon ha'Bitachon* or *Mabat*. Its commander, Colonel Akel Hashem was known for his uncompromising attitude towards the Islamic Resistance and its benefactors. Regarding Hizbollah as a mere proxy of Damascus, Hashem believed in the extreme application of punitive measures against villages suspected of harbouring the *al-Muqawama*.[25] *Mabat* coordinated intelligence collation and dissemination with the IDF through *Yakal*, the liaison unit of the IDF whose personnel were drawn mainly from the ranks of *AMAN*. Its centre of operations, located in the predominantly Christian town of Marjayoun, was concerned primarily with field or contact intelligence. Indeed, the primacy placed upon the gathering of such intelligence provides a prime example of adaptive rationality determining policy towards the *al-Muqawama*.

In 1995, *Shin Bet* oversaw the establishment of its mirror image, *Shabbak* Section 501. Its recruits were drawn mainly, though not exclusively, from the Maronite communities. It was tasked not only with establishing a network of HUMINT sources among both Christian and Shi'a villages of south Lebanon, but also with collating tactical intelligence on Syria's military dispositions throughout the rest of the country.[26] Those working for 501 were paid considerably more than the average SLA soldier's salary of between $300 and $500 per month. Given the frustrations of sustaining even a modicum of economic well-being in south Lebanon, a salary in excess of $1,000 per month paid to a *mukhabarati* (intelligence agent) proved incentive enough for many to take the Israeli shilling.[27] In time however, the transient loyalty purchased by financial inducement proved an Achilles heel in Israel's attempts to sustain its HUMINT assets.

The effective use of HUMINT is axiomatic to the successful prosecution to any LIC, remaining as it does crucial to distinguishing between intent and capability. Ensuring the loyalty of HUMINT assets in such conflicts remains, nonetheless, problematic where communal loyalties collide or overlap.[28] The fact that some 30 per cent of the 2,300 soldiers in the SLA were drawn from among the Shi'a community allowed Hizbollah to exploit competing identities and loyalties to undermine the morale and political allegiances of these soldiers in particular. By 1999, the porous nature of SLA field intelligence – from the sale of maps detailing IDF positions and routes through mine fields to information concerning planned IDF/SLA ambush operations – had become an accepted fact in operational planning among IDF commanders in south Lebanon. From being an organization that incurred crippling losses on naïve and all too bloody assaults on IDF/SLA positions in south Lebanon in the 1980s, *al-Muqawama* had, by 1996, developed into a disciplined and tenacious group of fighters whose excellence in tactics and field craft was underpinned by access to real-time intelligence. When, in October 1997, members of *al-Muqawama* were able to place explosive charges 150 meters from the border fence with Israel, which killed two IDF soldiers, the lesson was clear: Hizbollah had the proven capability to threaten Israel proper, but had chosen not to do so. Moreover, to have come so close to the 'Good fence' had required inside information on IDF force deployment and movements.[29]

Such operations leant credence to the old adage that nothing succeeds like success. As *al-Muqawama* became more adept at attacking SLA and IDF targets, the casualty rate among both sets of troops rose exponentially. If, for example, IDF casualties alone are taken for the years May 1993 to May 1997, and assuming that 4,000 soldiers served in the security zone throughout this period, then Israel incurred an 8 per cent casualty rate in south Lebanon. If one also includes the 73 IDF soldiers killed during the crash of a troop-carrying helicopter bound for the security zone in February 1997, then the figure rises to 10 per cent. This proved a high attrition rate given the small number of combatants involved, and was crucial in opening up a vociferous debate in Israel over the sagacity of Israel's continued presence in south Lebanon.[30] In turn, such debates fuelled doubts about the future of the SLA and hardly did much to assuage the growing perception that its members were merely sandbags for the Israeli bunker.

By 1995, Hizbollah's intelligence was of sufficient quality that it could engage in periodic bouts of psychological warfare against the SLA, threatening retribution on individual officers while offering periodic amnesties to those willing to desert the militia. The abduction and assassination of Tony Nahara, a senior SLA commander in 1996 was matched the following year with the death of Salim Risha, a leading figure in *Mabat* by a well-placed roadside bomb. Risha was known for his close contacts with both *AMAN* and *Mossad* and the fact that his travel plans were disclosed only to a select few suggested that *al-Muqawama* had a source among the coterie of advisors surrounding Risha.[31] The most apposite example of the extent to which Hizbollah penetrated the hierarchy of the SLA command remains the killing of Akel Hashem on 30 January 2000. Coming as it did among increased speculation in Israel of an impending withdrawal, Hashem met his bloody end in yet another roadside bombing. When, in May of that year, the former headquarters of *Yakal* in Marjayoun was taken over by Hizbollah, a former SLA commander and close friend of Hashem was duly installed in the building at the behest of the *al-Muqawama*. Treachery within the ranks of the SLA, it would seem, went to the very top.[32]

In other cases, sheer bad luck played the main part in unravelling Israel's HUMINT capability. In July 1998, a court in Beirut charged over 70 Lebanese with espionage for an 'enemy state'. The indictments followed the defection of an SLA intelligence officer, Raja Ward, to the Lebanese authorities where he handed over a list of Lebanese individuals alleged to be working for *Shabbak* 501. Ward's defection was, in the best tradition of the spy genre, motivated by passion alone. He had fallen in love with a Beirut woman whose family, staunch supporters of the small leftist Syrian National Socialist Party, disapproved of the relationship. The defection was, therefore, as much about proving his political loyalty as his emotional fidelity. Those involved with 501 had been tasked by their handlers with identifying main areas of Syrian military activity, as well as the location of Hizbollah targets – both human and material – within Beirut itself. It is thought that intelligence gathered by these operatives was used during Operation 'Grapes of Wrath', Israel's mass bombardment of south Lebanon in April 1996.[33]

While guarding against the vagaries of human emotion can prove all but impossible, the ability of Hizbollah to turn agents and penetrate Israeli field intelligence produced two bloody coups for *al-Muqawama* that impacted directly upon increased public and political unease in Israel over the sagacity of continued entrenchment in Lebanon. On the night of the 4–5 September 1997, a force from *Shayetet 13* (Flotilla 13, IDF naval commandos) were ambushed on their way to attack what is believed to have been a Hizbollah leader staying in the small village of Ansouriyeh located just south of the Lebanese port of Sidon. Having landed from inflatable dinghies, the commandos walked into a well-prepared, and in the truest sense of the word, executed ambush which left 12 of their number dead. *Al-Muqawama* knew the precise route that the commandos would take to their target because they had used a double agent to feed false information, complete with a detailed map, to the Israelis.[34] Moreover, because the Israelis were operating outside of the security zone, Hizbollah was quite willing to enlist the help of the regular Lebanese army who, once the ambush had been sprung, illuminated the ambush site with flares.[35]

The IDF proved markedly reluctant to concede that it had walked with its eyes wide shut into the Ansouriyeh debacle. To have done so would have been tantamount to admitting the extent to which Hizbollah was capable of manipulating Israel's intelligence apparatus. With a certain hit placed within its grasp, but faced with the constraints imposed by a limited window of opportunity, intelligence officers attached to the IDF's Northern command should at least have tried to corroborate the intelligence with other sources. In the immediate aftermath of the debacle, explanations for its failure ranged from detection by coastal radar, to monitoring by *al-Muqawama* of the cellular phone conversations of young IDF soldiers. Both explanations appear unlikely. Even if the force had been detected by coastal radar by chance, it is unlikely that *al-Muqawama* would have known precisely where to place its explosive charges or have had the time to lay them. Second, given that Special Forces were employed to raid Ansouriyeh, it is also unlikely that the rank and file of conscripts doing their tour of duty in the security zone would have had prior knowledge of such an operation. The impact of the failure of the Ansouriyeh raid – the bloodiest single loss suffered by the IDF in Lebanon since the 1982 invasion – resulted in Israel terminating further ambush operations for over a year as it attempted to locate the root cause of the failure and implement corrective measures.[36]

These measures included the confiscation of cellular phones from SLA soldiers and the dissemination of false intelligence information among SLA officers in the hope that disclosure of details about fictitious operations would expose double agents. While necessary for the maintenance of effective field security, the fact that such casuistry was deemed necessary highlights the profound difficulties faced by the Israelis in the production of reliable contact intelligence. Moreover, the collation of background intelligence required to construct a picture of Hizbollah movements proved increasingly problematic as IDF commanders, mindful of growing public distaste for Israel's presence in the security zone, proved reluctant to commit troops to long range patrols. Holed up for the most part in heavily defended bunkers around the security zone the IDF handed the tactical initiative in the conflict to the guerrillas of *al-Muqawama*.[37]

The result of this was seen in the death on 28 February 1999 of Brigadier-General Erez Gerstein, commander of *Yakal* (South Lebanon Liaison Unit) and the highest ranking IDF officer to be killed in Lebanon since 1982. Gerstein was know for his uncompromising approach towards the problem of Hizbollah and according to one IDF officer even considered them 'third-rate terrorists'. Such hubris proved tragically misplaced. Even though travelling in a heavily armed convoy within the security zone, the roadside bomb which ripped apart his armoured-plated Mercedes was detonated by guerrillas in line of sight of their intended target.[38] The audacity of the attack was compounded by the fact that the assailants were able to blend in with the local population and make good their escape.[39] Once more, an intelligence leak within *Mabat* was suspected, but never proved. In an ironic twist of fate, Gerstein met his death having just paid his condolences to the family of an SLA intelligence officer who had himself been killed by similar means. As one IDF officer noted in the immediate aftermath of the attack, 'His [Gerstein's] death is a slap in the face to the military doctrine in Lebanon. It once again proves how the IDF has fallen victim to those same patterns of action that repeat themselves in a sort of recurring ritual'.[40]

Deprived of effective HUMINT assets, the IDF retreated to the bunkers both physically and mentally. Between 1996 and 1998 recorded attacks against IDF/SLA targets rose from 460 to over 1,200.[41] Such statistics fuelled the growing debate in Israel over the future of the security zone. Foremost among those advocating a unilateral Israeli withdrawal from Lebanon were the *Arba Imahud* (The Four Mothers Movement), formed in the aftermath of the February 1997 helicopter crash. Their activities, scorned by many within the IDF itself, were crucial in persuading a critical mass of the Israeli public to embrace their agenda as the best means to release Israel from the Lebanese imbroglio. The views of the Four Mothers were lent further credence by both serving and former members of Israel's security establishment. Brigadier-General (Res.) Haim Yifrah, a former military intelligence officer openly questioned the received wisdom of Hizbollah's two-fold strategy, arguing that no objective intelligence existed that clearly demonstrated intent on the part of the Islamic resistance to take their struggle into Israel proper in the event of an Israeli withdrawal.[42] Moreover, even within the IDF, there were those prepared to go beyond the styptic notion of 'terrorist' that had conditioned its organizational culture towards dealing with the Islamic resistance. In the summer of 1997, the History Division of the IDF published a booklet that, for operational reasons, recognized Hizbollah as engaged in guerrilla activity, rather than terrorist operations associated with the Palestinian Islamist movement Hamas. This suggested that at least some within the IDF were willing to confer legitimacy upon Hizbollah's military activities, if not the more extreme tenets of its ideo-theology.[43]

The need to cultivate HUMINT sources close to Hizbollah saw *AMAN* and *Shin Bet* push the boundaries of legality within Israel itself. In December 2000 it was disclosed that two Israeli police officers from the Lebanon Border Unit tasked with countering drug smuggling from Lebanon had been arrested on charges of corruption. The smuggling of drugs across the border was nothing new: in November 1999 it was revealed by one IDF officer that between one to three tons of heroin were smuggled over the border annually.[44] The arrests themselves were however significant because they shed light on the willingness of *AMAN* to condone such activity on the part of one Lebanese individual, Ramzi Nahara. He was well known to the Israeli police for his nefarious activities but he had, in the past, supplied useful information on the activities of the Islamic resistance.

Nahara, a Lebanese Shi'a, hailed from the village of Abel al-Saki. Following Israel's invasion of Lebanon in 1982, he began to ply his trade in narcotics across the Good Fence. It would appear that he worked for both the Lebanon Border Unit and Unit 504, *AMAN's* main HUMINT unit, supplying both with details on corrupt police officers and the activities of *al-Muqawama*. His evidence had already led to a number of convictions, most notably that of Major Haim Shahar who was sentenced to 13 years imprisonment in 1991 for trafficking in heroin. Given his value as a source of information, the police ignored Nahara's own criminal activities. Even when, following an audacious attempt to smuggle three tons of hashish into Israel in 1989, his activities could no longer be overlooked, the terms of his lenient three-year sentence were such that he was allowed out on day release from prison in northern Israel. It is of note that a character witness at his trial was the commander of the SLA, Antoine Lahad.[45]

On completion of his sentence, Nahara returned to the village of Kila in southern Lebanon where he became a key actor in a tale whose outcome highlights all too well the human cost of the intelligence struggle in south Lebanon. Israel's intelligence community had been desperate to locate the whereabouts of Imad Mugniyeh, a key figure in *al-Muqawama* and believed by Israel to be responsible for the bloody attacks in March 1992 against the Israeli embassy in Buenos Aires, and a Jewish community center in the Argentine capital in July 1994. In their attempts to locate Mugniyeh, either *Mossad* or Unit 504 agents – it is unclear who had operational responsibility – posing as United States government officials investigating currency fraud in Lebanon recruited Ahmed Khalek, a former guerrilla with the PLO who was known to have contacts with Mugniyeh. Needing money to support his family, Khalek took the bait. Only in 1993, having worked for nearly a year under the 'Americans', did he discover the true identity of his patrons. Entrapped, Khalek was taken to Israel and given training in the finer points of intelligence and sabotage. He was then returned to Lebanon and tasked with trying to recruit Imad Mugniyeh's brother, Fuad, a store owner in south Beirut. His attempt floundered, not least because of Fuad's loyalty to both his brother and Hizbollah. On 24 December 1994, under instructions from his handlers, Khalek detonated a powerful car bomb outside the store owned by Fuad Mugniyeh, killing him and two innocent passers by instantly, but not, to the chagrin of his Israeli handlers, Imad Mugniyeh who, they believed, was present in the store at the time.[46]

Khalek was spirited out of Lebanon, only to return five months later to the village of Klea in the security zone under the pseudonym of Michel Hir Amin. Though Khalek was accorded round-the-clock protection by the SLA, Hizbollah, through a contact in the militia learned of his true identity and set in motion a plan to abduct him back to Beirut to stand trial. To do this they decided to 'double' Nahara, offering him immunity for his crimes of drug trafficking and collaboration with Israel. Given the alternative fate *al-Muqawama* had planned for him at a more opportune moment, it was a deal Nahara could hardly refuse. Nahara arranged a drinks party to which he invited Khalek. Among the guests was Salim Salameh, another known collaborator with Israel, but one who, like Nahara, had agreed to partake in the operation albeit under duress: *al-Muqawama* held his sister as surety. His presence undoubtedly assured Khalek that the guest list was in a truly mortal sense, politically correct. At the party, he was drugged and pistol-whipped before being bundled into a car and driven north away from the security zone. SLA complicity in the abduction was confirmed with the involvement of Bassam Hasbani, a security official ostensibly in charge of a border control point between the security zone and the rest of southern Lebanon. Hasbani ordered the troops manning the barrier not to stop the car as it sped on its way to Beirut. In June 1996, a military court in Beirut sentenced Khalek to death. The sentence was duly carried out by firing squad on 21 September 1996. His wife received a jail sentence of 15 years imprisonment.

This exemplar of human tragedy is worth retelling at length for three reasons. The fact that Khalek was tried in a Lebanese military court and *not* by Hizbollah demonstrates the extent to which the organization accepted the existing state dispensation and its legal process. Second, what limited HUMINT assets Israel was able to cultivate, became harnessed towards aiding and abetting a counter-terrorist campaign, rather than towards constructing a macro-picture of Hizbollah as a socio-political movement and its wider links to the Shi'a community. Third, the fact that Israel became reliant upon convicted criminals to sustain a HUMINT effort in southern Lebanon demonstrated not only the vulnerability of such agents to being 'turned', but also begged serious questions about the efficacy of recruiting such assets using methods developed in the more benign environment of the West Bank and Gaza Strip, where physical control and manipulation of the population could be imposed more easily. Again, the legacy of fighting 'terrorism' according to a bounded rationality undermined any serious analysis of how Israel employed its HUMINT assets.

Other methods used in south Lebanon that had their origins in the fight against Palestinian nationalism included detention without trial and abduction of those suspected of aiding and abetting Hizbollah. In July 1997, Amnesty International issued a report detailing allegations of torture and ill-treatment of detainees held at the al-Khiyam prison in south Lebanon, an establishment clearly visible from the border with Israel. Methods of interrogation used were multifarious, but ranged from sensory deprivation through to beatings and the use of electric shock treatment. Because they did not fit with the legal definition of a Prisoner of War as outlined under the Geneva convention, those incarcerated at al-Khiyam existed in a judicial limbo, with no legal rights or status. Most had no idea as to the length of their sentences or in some cases, the alleged crime for which they were being held. Israel refused to accept responsibility for the running of the prison or the conditions in which prisoners were kept directing concern expressed by human rights groups to the SLA head quarters at Marjayoun. This bureaucratic subterfuge failed to disguise the obvious: Israel remained the occupying power in its own self-declared 'security zone', irrespective of the fact that the SLA retained daily control over the affairs at *al-Khiyam*. In addition, enough evidence from former inmates emerged to suggest strongly that Israeli intelligence officers, probably from *Shin Bet* were regular visitors to the prison, and even on occasion participated in the physical maltreatment of prisoners.[47]

The length of incarceration endured by many prisoners could not solely be explained in terms of their links, however firm or tenuous with either Hizbollah or Amal. What useful operational intelligence they may have possessed would have had limited utility and be circumscribed by the rigid cell structure adopted by *al-Muqawama* in the field. Rather, their true value lay as human bargaining chips as Israel pressed for information regarding the fate of missing IDF servicemen in Lebanon. The abduction in July 1989 of Shaykh Abdul Karim Obeid, and the kidnapping of Mustafa Dirani in May 1994 to Israel proper were designed clearly to pressure Hizbollah for such information, most notably over the fate of Ron Arad, an Israeli Air Force navigator who had been shot down and captured over south Lebanon in 1986. When, in the summer of 2000, Israel allowed 12 Lebanese nationals held in detention inside Israel to be freed, Jerusalem continued to block the release of Obeid and Dirani on the grounds that it would be damaging to Israel's national security. The logic of this decision was hard to discern. Continued detention could not be justified on operational grounds implied in the term 'national security' – any information Obeid and Dirani may have possessed concerning Hizbollah or *Arad's* whereabouts was long past any intelligence sell-by date. As Zvi Ba'rel noted, the decision to hold the two men even after Israel's full withdrawal from Lebanon in May 2000 was flawed, making it increasingly likely that Hizbollah would seek some form of redress to exert leverage over Israel.[48] When on 7 October 2000 three IDF soldiers were snatched by members of *al-Muqawama* just inside the northern border, Israel had, in the most ironic sense of the term, made its own national security hostage to fortune.[49]

Regime targeting and technical intelligence

The failings identified in Israel's HUMINT effort were perhaps disguised, though not ameliorated by a long-held preference for regime targeting. The most notable example of this policy remains the assassination of Shaykh Hussein Abbas Musawi on 16 February 1992. From the perspective of the IDF, Musawi represented a prize target. As the then spiritual head of Hizbollah, he had largely been responsible for its growth and development, including its adoption of an anti-West and anti-Israel platform from 1982 onwards. His position at the apogee of the movement led Israel's political and military elite to conclude that his removal would represent a devastating blow, both militarily and psychologically, to *al-Muqawama*, allowing Israel to reassert its hegemony over the security zone. Moshe Arens, then serving as Israeli Defence Minister in a Likud coalition government led by Yitzhak Shamir, justified the attack in terms of deterrence, it being cited as a warning to all groups, be they Palestinian or Lebanese that they remained vulnerable to the reach of the IDF.[50] The decision to kill Musawi was taken on the spur of the moment. The initial intention, as with Obeid, had been to abduct him from his car, but given the security surrounding his entourage and in lieu of any wider cabinet consultation, Shamir, Arens, former Chief of Staff Lieutenant-General Ehud Barak, and the then serving director of *AMAN*, Major-General Uri Saguy, condoned the immediate assassination of the Shaykh before he slipped from their grasp.[51]

The operation itself was precise, demonstrating for once not only possession of high grade intelligence on the part of *AMAN*, but also considerable skill on the part of IDF helicopter pilots who launched the guided missiles at the convoy in which Musawi was travelling. With hindsight, the killing of al-Mussawi crossed a Rubicon of restraint that had been tacitly acknowledged by all sides. Despite the repeated call for the liberation of *al-Quds* (Jerusalem), Hizbollah had refrained from launching missile attacks on Israel proper, confining its operations to attacks on IDF/SLA targets within the security zone. Passions aroused by the killing of the Shaykh were, therefore, inflamed further by the knowledge that the attack had taken place outside the security zone. The response of *al-Muqawama* was to launch a salvo of Katyusha rockets on Israeli conurbations in the Galilee panhandle for the first time. Though inflicting little collateral damage, the retort of the IDF four days later was to launch a mass artillery bombardment of the Lebanese villages of Kafra and Yatar, just north of the security zone and identified by *AMAN* as centres of Hizbollah activity. According to one source over 3,000 shells were fired in a 24-hour period. Moreover, homes of people suspected of harbouring Hizbollah activists, were – in a practice adopted from policing operations in the West Bank and Gaza – destroyed. It was a policy that was both heartless and mindless.[52]

The price incurred by Jerusalem in killing Musawi – increased tension along the northern border as well the retaliatory bombing of the Buenos Aires embassy that left 28 dead – denied the very achievements that the IDF hoped to accrue by his removal. In a frank moment of reflection, Saguy noted, 'I don't know [how] to judge our operation at that time – is it the right thing to get it done because we paid our penalty in Argentina and other places as well? I don't know'.[53] A carbon copy of the assassination of Musawi occurred with the killing some three years later of Rida Yasin, a high ranking field commander, whose car was also hit by a missile fired from a helicopter, just east of the port city of Tyre but, again, well outside the security zone. The assassination was met with the almost ritual bombardment by Hizbollah of northern Israel, in which one Israeli civilian was killed and 15 wounded. If the security zone was about protecting the inhabitants of northern Israel, the policy of regime targeting clearly contradicted this self-declared aim.

Moreover, it failed to deter the increasing levels of proficiency that came to mark the operations of *al-Muqawama*.

On 27 October 1994 in a daylight assault filmed by Hizbollah, 20 guerrillas stormed the outpost of Dabshe in the security zone, tearing down the Israeli flag and replacing it with the banner of Hizbollah. Some 70 soldiers from the IDF's Givati infantry brigade were reported to have fled during the assault or cowered in adjacent bunkers until the attack had been completed. The impact of such attacks lay not in the material damage inflicted, but in their psychological impact upon the IDF itself and the wider Israeli public. Following the debacle at Dabshe, Yoav Gelber, a noted military historian remarked that the 'spirit of self sacrifice' that had served Israel so well in its previous wars was now sadly lacking among many of Israel's frontline combat troops.[54] With the bulk of IDF soldiers confined increasingly to fortified positions in south Lebanon, greater use came to be made of a new Special Forces unit tasked specifically with conducting long range reconnaissance patrols in south Lebanon in an attempt to thwart the activity of *al-Muqawama*. This unit *Egoz* (Hebrew for 'almond') comprised volunteers from the Golani Infantry Brigade, and unlike other units who served in the security zone on a rotational basis, it remained a permanent fixture in the IDF order of battle in south Lebanon. According to the limited publicity surrounding the unit, it was tasked mainly with interdiction along routes identified as likely supply lines for the Islamic resistance.[55] While *Egoz* soldiers were undoubtedly of high calibre, its ability to close with *al-Muqawama* remained dependent as much upon chance as good intelligence. Given the physical area to be covered, it would appear that their use was as much a psychological boost for the battered pride of the IDF, than as a potent tool with which to bring its nemesis to account.[56]

With the attritional toll imposed upon its HUMINT assets, *AMAN* came to rely increasingly upon technical means to acquire real-time intelligence on Hizbollah. While undoubtedly providing Israel with much useful data, such dependence upon technical means to gauge intent *and* capability was in itself a tacit admission that Israel was losing the intelligence war. The closed nature of guerrilla organizations makes the gathering of intelligence – either through ELINT (Electronic Intelligence) or signal's intelligence (SIGINT) – notoriously difficult.[57] The filming of the attack on Dabshe demonstrated the importance Hizbollah placed on the propaganda value of such assaults, but the actual planning of such operations remained closed to the prying ears of Israeli SIGINT because the use of telecommunications, even if encrypted, remained anathema to the high levels of field security imposed by the Islamic Resistance. Indeed, the introduction of a tight cell structure among its operational units by the end of 1992 had made *al-Muqawama* all, but impervious to penetration, a fact recognized by the more discerning among Israel's military correspondents.[58]

Much reliance came to be placed upon Unmanned Airborne Vehicles (UAV) to offset deficits in HUMINT and SIGINT collation of real-time field intelligence, most notably in attempts to hit launch sites of Katyusha rockets. However the range and mobility of these rockets, often launched from a single man portable tube, made it extremely difficult for even these pilotless drones to locate accurately suspected firing points within the security zone. This in part explains the tragedy that befell Lebanese civilians at al-Qana on 18 April 1996 during Operation 'Grapes of Wrath'.

An operation that was designed to place pressure upon Damascus and Beirut to control the activities of Hizbollah in the security zone, 'Grapes of Wrath' turned sour for Israel when an artillery shell landed in the middle of the UN compound at al-Qana, slaughtering 102 Lebanese civilians who had taken what they believed to be safe refuge from Israel's mass aerial and artillery bombardment. The IDF version of events was that one of its UAV's had spotted the *al-Muqawama* preparing to fire a rocket some three hundred meters from the compound, and opened fire. The deaths of so many were blamed not only on a misdirected shell, but on the Islamic Resistance using the compound as cover for their activities.

Under the weight of international opprobrium, Jerusalem was soon forced into a unilateral cease fire, much to the disgust of Major-General Herzl Budwinger, head of the Israeli Air Force who opined that Israel had been close to breaking Hizbollah had it not been for the 'tragic mishap' of al-Qana.[59] Such hubris was not reflected in the acrimony which emerged between *AMAN* and the head of IDF Northern Command, Major-General Amiram Levine. Levine accused military intelligence of providing injudicious assessments regarding Hizbollah capabilities, not least the time it would take to 'break' the Islamic Resistance as Katyusha rockets continued to fall on towns and villages in northern Israel.[60]

'Grapes of Wrath' was an undoubted intelligence failure in two key respects. It failed in its wider political aim of using the mass exodus of Lebanese, fleeing north to escape the bombardment, as a means to place pressure upon Beirut and Damascus to control Hizbollah. Second, the very scale of the bombardment merely served to entrench support for Hizbollah even further among all confessions in Lebanon, best expressed in the aid proffered freely by both Christian and Muslim communities to those fleeing the onslaught. The symbolism of *al-Muqawama* defending Lebanese national honour as opposed to a purely confessional identity was summed up in the words of one Shi'a resident of Tyre who noted that 'at least our boys are defending our land'.[61]

In the aftermath of 'Grapes of Wrath', a number of studies were produced by IDF officers seeking more efficient ways to deal with Hizbollah and the problem of south Lebanon. Colonel Shmuel Gordon recommended the creation of a new command structure that could coordinate a three-pronged strategy designed to deal with Hizbollah. The study is of interest precisely because of the language used. While noting the difficulties associated with COIN operations and LIC, the measures advocated remained purely military in their orientation with intelligence activity confined to providing real-time operational information for an interdiction capability organized around heli-borne forces. Indeed, all too often Hizbollah and 'terrorist' are employed in symbiotic terms with little appreciation of the wider political context in which the conflict was being played out.[62] Once again, the microscope appeared to retain its myopic hold among IDF officers over the choice of methodologies in dealing with Hizbollah.

Other, more subtle technologies were introduced to gather information. These reportedly included the planting of remote sensors along suspected guerrilla routes throughout south Lebanon, the use of multiple radio frequencies to either jam or detonate roadside bombs prematurely, as well as reported requests to Washington to provide satellite data on south Lebanon.[63] But such measures, however effective in a tactical sense, could never replace HUMINT assets, the paucity of which forced Israel into reactive, rather than proactive measures. Nor, more importantly, could they offer a broader perspective of the conditions that had allowed both Hizbollah and its support to flourish among the hills and wadis of southern Lebanon. As Danni Reshef, a former intelligence officer with *AMAN* noted:

> In summary, the IDF is fighting in Lebanon [in 1999] in order to protect the northern settlements from an enemy who has never tried to cross the border into Israel, and is doing this in the framework of rules and under-standings that bring a threat to the northern settlements only when the war brings the inevitable civilian casualties in Lebanon. This threat cannot be answered by the existence of the security zone. The reality in which the security zone was established, no longer exists. The Middle East has changed time and again. But the [successive] Israeli governments did not change their perceptions. They did not re-examine the facts, and did not seriously examine other alternatives, including that of immediate withdrawal in south Lebanon.[64]

Conclusion

On 25 May 2000 the last IDF soldiers crossed the border back into Israel, bringing an end to nearly 18 years of continuous occupation of their security zone. Without the physical protection of their main benefactor, the SLA dissolved overnight. Much to the surprise of many observers, the feared blood-letting against its rank and file members did not occur. The more senior members had already made good their escape, Lahad to France, his subordinates to northern Israel and beyond.

Until the end, the IDF high command proved resistant to the idea of a unilateral withdrawal, it being consistently argued that in the absence of a written agreement with either Beirut or Damascus, Hizbollah attacks into Israel proper would result. These reports, collated and presented by *AMAN* have proved to be unduly alarmist. Aside from the October 2000 abduction of three IDF soldiers, and a brief Katyusha and artillery duel prompted by the kidnapping, the northern border proved remarkably quiescent until the 2006 Summer War.[65]

In explaining the obtuse position of the IDF, it was noted that a unilateral withdrawal in the absence of an agreement would undermine the conventional deterrent capability of the IDF. The use of roadside bombings by Palestinians against Israeli targets in the West Bank and Gaza Strip during the *al-Aqsa Intifada* was proof that organizations such as the *Tanzim* and *Fatah* were attempting to ape the methods that proved so successful for *al-Muqawama*. While his name remains pilloried among some commentators of Israel's domestic political scene, Ehud Barak's decision as Prime Minister to press ahead with the unilateral withdrawal from Lebanon against military advice proved a brave political act. As one commentator noted, for the IDF, Lebanon became a habit, a cockpit of violence in which it remained the main arbiter of what was, or was not good for the security of Israel's northern border. This hegemonic position allowed the IDF not only to frame the consensus over Lebanon, but to gainsay government policy towards the conflict.[66]

It is often said that hindsight is the only precise science. This aphorism is certainly true of Barak, who during his tenure as Chief of Staff, opposed any withdrawal from the security zone. It is quite clear that however good Israel's operational or field intelligence may have been in south Lebanon, its overall intelligence effort remained flawed conceptually. The inability to regard Hizbollah as anything more than terrorists, or to look beyond the more extreme rhetoric at their emergence into the mainstream of Lebanese politics produced erroneous intelligence assessments. Such assessments and the resulting actions remained a product of a national security doctrine built around a construction of the 'other'. As such, they all too often became self-fulfilling prophecies, rather than being objective analyses of both the political *and* military situation in south Lebanon. Given close ties that define civil–military relations in Israel, objective intelligence was undermined by being a product of the very strategic culture from which it had emerged. Replication of methods used to deal with the PLO, or decisions based on a cultural perception of 'pain thresholds' proved myopic in the extreme and often undermined the very national security it claimed to uphold.

The wider context of the conflict in south Lebanon should never be forgotten. Undoubtedly, the support of Tehran and Damascus remained crucial to the ability of Hizbollah to sustain its campaign. Equally, one should not suggest that a radical revision of Israeli LIC could have supplanted the appeal of the Islamic resistance among the Lebanese Shi'a. It is, however to suggest that more judicious intelligence assessments, including an appreciation of the changing nature of Hizbollah as a political organization may have restricted the political and military space available to the organization, and allowed Jerusalem greater latitude in shaping the preferences and choices of its Arab neighbours. But as their experience of Lebanon demonstrated, the operational reach of Israel's intelligence community was always to remain greater than its strategic grasp.

8 The pragmatic and the radical
Syria and Iran and war by proxy

Hassan A. Barari and
Hani A. M. Akho-Rashida

Introduction

Proxy wars have been fought in different parts of the world throughout modern history. It was particularly so during the Cold War era when the United States and the Soviet Union, fearful of the devastating impact of a nuclear exchange but unwilling to forego competition for global power and influence, resorted to war by proxies. But such conflicts have not been the exclusive preserve of the former superpowers, nor indeed, did they fall into abeyance with the demise of the Soviet Union and the end of the Cold War. Tehran and Damascus are often said to be in a proxy war with Israel, perhaps best exemplified by the 34-days war in the summer of 2006 between Israel and the Iranian-backed militia Hizbollah. Even the most optimistic Hizbollah supporters never imagined that the group could have withstood the might of the Israeli army for as long as it did. Given the perceived supremacy of Israel's army and the obvious military imbalance between the two sides, Israelis and Americans alike were stunned by the war's outcome; Hizbollah guerrilla fighters not only managed to resist the Israeli ground offensive, but also inflicted a relatively high casualty toll on the Israeli army.[1]

Given the apparent friendship between Hizbollah, Syria, and Iran, the term proxy is often employed by analysts to characterize the power dynamics between Hizbollah on the one hand and Damascus and Tehran on the other with Hizbollah often referred to as a pawn that either Syria or Iran (and sometimes both) manipulates for regional gain.[2] While both Iran and Syria have indeed supported Hizbollah for decades, categorizing the different players in such black and white terms of client/proxy and patron is somewhat misleading. It is true that both Syria and Iran support Hizbollah and influence some of the party's important decisions, but relations have not been a one-way street, especially in the last decade. Far from being a proxy for either Iran or Syria, Hizbollah has demonstrated that it is a quintessentially Lebanese movement, and clearly engages in the push and pull of Lebanese politics. Equally important, the 'Divine Victory' of which Hizbollah boasts deserves closer scrutiny. What role have Syria and Iran played in conducting war? What is the nature of Hizbollah's relations with those two regional powers? Historical evidence suggests that Hizbollah had been a proxy for either Iran or Syria, but the 2006 war has challenged this strongly held belief.

It is widely asserted that Hizbollah's ability to function as a military and social organization has been contingent upon financial, material, military and ideological support from Tehran and Damascus. Israel sees that support as consistent with an aggressive intent on the part of Syria and Iran – an intent that denies the very basis of Israel as a 'Jewish State'. The costs to Syria and Iran in supporting Hizbollah have been negligible, given that their support of the party furthers their own particular foreign policy goals. For Iran, Hizbollah symbolizes an Islamic rejection of Israel's right to exist within borders that are seen as *waqf*, the preserve of Muslims. For Syria, military and political support for a movement whose religious basis negates the secularism of the Ba'athist state has always been directed towards extracting concessions from Israel over the occupied Golan Heights.

While this blend of realpolitik and ideological affinity defined the boundaries of engagement with Hizbollah, Syrian and Iranian support for the movement has also been dependent upon their changing political leadership. This chapter examines the changing nature of support given to Hizbollah and the extent to which the movement has managed to remain an autonomous actor despite its logistical and political reliance upon Damascus and Tehran. The first section of this chapter outlines the historical, social, and economic background behind the establishment of Hizbollah. The second section examines the complex relations between the party and Syria. The third section examines the power dynamics in the relationship with Iran. The fourth section sheds light on how the power dynamics played out during and after the last confrontation between Israel and Hizbollah, especially within the shifting Lebanese political scene. The final section presents the findings of the study and accounts for the role of the confessional system in facilitating or impeding the regional schemes of external actors.

The wretched of the earth

Analysts often refer to Hizbollah as nothing but a surrogate of either Iran or Syria. Many Lebanese writers make this false assumption.[3] While it is hard to deny the organization's strong connection with both Syria and Iran, Hizbollah's rise should be seen as an attempt to meet the needs of the marginalized and excluded Shi'a community in Lebanon. Presenting Hizbollah as a tool or pawn of Damascus or Tehran, therefore, distorts the way the movement works. The *raison d'être* of Hizbollah is not to benefit regional patrons, but to meet the demands of the Shi'a community that, as a result of sectarian differences, have given up on the state as a provider of social and economic benefits.

There are historical reasons for the impoverishment of the Shi'a community in many of the Sunni Arab states. When the Ottomans ruled the region, many leaders saw Shi'as as a stalking horse for Persia. More recently, even

Egyptian President Hosni Mubarak stated that the Arab Shi'a loyalties are to Iran rather than to the predominantly Arab dispensations in which they live.[4] Although this statement reflects the fear of Iran's ascendance in the region following the breakdown of the balance of power, as a result of Saddam Hussein's removal in 2003, it indicates profound sectarian divisions, ones that could be used for political ends. Indeed, the Sunni–Shi'a divide dates back centuries before the Safavids decided to transform Persia into a Shi'a state.

The Shi'a community in Lebanon was further suppressed when Sunni leaders and their Maronite counterparts signed the National Pact of 1943, which divided political power among the different sects. The Shi'a*s* were given the position of speaker of the Lebanese parliament, a largely symbolic post that wielded relatively little power in relation to the growing demographic weight of the community. As a result, their political rights remained circumscribed in comparison to those of the Christian Maronites and Sunnis. During much of the 1950s and 1960s, the Shi'a community was attracted to leftist parties, especially the Syrian Social Nationalist Party and the Communist Party, since these parties condemned 'the tribal, religious, or ethnic bases of discrimination'.[5] The Shi'a attachment to these secular parties came as a result of the political, social and economic marginalization that had characterized their status for decades. This exclusion led to a new realization in the 1970s and the emergence of new political trends within the community that broke with their leaders' old mentality.[6]

Within this cauldron of simmering identities and ethno-religious animosity, a new political agency had begun to emerge among the Shi'a community. An Iranian-born cleric, Sayyed Musa al-Sadr, whose ancestors hailed originally from south Lebanon, arrived in Tyre in 1959. A man of exceptional organizational ability and charisma, al-Sadr set about challenging the sectarian constraints imposed upon the Shi'a by the confessional system. This included attacks upon the traditional role played by the Shi'a *zu'ama*, families whose control of land and resources allowed them to benefit from the confessional system, while imposing a feudal order on the mass of their co-religionists.[7] His proselytising in the mosques, as well as the organization of strikes among predominately Shi'a communities, brought him to the attention of the authorities in Beirut. While unwilling to reform the political structure that imposed such hardship among the Shi'a, the political activism of al-Sadr began to attract increased funds for infrastructure projects among his natural constituency. Accordingly, al-Sadr has been credited with reinvigorating 'Shi'a*ism*' as the means to challenge the social and political hegemony of the confessional order, rather than just remaining an identity associated with cultural inferiority and political servitude.

The shifting contours in the confessional makeup of Lebanon manifested itself in increased sectarian tension and violence throughout the early 1970s. For the Shi'a of south Lebanon, this tension was related to the political and military influence wielded by the PLO in the refugee camps in and around the southern cities of Sidon and Tyre. Inevitably, the activities of the PLO, particularly its cross border raids into northern Israel, drew the violent ire of Jerusalem. While professing support for the Palestinian cause, the scale of retribution visited upon south Lebanon meant that Shi'a communities often became the unwitting victims of this undeclared border war. Moreover, many Shi'a came to resent the heavy handed methods of PLO guerrillas in enforcing their writ on the communal life of south Lebanon. The epithet *Fatahland*, used to describe the hegemony exercised by the PLO in south Lebanon, was yet another reminder that other forces continued to be masters of the Shi'a house. By 1975, the need for the Shi'a community to organize an effective defence force amid the tide of rising confessional tension was all too apparent. With the outbreak of the Lebanese Civil War in June of that year, that need became an absolute necessity. Accordingly, in July 1975 Sayyed al-Sadr oversaw the establishment of the *Afwaj al Muqawama al Lubaniyya*, the Lebanese Resistance Brigades or Amal.

Amal came to dominate Shi'a politics between 1975 and 1982. Its prestige was helped immeasurably by two main events. Its protection of the Shi'a from the vicissitudes of the civil war – including Israel's incursion into south Lebanon in March 1978 – and the mysterious disappearance of Musa al-Sadr during a visit to Libya in August of that year. Though denied by Tripoli, most believe that al-Sadr was murdered. But his 'disappearance' had a wider religious significance for the Shi'a of Lebanon, and one that came to acquire a symbolism that radicalized many associated with Amal. As James Piscatori explains

> [T]he Shi'a public associated al-Sadr's disappearance with one or the other two venerable Shi'a traditions: martyrdom (*shahada*), or occultation (*ghayba*), the process whereby the Imam, or messianic leader, goes into hiding and is expected to return in the fullness of time.[8]

Events following the disappearance of Musa al-Sadr – the Iranian Revolution of 1979, the Shi'a's awareness and political manifestation of their social, economic, and political exclusion, and the Israeli invasion of Lebanon in 1982 – triggered a marked change in Shi'a politics. Designed to remove the immediate guerrilla threat posed to Israel's northern border by the PLO, the political aims of the invasion were far more radical: the destruction of the PLO as a symbol of the national aspirations of the Palestinian people, and the placing of the Lebanese political map once more under a Christian Maronite ascendancy.[9]

Somewhat surprisingly, Israel's invasion was welcomed initially by some Shi'a villages, grateful for the immediate relief it offered from the overbearing influence of the PLO. Such gratitude was to be short-lived. It quickly became clear that Israel's presence in south Lebanon would not be transient – that is, limited to the destruction of the PLO – but long-term as it tried to promote Christian Maronite hegemony. Moreover, whatever animosity existed between the Shi'a Lebanese and the Palestinians was dissipated by the shock registered by both communities at the massacre of Palestinians in the refugee camps of Sabra and Shatila by Christian militiamen under the nominal control of the Israel Defence Forces (IDF).[10] The impact of Israel's invasion on the Lebanese Shi'a brought to the fore the long-simmering tensions in Amal over how to deal with Israel's occupation of south Lebanon. A splinter group, Islamic Amal, emerged in the ancient city of Ba'albek in the immediate aftermath of the invasion, led by a former school teacher Hussein al-Mussawi. The inspiration behind this group was the Iranian Revolution, an event that demonstrated to men like al-Mussawi that Islam could be the vehicle for radical change in the political and social structures of Lebanon. Accordingly, al-Mussawi called for the establishment of an Islamic state throughout Lebanon, one that was clearly to be based upon the Iranian model.

It was Iran's influence, however, that was central to the emergence of Hizbollah. Tehran dispatched members of the Islamic Revolutionary Guard Corps, the *Pasdaran*, to the Beqaa valley as advisors to the emerging resistance to Israeli occupation. The ability of Iran to oversee the merger of a number of disparate groups in Lebanon, including Islamic Amal, gave birth to Hizbollah, the Party of God, in 1982. A key role was played by the Iranian ambassador to Damascus, Ali Akbar Motashemi, who arranged not only financial support for the organization, but also encouraged Lebanese Shi'a clerics to participate fully in recruiting followers to Hizbollah while providing spiritual guidance to those resisting Israel's occupation of Lebanon. This brought to prominence men such as Sayyed Fadlallah, who in Hizbollah, found a particularly apposite platform for the propagation of a radical ideo-theology that relied heavily on the symbolism of the Iranian Revolution. In making continued reference to the leadership of Ayatollah Khomeini, men such as Fadlallah cloaked Hizbollah's struggle in a meta-historical language.

Continued reference was made to the continuing struggle between the 'arrogance of the world' (*mustakbirin*) and the 'downtrodden of the world' (*mustafadin*). Consequently, whatever violent acts came to be associated with the movement, these remained, according to Fadlallah's worldview, defensive acts in the name of Islam and were, thus, to be condoned. As such, the struggle that Hizbollah now engaged upon was seen as inseparable from the wider confrontation between *dar al-harb* (House of War) and *dar al-Islam* (House of Islam). The struggle against Israel was seen as an inevitable catalyst to the destruction of the Jewish State and the liberation of *al-Quds* (Jerusalem) from 'Zionist occupation', and the removal from Lebanon of a confessional order that suppressed the people and served only the interests of Western intervention. Hizbollah also placed strong emphasis upon the creation of an Islamic dispensation in Lebanon, to be achieved in coordination with the wider Islamic community or *umma*.[11] Accordingly, Hizbollah deliberately eschewed the previous symbols of the Lebanese state, instead adopting their own iconography that impressed loyalty to their radical view of Islam upon Lebanon's fragmented political scene. To quote Frantz Fanon, it was the 'wretched of the earth' who laid the groundwork for the emergence of a more assertive Shi'a political movement.

Syria now allowed Iran to dispatch around 1,000 *Pasdaran* to the Beqaa Valley, which was until then controlled entirely by Damascus. The Syrian policy shift was caused by the Israeli invasion of Lebanon and concern that Israeli designs in Lebanon – not least the establishment of a Christian client in Beirut – represented a strategic threat to Damascus. As such Iran's involvement, the Syrians reasoned, could serve to counter Israeli influence in Lebanon. Hence, Syria was driven, by and large, by its tactical need to confront Israel. Equally important, Iran was supplying Syria with much-needed oil at a very favourable price. These two factors greatly influenced Syrian decision makers when they allowed Iran to penetrate the south, thus, supplying the impetus to strengthen the ongoing relations between Hizbollah and Iran.[12]

Therefore, while the origin of Hizbollah should be seen against the backdrop of the impoverishment of the Shi'as, its rise to prominence in the Lebanese political scene would have been almost impossible without the military and economic aid it received from both Syria and Iran. Iranians offered the party the necessary weapons and funds to provide services for the needy. In addition, as will be seen below, the party managed to establish objectives that it could deliver. Its readiness and desire to confront both the Israelis and the American-led Multi-National Force in Beirut (MNF) – a force deemed by Damascus and Tehran to be but a cloak for Washington's regional ambitions – conflated with Syrian and Iranian objectives.[13]

However, after the withdrawal of the MNF and the Israeli withdrawal from central Lebanon, the relationship between Syria and Hizbollah took on a new twist. Syria began to feel somewhat emboldened and confident about handling matters in Lebanon. Therefore, Syria's patience with a revolutionary group, which was seen as a threat to the entire Lebanese political system, was not without limit. Their relationship deteriorated into armed clashes, especially when Syria's other proxy Shi'a movement, Amal, stepped up its violent campaign against the Palestinians.[14] Iran has had more to do with the emergence of the Shi'a movement than Syria, but the three players have become involved in a triangular relationship that has led many pundits and politicians to claim that Hizbollah is nothing but a pawn for either Syria or Iran. Is this the case?

Who calls the shots? The case of Syria

The statement 'no war without Egypt, and no peace without Syria', has almost become an axiom. Israelis make the case that the most hostile regime to Israel is the Syrian Ba'ath regime, since it has been in conflict with Israel since the war of 1948 and the very basis of its Ba'athist ideology denies legitimacy to any Jewish polity in Palestine. Although the Golan Heights as a theatre of conflict has been quiet since the October 1973 war, Syria has fought

Israel continuously through proxies, particularly from within Lebanon. Within that context, Hizbollah has furthered Syria's strategy vis-à-vis Israel repeatedly, but to categorize the bilateral relationship between Syria and Hizbollah as one of patron–client or patron–proxy is misleading. One can see this by analysing the important stages in the history of the shifting power dynamics between the two.[15] Syria became the undisputed arbiter in Lebanese politics in the 1990s, and took advantage of the regional developments following Saddam Hussein's ill-fated decision to invade Kuwait in August 1990. Syria realigned itself and joined the American-led coalition to oust Saddam's forces from Kuwait. But as a quid pro quo for supporting America's regional efforts, Syria was given free reign in Lebanon. That was the first significant turning point in the relationship between Hizbollah and Syria.

The Syrian presence in Lebanon seemed the only way to guarantee the implementation of the Taif Agreement of 1989, which ended the bloody 15-year civil war, and reinforced sectarianism as the basis for power sharing in Lebanese politics. This agreement put an end, albeit for an undetermined period, to Hizbollah's ultimate goal of an Islamist state in Lebanon. Syria started calling the shots in Lebanon, Hizbollah realizing that realpolitik dictated accommodation of – rather than confrontation with – Damascus. Indeed, the Taif agreement of 1991 that brought about an end to the Lebanese Civil War and the role it assigned Syria forced Hizbollah, after much internal debate within the movement, to finally accept the confessional system on which the Lebanese state is based.[16] More than at any other time, Hizbollah realized the necessity to work out an arrangement regarding its armed wing, *al-Muqawama* given that the Taif Agreement calls for disarmament of all militias.[17] In addition, the death of the Ayatollah Khomeini in 1989 freed the movement from its deep-seated attachment to Iran. Mohammed Hussein Fadlallah, Hizbollah's spiritual leader, did not hold the emerging religious order in Tehran in any great esteem, thereby loosening the hitherto strong fidelity to the Iranian revolution that had marked the emergence and development of Hizbollah in the early 1980s.

With the expulsion from Lebanon in 1991 of the Iraqi-backed Christian warlord, General Michel Aoun, Syria once again emerged as the dominant hegemonic power across most of the country. This position of power presented Syria with an opportunity to confront Israel through Hizbollah. President Hafez al-Assad, a shrewd strategist, sought an approach through which he could harass Israel by using Hizbollah as a means to restore the Golan Heights once more to Syrian sovereignty. Therefore, during the 1990s, the interests of al-Assad and Hizbollah converged into what became a marriage of convenience. Hafez al-Assad sought to liberate the Golan Heights, and Hizbollah sought to liberate the south of Lebanon. For Damascus, Hizbollah represented a tool from which to exact territorial concessions from Israel and as such, Hizbollah's right to resist Israel became a position that al-Assad championed vociferously, not least at times of particularly bloody encounters between the IDF and Hizbollah.[18] This was particularly so when, much to the chagrin of Damascus, the Palestinians went their separate way by signing the Oslo accord with Israel in September 1993, the Jordanians soon following suit by signing a full-fledged peace treaty with Israel in 1994. The only country left was now Lebanon, and al-Assad was determined to keep it staunchly behind him in order to negotiate with Israel from a position of relative strength.

Throughout the 1990s, Syria imposed military and political constraints on Hizbollah. While Hizbollah justified its possession of weapons on the grounds that it was Lebanon's only true resistance force, the party never enjoyed a free ride, since Syria had the last word at the strategic level. Unsurprisingly, Syria directed the party in a manner meant to serve Syrian objectives. This logic did not escape peace mediators. Therefore, when Israel launched the ill-advised 'Grapes of Wrath' campaign, Syria's status was accentuated accordingly. Warren Christopher, then US Secretary of State, employed a very active form of shuttle diplomacy between Jerusalem and Damascus to discuss and mediate the 'April Understanding' between Hizbollah and Israel.[19] In addition, Hizbollah had to coordinate with the Syrian military and intelligence personnel working in Lebanon. Syria's prominence was further enhanced because of its strict monitoring of weapons shipments from Iran. On a political level, Syria curtailed the aspirations of Hizbollah, resulting in the party's disproportionate representation compared to its popular base in the Shi'a community. This arrangement benefited the less popular movement Amal, which was a proxy of Syria.

Paradoxically, the Israelis, who came under heavy domestic pressure to withdraw from south Lebanon, injected another factor into the Syria–Hizbollah power dynamic.[20] It was obvious to the Israelis that Hafez al-Assad's ability to use Hizbollah as a proxy and as a bargaining chip was contingent on the continued Israeli occupation of south Lebanon. All Israeli attempts to reach an understanding with the Lebanese government failed because they simply ignored the Syrian factor. Therefore, once the Israelis realized that their occupation of Lebanon gave al-Assad a legitimate excuse to stay in Lebanon and to use Hizbollah, they opted for a different course of action. The Israeli government, under Ehud Barak, hoped to nip this arrangement in the bud by unilaterally withdrawing from south Lebanon in May 2000. This move, in Emile El-Hokayem's words, 'explains why the Lebanese government and Hizbollah, with heavy Syrian prompting, raised the contentious issue of the Shebaa Farms, a strip of land whose real ownership remains unclear but which Lebanon claims'.[21]

It is important to note the regional prestige that Hizbollah achieved as a result of its military success in 1993 and again in 1996, with the cumulative impact of the resistance that led to the expulsion of the Israeli forces from south Lebanon. Hassan Nasrallah became a hero in Lebanon and the Arab world. Therefore, one can argue that there was a subtle shift in the power dynamic between Syria and Hizbollah by the turn of the century. This gradual shift was difficult to sense, but when Bashar al-Assad, Hafez's son, assumed the presidency of Syria, it had become obvious that Hizbollah had changed from a proxy to a more autonomous player. This trend was strengthened by the fact that Bashar did not enjoy the same credentials his father had, and he showed admiration for Nasrallah and dealt with him accordingly. This was an attempt on the part of Bashar al-Assad to enjoy 'legitimization by association' to make up for his lack of credentials at the beginning of his presidency, a marked departure from his father's shrewd way of dealing with all of Lebanon's competing factions.[22]

Accordingly, the death of Hafez al-Assad marked a turning point in the Hizbollah–Syria relationship. Bashar began to deal with the leader of Hizbollah as an equal. Posters with the pictures of Bashar, Hassan, and Hafez appeared all over Lebanon, serving as tangible evidence of al-Assad's method of bolstering legitimacy. Nevertheless, following Hizbollah and praising its steadfastness hampered Syria's ability to manoeuvre. As events unfolded in the wake of the Iraq war in 2003, Syria became more dependent on Hizbollah, especially inside Lebanon. The Syrian regime came under heavy scrutiny by the international community and some key Arab states. In addition, some influential Lebanese became overtly critical of Syria. Indeed, there has been no love lost between the Syrian regime and Lebanese factions associated with Christian and Sunni confessions who felt increasingly marginalized by three decades of Syria's overt control of Lebanon. The assassination of the former Lebanese Prime Minister Rafiq Hariri, a Sunni, in 2005 prompted a mass outpouring of both grief and anger against the Ba'athist regime in Damascus, whose agents were widely regarded as responsible for the bloody demise of a popular, if controversial figure.[23] As such, the mass demonstrations that followed in Beirut, the so-called Cedar revolution that enjoyed the support of Washington, was nothing short of an anti-Syrian revolt. Under international scrutiny for its alleged role in the murder of Hariri, and sensitive to the wider neo-Conservative agenda in Washington that attributed much of the bloodshed in Iraq to the malfeasance of Damascus, Bashar al-Assad probably felt that he had few options other than to withdraw all Syrian forces from Lebanon.

When numerous Lebanese factions celebrated the forced departure of Syrian forces from Lebanon in May 2005, Nasrallah organized a massive and impressive 'good-bye but thank you' parade for Syria.[24] He made it clear that the Lebanese owed Syria for its unfettered support for their victorious resistance. As a token sign of gratitude, Nasrallah presented the Syrian forces with a gift: an Israeli rifle that had been seized by Hizbollah. This demonstration of gratitude helped drive home the message to al-Assad that his forces were not driven out of Lebanon in humiliation. Moreover, the association with Hizbollah paid off domestically for the Syrian regime. This mobilization of support undoubtedly stiffened the resolve of Damascus to face the mounting pressure from the Bush administration for the establishment of an International Tribunal to investigate Hariri's death. For Syria such a tribunal was politically motivated, and was perceived as little more than a Trojan horse for the US to undermine still further the Ba'athist regime; Hizbollah's rejection of the tribunal, therefore, was important in that it polarized opinion in Lebanon, depriving the idea of the international tribunal of any semblance of pan-Lebanese legitimacy.

Given the complex interaction and partnership between Syria and Hizbollah, the question of who is a proxy to whom is perhaps obsolete. As this study argues, both actors have used each other to further their own interests. An alliance of convenience rather than conviction, it has nonetheless helped counter the regional machinations of both Israel and the US, ensuring that whatever else, no regional settlement can ever be reached that denies the interests of either Damascus or the Party of God.

Iranian connection

If Hizbollah cannot be regarded as a Syrian proxy, is it an Iranian one? The conventional wisdom in both Washington and Jerusalem is that Hizbollah is an Iranian creation meant to further Iran's regional ambition and to serve as part of a Middle Eastern Shi'a bloc.[25] While the Iranian–Hizbollah link is firm, it is rather inaccurate to present Hizbollah as a pure proxy, given the origin and development of the party itself. Graham Fuller rightly argues that Hizbollah is a function of a growing trend in the Middle East's socio-political development that has shaped, and will continue to shape, the region in general: the long-term Muslim/Arab resolve to oppose Western domination, and the region's minorities' new assertiveness.[26] Hizbollah is clearly a function of these cultural and psychological forces, which, in one form or another, have persisted throughout the region for decades.

There are historical ties between Iran and the Shi'as of Lebanon, dating back to the beginning of the 'Shi'a*fication*' of Iran under the Safavids in the early sixteenth century. Lebanese Shi'as provided Iran with the jurists it badly needed to educate Sunni Iranians. However, ties were strengthened in the early 1980s, and Iran has helped fund, equip, and train Hizbollah ever since. Indeed, it would not have been possible for Hizbollah to assert itself the way it has been doing were it not for Iran's key role. Given the primacy of the Iranian role in empowering Hizbollah, one might ask to what extent Iran dictates policy. In other words, how much influence does Iran have in Hizbollah's decision-making process?

From the beginning, Hizbollah has declared that its ultimate goal is the expulsion of Israeli forces from Lebanon. Indeed, Hizbollah's *raison d'être*, which justified the party's attempt to transcend confessional structures, is to liberate Lebanon from Israeli control. Hence, Hizbollah was not created to be Iran's tool, but rather to strengthen the Shi'a community's independence and to meet its genuine security needs before and during the civil war. Yet, both Hizbollah and Iran consider Israel an enemy and a challenge with which they must contend. This is their common vision, and it follows that some important geopolitical repercussions flow from this commonality. Since Syria controlled Lebanon's confessional politics in the 1990s, Iranian influence on Hizbollah was controlled by Syria. The geopolitics of the triangle is interesting but cannot be fully understood without comprehending the nature of the alliance between Damascus and Tehran, which has been solid since the early 1980s.[27]

With Iran and Iraq at war throughout most of the 1980s, President Hafez al-Assad found in Iran a precious geostrategic ally. Iran supported Syria in Lebanon, not least because Damascus remained an important counterweight to Saddam Hussein. Despite adherence to the shared ideology of Ba'athism, relationships between al-Assad and Saddam Hussein had been marked by a mutual suspicion born from a combination of personal animosity and regional competition that had witnessed Baghdad support the Lebanese Christians during the Civil War.[28] The alliance between Damascus and Tehran has, therefore, endured, despite the Islamic basis of the Iranian state to appear seemingly at odds with the staunch secularism of Syria. Shared interests, rather than values have, nonetheless, underpinned the pragmatism of both towards regional issues.

This triumvirate, therefore, (Iran, Hizbollah, and Syria) need each other for political and strategic considerations. Hizbollah's existence is not a result of Syrian or Iranian decisions. From the outset, Hizbollah has sought Iran's help, and Iran has provided Hizbollah with the necessary means to address the societal needs of the Shi'a community and the weapons and training to confront Israel. Moreover, Iran has been adopting popular issues, such as anti-Israel rhetoric, which resonate well with the Arab masses. The Shi'a community of Lebanon, which suffered from the Israeli occupation of southern Lebanon, is no exception. Iran's support enabled Hizbollah leaders to confront Israel and to achieve popularity among the Shi'a community for the services they have been providing to the needy.

Iran's support for Hizbollah, however, has not been entirely philanthropic, and it would be naïve to assume that Iran wields no clout over Hizbollah. In fact, Nasrallah follows the theological guidance of Iran's Supreme Leader, providing Tehran with political leverage over the organization. Iran is not helping Hizbollah out of a sense of charity alone, but also in order to realize its own regional interests. Equally, it is such alliances that many see as promoting instability across the region. This is why the Islamic Revolutionary Guard Corps has been training Hizbollah forces in Lebanon. Iran also provides Hizbollah with much-needed financial support, thus, enabling the party to provide a wide range of social services to its constituency, the Shi'as in the south. This financial support, however, has a price. Many analysts, especially in Israel and the United States, argue that Hizbollah's decision to initiate the war with Israel in July 2006 was made to buy Iran time and distract the international community from Iran's nuclear ambitions.[29] While this interpretation has some logic, it remains a supposition rather than a statement of political and strategic fact. There undoubtedly exists a marriage of interests between Iran and Hizbollah when it comes to Israel, but labelling 'Hizbollah as a proxy of Iran' denies agency to a party and movement that remains located and legitimized within a particular Lebanese milieu.

Shifting power dynamics: Hizbollah at war with Israel

While it is not clear yet whether the 2006 war in Lebanon was a proxy war, the support of the United States for Israel should not be forgotten. In this sense, Lebanon became a battleground for the competing regional ambitions of Washington and Tehran. The US Secretary of State Condoleezza Rice declared openly that she hoped the war provided the 'birth pangs of a new Middle East.' If so, the resultant order was not one Washington, and indeed much of the Arab world, could have wanted. If Israel failed in this war, that failure was equally shared in the corridors of the White House where, much before the emergence of al-Qaida, Hizbollah had long been regarded as Washington's main nemesis in the Middle East. That Hizbollah withstood the Israeli onslaught came as a bitter surprise to the Israelis who managed the war poorly having underestimated the capabilities of *al-Muqawama* to continue to fire rockets into Israel.[30] For Washington, Hizbollah's apparent victory not only undermined the pro-Western government of Fouad Siniora in Beirut but equally, threatened to embolden the Shi'a of Iraq as they struggled to control a growing insurgency that to all intents and purposes, was fast descending into civil war.

But amid the apparent hubris of victory, the future of Hizbollah and its armed wing remains unclear in the aftermath of the 2006 war. Almost half of the Lebanese population thought Hizbollah was irresponsible for provoking Israel and triggering an unnecessary war. Nasrallah himself tacitly admitted as much, saying that had he known Israel would react as it did, he would not have ordered the abduction of the Israeli troops. Yet the war ended in a way that enabled Nasrallah to declare victory. In the eyes of the majority of Arabs, Hizbollah emerged from the war with increased popularity. According to an Ibn Khaldun Center poll conducted in Egypt after the outbreak of the war, Nasrallah was ranked more popular than President Mubarak in Egypt.[31] Paradoxically, Nasrallah does not enjoy the same level of popularity in his own country. Indeed, the Lebanese were divided over the war because of the high costs associated with it. Many argued that the power to declare war should remain the prerogative of the state, and not of a particular party.

Nevertheless, Nasrallah is intent upon exploiting his 'divine' victory. Gone are the days when Hizbollah subordinated its Shi'a agenda in Lebanon for the sake of resistance; now Nasrallah wants to keep the option of resistance open, an option that he believes transcends all sectarian divisions while concurrently, advancing the political interests of his sect.[32] Thus, the war transformed the internal political debate in Lebanon. Hizbollah has long felt that its representation in parliament was not commensurate with its popular base, thanks to the Syrian intervention in the 1990s which restricted the parliamentary role that Hizbollah could play in Lebanese politics.

This now appears to have changed. After Syria's forced withdrawal from Lebanon, Bashar al-Assad's regime started to rely heavily on Nasrallah's position in blocking the progress towards the effective functioning of the international tribunal, established by the United Nations to investigate the murder of Rafiq Hariri. Fingers immediately pointed toward Syria, since it is the only actor that stood to benefit from the murder of a figure who opposed Syrian policies in Lebanon.[33] Not surprisingly given the nature of the US–Syrian relationship, al-Assad's regime remains concerned at the prospect that such a tribunal might be used as a tool to put more pressure on Syria. Certainly, few Syrians believe the investigation, let alone any eventual outcome, will be limited in scope to individual culpability for Hariri's death.

In sum, the party's relationship with Syria is different from that with Iran. With Syria, Hizbollah is more independent. The forced Syrian withdrawal from Lebanon and the war in 2006 allowed Hizbollah to adopt a more assertive and stronger position vis-à-vis Syria. Equally, Iran remains an ideological and a strategic ally and upon whom Hizbollah relies for military assistance, training, and economic aid. While Hizbollah receives monetary donations from wealthy Shi'as, the largesse provided by Iran remains indispensable to the party's capacity to contend with regional and internal socioeconomic and political challenges. This clearly makes the party less autonomous in its relations with Tehran, but by no means equates it to the role of puppet or proxy.

Conclusion

Categorizing the power dynamic between Hizbollah, Iran, and Syria in simplistic terms – a proxy–patron relationship – is inaccurate. Their relations are complicated, and as this chapter argues, there have been many twists and turns. Perhaps one should look at the two main factors shaping Hizbollah's position vis-à-vis Iran and Syria, especially at times when it appears that Hizbollah is working extraordinarily hard to serve its two 'patrons'. The first is the fact that the Lebanese state has not served the Shi'a community well throughout history. The need for external help was necessary in order for the community to achieve an acceptable standard of living and a reasonable level of political influence. Second is the confessional political system, which has enabled both Syria and Iran to exert influence over Hizbollah to an extent commensurate with the help they offer the party.

When the confessional pie was divided up in 1943, the Shi'a community was subjugated to the Christian Maronites and the Sunnis. The Maronite–Sunni political supremacy resulted in socio-economic policies that impoverished the Shi'a community. During the 1950s and 1960s, leaders of the Shi'a community did not stand up to the state to extract concessions for their sect; rather, they sought to improve their own status. This paved the way for the re-emergence of a more assertive generation, starting in the 1970s.

Given the situation, the Shi'a community was ready to break with the past and assume a new orientation in their relationship vis-à-vis the Lebanese state. At this juncture, the revolutionary Islamic Republic of Iran stepped in and started to assist the Shi'a community through Hizbollah. The party's ability to maintain a network of economic and social services to the almost disenfranchised community hinged, by and large, on financial help from Iran. Furthermore, the military aid to Hizbollah enabled the party to stand up to the Israeli occupation and to appear invincible within Lebanon. Following the war in 2006, Hizbollah demonstrated its military prowess when it swept through Beirut, besieging the government until it caved in.[34]

One cannot argue, therefore, that the relationship is a one-way street, with Iran issuing orders as though Hizbollah were an Iranian military division. Although there is ideological and religious affinity between Iran and Hizbollah, both loathe Israel, so Hizbollah sees itself primarily as defending Lebanon. Hizbollah can be viewed as a religious national movement that has exploited the animosity between Israel and Iran to get more weapons and economic aid to further its own sectarian and national interests. Seen in this way, the party is similar to certain third world countries during the Cold War, playing one superpower against the other to extract more aid.

Syria's involvement in Lebanon is different from Iran's. Damascus decided to get involved in Lebanese politics during the second half of the 1970s, mainly because of security interests. The existence of Syrian forces in Lebanon also gave Syria significant leverage over the confessional system to Syria's benefit. Unlike Tehran, any marked internal change in Lebanon could influence the security interests of Syria. In other words, Syrian involvement in Lebanese politics predated the creation of Hizbollah. Furthermore, the Syrian regime supported the other Shi'a movement, Amal, against Hizbollah in the second half of the 1980s. Even during the 1990s, when Syria was the ultimate arbiter of political power in Lebanon, Hizbollah did not act as a mere proxy. While the party's provocation of Israel helped Syria, Hizbollah was acting on its own ambitions of liberating Lebanon from the Israeli occupation.

The second observation pertains to the extent to which the Lebanese confessional system helps or hinders the pursuit of regional hegemony for key state actors. All along, Lebanon has been a porous country; even Israelis have managed to cultivate close relationships with some leaders of the Maronite sect.[35] The confessional system allows all sects to ask for help from regional powers without impediments, and almost every sect has received economic and military assistance from abroad. Lebanon is also a state where the government has never had a monopoly over the use of force.

This sectarian system has helped external powers penetrate Lebanon, but at the same time the system restricts the influence of those external powers to achieve their goals. In other words, the internal system balances itself.

However, when Syria was in full control in Lebanon (some would call this 'occupation'), it was difficult for any sect to behave in a manner that frustrated Syrian interests. Syria tried to use Lebanon to further its regional standing vis-à-vis Israel. Nonetheless, Syria failed to realize its objective of recovering the Golan Heights by using Hizbollah and Lebanon as a staging point to attack Israel indirectly.

Following the assassination of Rafiq Hariri, Syrian forces were forced to withdraw under great popular pressure from the Lebanese, the West and moderate Arab states. Although this withdrawal has emasculated Syria and led to its regional isolation, the United States has failed to provide the elected Lebanese government with hegemony in Lebanon due to the confessional system that still allows other powers to interfere. Both Iran and Syria have stepped up their assistance to Hizbollah to bring the government to its knees. Indeed, the 2007 Doha agreement reflects the fact that in Lebanon, there can be no hegemon.[36]

The geopolitical relationship between Iran, Syria, and Hizbollah is complicated, but, as this chapter has argued Hizbollah does not play an inferior role. The three actors will remain dependent upon each other in the short to medium term, but it remains to be seen how this triumvirate can continue to function should Syria ever achieve peace with Israel. Will Syria realign and reorient its foreign policy the way Egypt did in the 1970s? Will Lebanon sign a peace treaty with Israel if Syria does? What will happen if Israel withdraws from the Shebaa Farms? Will Hizbollah lose its pretext and indeed legitimacy for maintaining *al-Muqawama*? More dramatically, what would happen if a war was to break out between Israel and Iran? These remain debates for the future. For now, however, the pragmatic and the radical continue to support the Party of God in its struggle with Israel.

9 Forever at the crossroads

Hizbollah's combined strategies of accommodation and resistance

Mats Wärn

Introduction

In the unfolding drama of Lebanon, Hizbollah displays an enigmatic nature, consistently puzzling observers by oscillating between revolutionary passion and calls for calm and moderation. Hizbollah's sweeping takeover of Beirut in May 2008, when its fighters stormed the streets of the capital, besieged government buildings and closed down the station of *Future TV* (a political antagonist to the party), even engaging in gun battles that caused over one hundred casualties, might be seen as the extreme expression of one such 'moodswing'. To some Lebanese, it revealed the more sinister apprehensions of the Lebanese Islamist movement, long pending, since it finally, and despite assurances to the contrary, had turned its guns 'inwards', against the Lebanese state institutions and indeed, its critics argued, against Lebanon itself. Others regarded the turbulent events and Hizbollah's storming of the downtown area of the Lebanese capital as the inevitable culmination of the severe tensions and divisions tormenting the country ever since the Syrian troops and security services (*al-mukhabarat*) were pressured to leave Lebanon after the assassination of former Prime Minister Rafiq Hariri on 8 February 2005.

The killing of Rafiq Hariri, a tycoon and statesman, both revered and scorned by the multitudes of Lebanese confessions and politicians, was one of those watershed events that had placed the country's players 'at the crossroads', not the least Hizbollah. After all, the assassination took place amid increasing domestic and international pressure upon the Syrian forces, present in Lebanon since 1976, to leave Lebanon in line with United Nations Security Council Resolution (UNSCR) 1559, drafted in early September 2004, after Damascus had enforced its clout by seeing to it that the Syrian-friendly Lebanese President Emile Lahoud's mandate was extended for another three years. UNSCR 1559 called 'upon all remaining forces to withdraw from Lebanon' (meaning Syria) and the 'disbanding and disarmament of all Lebanese and non-Lebanese militias', meaning Hizbollah and the Palestinian guerrillas residing in the country.[1] Correctly or not, Syria was widely blamed for being behind Hariri's assassination and raging street demonstrations around Lebanon demanded Syria's departure from Lebanon as well as an international court to sentence the culprit.

During this furore, Hizbollah – a long term ally of Syria – at first kept silent. However, after Syria's President Bashar al-Assad declared his commitment to withdraw all Syrian troops from Lebanon, Hizbollah, along with a number of its Lebanese allies, arranged a large demonstration of more than half a million supporters in downtown Beirut, waving banners that read 'Thank you, Syria', 'No to 1559', and 'Who Killed Hariri?'. To Hizbollah, ever carrying a deep grudge towards US policies in the Middle East and Lebanon, the murder of Rafiq Hariri and the drafting – and the strident demands for implementing – UNSC resolution 1559 were mere pretexts for sowing divisions in Lebanon that in the end might undermine Hizbollah's national standing. Crowning the large-scale gathering, Sayyed Hassan Nasrallah, Hizbollah's secretary-general, defiantly addressed the US administration:

> Your calculations in dividing this country are wrong. Lebanon cannot be divided nor defeated. Lebanon will neither change its name, nor its history, nor its identity . . . I tell the Americans: Do not interfere in our domestic affairs. Let your ambassador relax in his embassy . . . and leave us alone.[2]

True, Hizbollah's anti-American fervour was well-known and predictable, but observers were puzzled by the explicitly expressed support and gratefulness for – in Nasrallah's words – 'Bashar Assad's Syria, the resisting Syrian people, and the steadfastness of the Syrian Arab Army who accompanied us, and still does, throughout years of defiance and resistance'.[3] Amid the prevailing anti-Syrian moods and sentiments, Hizbollah's stand appeared provoking and to an extent incomprehensible. Indeed, the week following Hizbollah's pro-Syrian manifestation, the anti-Syrian opposition forces – the so-called 14 March group – gathered an even larger rally (perhaps prompted by Hizbollah's *act de force*) which numbered nearly a million demonstrators, near the tomb of the slain Rafiq Hariri. Many observers translate Hizbollah's persistent defiance and oscillations between radicalism and moderation, belligerence and friendliness, as indications of a party that is trapped in the 'impossible mission' of reconciling two ostensibly irreconcilable ambitions: to keep its ideological pledge to the tenets of Ayatollah Khomeini's Islamic revolution while at the same time becoming an congruent party of the very pluralistic and heterogeneous fabric of Lebanese politics. One of the party's most fervent critics commented on its pro-Syrian manifestation: 'Does it want to be local or does it want to be regional? It cannot be both . . . Lebanese society is under no obligation to accept permanent [Islamic] revolution and an open-ended Syrian domination so Hizbollah can remain regionally relevant'.[4]

A well-known *Washington Post* columnist also spoke for much of the international media coverage at the time when he wondered whether Hassan

Nasrallah was 'a man of the future or of the past. Is he a Lebanese patriot or a Syrian stooge?'[5] However, whatever Hizbollah's intentions, *Le Monde's* correspondent astutely observed that Hizbollah demonstrated it is 'a political force that cannot be circumvented'.[6] Obviously there were more components to the complex problems plaguing Lebanon and fuelling rage on the 'Lebanese street' than popular protests against a regime that for years had been governed by a repressive *mukhabarat*. Yet, in a way, Hizbollah brought a message: the Lebanese formula was founded on a delicate balance between varying forces, and a large number were, for different reasons, allied to Syria; neglecting that balance, the message went, could spell disaster, as the short history of the Lebanese republic had witnessed on numerous occasions – and as it would witness yet again.

This chapter attempts to understand Hizbollah's ambitions to reconcile the assumingly irreconcilable, that is, to remain a vanguard for the Islamic revolution while submitting to the pluralist confessionalist system that informs Lebanese politics, and which the party essentially rejects, but yet, for strategic reasons, embraces. This begs the question, however, over the nature of those strategic reasons. It also begs the question of the nature of the movement's so-called process of 'Lebanonization', starting off alongside the Taif Accord (or the National Reconciliation Charter, concluded in 1989, implemented in 1991), and which was an amended version of the National Pact of 1943. While this process enabled the movement to create an upsurge of Lebanese 'national' feeling – and finally even popular consensus – around its 'Islamic resistance' against the Israeli occupation of south Lebanon in the1990s, it lost much of that consensus once the Israelis were eventually ousted in May 2000. At that time, enjoying the height of popularity in Lebanon and the Arab world, Hizbollah decided to persist in fighting the Israelis. Hizbollah was backed by Beirut and Damascus in claiming that the Israeli withdrawal was incomplete (as Israeli forces remained deployed in the so-called Shebaa farms). Why did Hizbollah insist on challenging the Israelis, a bold – and, critics charged, reckless – posture that finally ended in the *harb al-tammuz* (the July war) in July 2006? Why did Hizbollah not call an end to the armed struggle after having been seen to defeat the once mighty Israeli armed forces and turn its attention to domestic issues, harvesting much of the kudos gained (itself an impressive achievement in a country as diverse and divided as Lebanon) for immediate political gain?

In contrast to those who argue that Hizbollah suffers from political 'schizophrenia' in its attempt to forge a precarious balance between its Islamic commitments to the radical doctrines of Ayatollah Khomeini and declared loyalties to the Lebanese state, it will here be argued that Hizbollah has been rather consistent in its ambitions since it emerged as a resistance against the Israeli invasion of 1982 and its ensuing process of blending Islamist zeal with nationalist fervour. As it will be argued, the perceived 'dualism' of Hizbollah's project rests upon an insufficient comprehension of the Islamist impulse as such and indeed the predicaments of a postcolonial state tragically squeezed in a regional conflict of international stature. Its so-called 'Lebanonization' process was not about adapting to an already given national identity of the Lebanese state, but rather it tapped into a historical contest over that very national identity of Lebanon, which still remains unresolved.

The disputed nature of Islamism and 'Lebanonization'

To begin with, the bewilderment over Hizbollah's assumed or disputed agency taps into a more general debate on Islamism, especially as many Islamists are investing their efforts in taking part in pluralist political systems, seemingly soft-peddling over alleged radicalism. Since the ultimate objective (and indeed often the very definition) of Islamism is to establish an Islamic state, that is, a state governed by the Islamic law, Islamists' submission to pluralist formulas of power-sharing invokes controversy and suspicion. Some observers see such attempts of integration as mere hoaxes, concealing strategies of prospective capture of the state and society 'from below', in a 'Gramscian' way.[7] Once within the system, and by their cultivating of devout 'communities' of believers and adherents – what has been referred to as *hala al Islamiyya* (Islamic space) – across society, often by running well-organised welfare services and social institutions, Islamists are cultivating politically assertive generations in preparation for an eventual grab of state power, by ballot or bullet, for the sake of institutionalising Islamic governance.[8] For instance, drawing his conclusion of what he refers to as an Hizbollah 'gradualist policy', Nizar Hamzeh argues that Lebanon is seemingly 'demographically destined toward a Shi'a majority' [where Hizbollah's popular constituencies are found], and '[n]othing then will prevent the establishment of a state dominated by the Shi'as, or Hizbollah from using the state apparatus for the realization of its Islamic order'.[9]

However, other scholars propose a more 'Weberian' understanding in which most radical impulses of Islamism have been inevitably absorbed by the empowering – or even 'secular' – logic of the nation state. Indeed, prominent observers have suggested that that we are witnessing the beginning of a 'post-Islamist' phase (or what is also referred to as 'Islamico-nationalism') in which the Islamists' ultimate aspiration – generally defined as the quest for an Islamic state, and which surpasses the border of the nation state to involve the whole Muslim *umma* (nation) – has stranded, even 'failed', as Islamists across the board are accepting pluralism and power-sharing.[10] Such approaches to Islamism may overemphasise its professed objective of establishing an Islamic state and overlook the various impulses from below that also often inform the Islamist project; the issue of identity and quest for dignity, forged and fought for in diverse dynamics of struggle; Islamism projects an assertive ambition to overcome an 'inferiority complex' imposed and absorbed by the Muslim world in the context of colonialisation.[11] Rooted in the writs of Islamic divinity, it also offers a certain ethico-political vision – and critique – upon the modern, rationalist order of the world.[12] From this angle, Islamism is to be understood more as an inclusive and dynamic approach of conviction, rather than a system. More than seeing the Islamic state as a declared goal, it poses the question: why an Islamic state in the first place? What are the perceptions and assumptions upon reality for demanding such an order? Equally important, how to understand the Islamist quest when an Islamic state is not possible to achieve?

Hizbollah's 'Lebanonization process' has been understood in that perspective, and prior to the Israeli withdrawal, it was widely believed that it was the Israeli occupation of south Lebanon that bred Hizbollah's radicalism and militancy. Hence, the withdrawal would temper its ambitions.[13] It was supposed (or hoped) that Hizbollah, having mastered the Israeli forces in combat, would turn its organisational expertise and commitment towards the centres of power in Beirut, especially towards the corrupted confessional system in Lebanon. Now we know, of course, that no such scenario came to pass. Hizbollah did not turn its fury against the crooked centres of the Lebanese nexus of political and economic power and privilege, even if the party would scorn the system as such. On the contrary, it deepened its ties to the Lebanese–Syrian security regime and turned much of a 'blind eye' to the ongoing corruption, preferring instead to continue to confront its nemesis in the south.

Of course, this somehow challenges the general assumption that Islamist parties would fall back and embed themselves in parliament and popular constituencies if given the opportunity. Nonetheless, it would be hard to deny that Hizbollah has not walked some distance from its earlier deeply radical and rejectionist position, perceived or real. For instance, Fawaz Gerges, in a very critical account, describes how Hizbollah in its early phase 'never shied away from its Iranian inheritance and served Teheran's regional and foreign policies', and how the movement, in the beginning, rejected:

> the very foundation of Lebanon's plural, secular, multi-religious, multi-ethnic experiment. Hizbollah was initially determined to subvert Lebanon's very existence and establish Allah's kingdom along the same rigid lines of those of Iran's Ayatollah Khomeini. It hoped to extend Iranian influence to Lebanon as well as to fertilize its secular soil with revolutionary Islam.[14]

Naturally, Hizbollah officials mostly disapprove of any such descriptions, even from the earlier years (one of its senior officials reacted in a very disdainful manner to this author when this early image of Hizbollah was proposed as a fact of history).[15] Its spokesmen argue that the main priorities of Hizbollah in this early phase were to resist the Israeli invasion of 1982 and the ensuing occupation that covered Lebanese territory all the way up to Beirut and the Beqaa Valley.[16] Hizbollah's hostility towards Israel always reigned supreme. According to the party's ideological manifesto, named 'The

Open Letter to the Oppressed in the World' (released in February 1985), the party considers Israel as both an imperialist tool, 'the American spearhead in the Islamic world', as well as the very essence of injustice, since it has driven away the Palestinians from their homeland. The manifesto states that Israel is:

> [A]n usurping enemy that must be fought until the usurped right is returned to its [Palestinian] owners . . . This enemy poses a greater danger to our future generations and to the destiny of our nation, especially since it embraces a settlement-oriented and expansionist idea that it has already begun to apply in occupied Palestine and it is extending and expanding . . . Therefore, our confrontation of this entity must end with its obliteration from existence . . .[17]

To be sure, while certain circles around Hizbollah advocated the imposition of an Islamic state in Lebanon, others saw this as irrelevant to the more pressing danger posed by the Israeli occupation. According to veteran member Mohammed Raad, currently the head of Hizbollah's parliamentary group, the early years witnessed disorder and confusion, especially as the Israeli occupation made everyday life difficult, but, he notes, the common desire among Hizbollah's militants of disparate cadres was *resistance*.

> For two or three years, we had contributed to the escalation of resistance operations. At the same time, we debated the political project of this resistance. The debate centred on one question: Should we elaborate on a detailed political project in the context of national liberation? A majority of us retained the consistent opinion to give priority to the resistance. All the same, our project of national liberation did not gainsay our Islamic intellectual and cultural identity. I think that this aspect of incomprehension or misunderstanding resulted from this fact. This media affirmed that our battle would end in the creation of an Islamic republic in Lebanon. But this goal was not our agenda. However, we do not deny that during the course of battle against the occupier, certain groups were carried away to the point that they claimed the creation of an Islamic republic. But we had no organised relation with them. During two or three years, we had no knowledge of everybody involved. Some Islamist groups resisted without having any organised relations with us.[18]

Around the time of the release of the movement's ideological manifesto in 1985, Sayyed Mohammed Hussein Fadlallah, a revered Shi'a cleric who exercised a profound influence upon the movement in the formative years, complained about those Islamists who are 'in a hurry' and who 'appear to think that Islamic rule is enough [of] an issue to arouse the masses' and who seem to have no qualms about imposing an Islamic state by violence, if need be; many people are incapable, he warned, of seeing 'the realities on the ground'.[19] Indeed, the manifesto itself also gave the impression of such caution. While making no secrets of its allegiance to Ayatollah Khomeini and the 'Islamic awakening' following the ongoing revolution in Iran, and while expressing a clear commitment to an Islamic state, it shows prudence over its feasibility in Lebanon (arguing that 'it cannot be imposed by force'). As a 'minimum aspiration', the manifesto advocates that Lebanon shall be '[rescued] . . . from subservience to either the West or the East' and the 'Zionist occupation' shall be expelled and will be followed by the 'adopting [of] a system that the people establish of their free will and choice'.[20] To this end, Hizbollah sought allies across the Lebanese confessions, calling for cooperation with all those groups who desired to end the Zionist project in Palestine and beyond. Domestically, its ideological ire was, nevertheless, directed at the Lebanese regime and its confessionalist system which it considers 'a fundamentally oppressive structure' beyond reform and that 'must be changed from the roots'.[21]

This stands of course in sharp contrast to the later ambitions of the party's process of 'Lebanonization'. Again, Sayyed Mohammed Hussein Fadlallah, who urged Hizbollah to change course around the implementation of the Taif Accord and become part of Lebanese political life, described this process as 'to examine the prevailing circumstances in Lebanon and formulate its strategy within that framework, making allowances for Lebanon's particular circumstances, its confessional sensitivities, its perception of its environment'. Fadlallah suggested, the Islamists needed to be aware of the wariness of the Lebanese Christians, they must not let confessionalist worries 'become a bone of contention that could lead to warfare among the Lebanese'.[22]

In a particular consistent way, Hizbollah has followed this strategic trajectory, through the various ups and downs, from the Taif Accord to the years of political participation under Syrian patronage in Lebanon, to the current phase of the 'post-Syrian' domination. Indeed, as Joseph Alagha even suggests, Hizbollah not only has accepted 'an engagement in the democratic process under a sectarian-confessional political administrative system', but '[m]ore dramatically, *Hizbullah*'s political program modified its demand from the abolishment of political sectarianism, to the adoption of the political [Christian] Maronite discourse, which stresses the abolishment of political sectarianism in the mentality, before abolishing it in the texts'.[23] As such, the movement has, ironically enough, embedded itself rather conveniently in the 'confessionalist realities' of Lebanon. Equally however, this does mean that Hizbollah has deviated from its original ideological ambitions.

The struggle for the 'soul' of national identity

In an important critique of Hizbollah's assumed 'Lebanonization' process, Jacob Hoigilt claims that the party's embracing of Lebanon's pluralism is sincere (meaning that Hizbollah does not carry any totalitarian ambitions in the sense of imposing Islamic rule by force), although this inclusive approach also is strictly conditioned by the question of Palestine, which determines much of the party's political and ideological agenda.[24] After the withdrawal from Lebanon in May 2000, Hizbollah radically increased its media coverage of the Palestinian struggle, giving particularly extensive coverage to the *al-Aqsa Intifada*.[25] Hoigilt emphasises that in this regard Hizbollah sees its own *resistance* in the south as its main priority, and 'connected to the issue of the Shebaa farms and Israeli air space violations, the word has been more and more connected with the Palestinian resistance against Israeli occupation'.[26] As such, Hizbollah is increasingly blurring the national borders that distinguish Lebanon from Palestine, although despite its calls for national unity in support of the Palestinian cause, Hoigilt argues that this is a road Hizbollah will most likely walk alone. He concludes that:

> The national unity that *Hizbullah* preaches is one where internal dialogue and discussion are suppressed in favour of the party's own views about the necessity and the aims of the resistance in Palestine . . . *Hizbullah*'s national unity includes only those who agree with its views about Palestine, and this notion of unity excludes a significant part of the Lebanese population.[27]

He also suggests that because Hizbollah deems the Palestinian issue a 'religious obligation' 'religious absolutes enter the national stage indirectly'.[28]

Hoigilt's remarks are worthy of consideration in the way they tap into the debate over the extent to which Islamist movements may submit to pluralist politics, especially as 'religious absolutes', which in his view, undermine pluralism. However, while Hizbollah's ideologists would welcome an opinion that ties Islamic piety with a greater commitment to the Palestinian struggle, it is not clear why a secular individual equally committed to Palestine would rally to the banner of Islam; nor is it clear why Hizbollah should be ploughing a lone furrow to show solidarity with the Palestinian cause (even if that involved military confrontation with Israel, something cherished by the Islamic resistance). After all, the Lebanese support for Hizbollah – both during the July 2006 war and afterwards – was impressive, cutting across political and religious barriers, even though Hizbollah's actions which precipitated the war remained a matter of considerable dispute both among and between confessions. And this is the point: the Palestinian issue has *always* divided the Lebanese across the political and ethnic spectrum. In fact, ever since the days of independence, if not before, the subject of the national identity, commitment, and direction, of Lebanon has been severely contested. As with the other Levantine countries, Lebanon's borders were drawn by France and Britain who, having emerged victorious from World War I, proceeded, 'under the cover of [the] League of Nations mandates . . . to build sectarian, non-Muslim states to solidify their control in the former Arab Muslim domains of the Ottoman Empire'.[29]

They did so, of course, with the cooperation of local elites, and since the French nourished historical ties of cooperation with the Christian Maronites, they also retained a favourable position in the transpiring confessional order. While the confessional order was one outcome of this agreement, another important issue was the 'Arab face' of the country's national identity. Deliberately vague, the 'Arab face' was meant to speak to 'two negations' that, needless to say, appeared conflicting – to be Arab by affiliation yet 'neutral' in position. In a region such as the Middle East, especially as the Palestinian trauma unfolded and first Palestinian refugees, then PLO guerrillas, started to crowd the south of Lebanon, the situation became almost consistently untenable, as the increasingly bitter conflict over Lebanon's national identity became deeply enmeshed with the question of Palestine.

Whereas the Lebanese 'isolationists' wished to abstain, claim neutrality, or even seek protection from the Western powers, the Lebanese Arab nationalists saw the Palestinian cause as central, not only in the way it illustrated a deep injustice committed against the Palestinians, but how Israel served the strategic schemes of division on the part of imperialist interests to keep the Arab world subjugated by a sense of defeatism, especially after the miserable Arab defeat in 1967. Even in its most radical phase, Hizbollah's ambitions, thus, tapped into this rather historical division, which *long preceded* the movement's advent. In this sense, Hizbollah's experience substantiates the reflection that today's Islamists are yesterday's nationalists.[30] In other words, these nationalist and Islamist currents might be understood as 'anti-systemic movements'; that is, while they may or may not share common ideological foundations and objectives, they do share a historical experience that is fostered in similar (dis)orders and asymmetric relations of power.[31]

Indeed, before embarking on its process of 'Lebanonization', Hizbollah would, in the early days, refer to Lebanon as 'colonial construction'. In a lecture given in July 1985, Hassan Nasrallah (at the time a young cleric within Hizbollah) referred to Lebanon as '10452 square km', that is, an entity established by France for the interests of sowing schemes of division and facilitating colonial rule. Lebanon had no real history as a 'political entity', Nasrallah pointed out, other than being the gathering of patches of land, which historically were part of a larger region, including Sham (Syria) and the rest of the *umma*. Both in terms of borders and the domestic political order (the confessional system) the Lebanese project was essentially an ambition of division, which also discriminated against Muslims. Interestingly, Nasrallah does not refer to the Shi'a Muslims, which were Hizbollah's constituency and indeed more discriminated against than the Sunni, most likely because he wished to undermine further sectarian division.

In this lecture, Nasrallah pulled no punches over the Maronite domination in Lebanon; not because he deplored Maronites as a community, but because their given political privileges expressed the colonialist scheme of a preserved Western dominance as well as the consequent denigration and the marginalisation of the Muslim community.

For the sake of the fear of the Christians [to be dominated by Muslims], they would sit in the house and the Muslims would remain outside of it, in heat as in cold. They also charged that the Muslims are not qualified to govern Lebanon because they were staying behind in their small villages and townships when the Maronites went to the universities of London and Paris . . .

He added, 'This creation of France is the fundamental reason for the injustice and deprivation we endure'.

Nasrallah went on to argue that the solution to the Lebanese predicament could not be found in Lebanon, only beyond its borders, because it was entangled in a regional problem. Nasrallah charged that it is demanded of the Lebanese elites to remain neutral in the Arab–Israeli conflict. Referring to events in the civil war, he argued that the Lebanese army was only to be deployed to suppress domestic opposition, not to fight against Israel. The failure of Israel's invasion of Lebanon in 1982 to reassert a Christian hegemony, a hegemony widely regarded as being but part of an attempt by Washington to roll back Syrian influence in Beirut had, Nasrallah argued, been defeated by the Islamic Revolution inspired by Iran which in turn, had boosted an 'awakening' among the oppressed. He continued:

> The question is what we can do for this [revolution] in Lebanon. We don't say that the Lebanese Muslims are able to take on regional challenges by themselves, but neither does this mean that they should relax and stay at home. Rather we say that the Lebanese Muslims should become part of a movement which encompasses the whole region . . . and the Islamic republic is the centre of it.[32]

The ambition, Nasrallah noted, was to build a generation of *mujahidin* to challenge this fate of the nation. Indeed, this is also what Hizbollah set out to do while rooting itself in the Shi'a community of Lebanon; disseminating the philosophy of 'Islamic resistance'.[33] Yet, Hizbollah would carefully pick its battles as time went by forging a strategy of adaptation to the confessionalist system even with its confessional bias against the Shi'a for the sake of promoting the resistance as an essential ingredient in an altering Lebanese identity grounded in an Arab and Islamic affiliation; this was necessary, as Nasrallah claimed, since the main Lebanese's predicaments were to be found outside the country.

The Islamic depth of a third worldist struggle

The argument is, thus, that the challenge in studying Islamist movements, is to account for the religious dimension of the movement's struggle without *reducing* the struggle to what has been referred to as 'religious absolutes'; yet neither should acclaimed religious attributes in those struggles entirely be understood as mere expressions for needs and desires that are in essence materialist and 'secular'. Scholars point out that Islamists promote an 'ethico-political' vision and critique of the modern world in which the belief in tran-scendence and revelation, for its adherents, is central and real, and indeed most compelling and influential.[34]

For Hizbollah, both in its military struggle and its ambitions to forge a 'resistance society' – or what has been referred to as al hala al Islamiyya (the Islamic sphere), a core community of believers and followers – the dimension of the al-akhira (the afterlife) and its connection to al-dunya (the worldly life) is absolutely central. However, these dimensions of Hizbollah are deeply rooted in the revolutionary dynamics and doctrines of Ayatollah Khomeini's Islamic vision which already at an early stage were understood by scholars as a novel version of 'third Worldism'. At an early stage of the Islamic revolution in Iran, Nikkie Keddie suggested that there was 'little in the way of compari-son of Islamic revival with other kinds of movements – comparisons that might make the Muslim revival appear less unique and incomprehensible', since it was partly 'one type of a movement that the world has already expe-rienced'. To her, Islamism, as expressed by Khomeini's revolution in Iran, should be understood as a particular version of 'Third Worldism'; that is, 'a viewpoint that sees the third world (roughly Asia, Africa and Latin America) as exploited and heavily controlled by the West' and that these countries 'must strive to rid themselves of Western control, influence and customs, and to set up ways of life with native and traditional roots . . . where Western power to profit from exploitation of the third world will be negated'.[35]

Embedded in Islam, Khomeini's revolution was one of many impulses of self-assertion and expressions of resistance in a neo-colonial world order. In his biography of Sayyed Muhammad Hussein Fadlallah, Jamal Sankari argues that the Shi'a mujtahid (Islamic scholar) did not see the most impor-tant development in the Islamic Republic in Iran as the way it instituted the Islamic law as a penal code system, but rather how it brought about 'the deliv-erance of the human will from a state of submission to iniquitous, aggressive, or infidel power'.[36] Fadlallah, Sankari argues, saw the Islamic revolution through a 'Fanonian' perspective as it 'provided the dynamism necessary for the awakening and the rebellion of the hitherto subjugated collective indige-nous spirit against conditions of resignation, enfeeblement and sub-servience'.[37]

Frantz Fanon, it should be recalled, was an anti-colonial ideologue elabo-rating upon the experiences of the Algerian war of independence. To him, the very ontology of the colonial world was *violence*; the colonial system of sub-ordination was shaped and sustained by the violence that the colonisers imposed and which the colonised internalised through their own sense of weakness and lack of self-esteem. 'It is not possible to enslave men without logically making them inferior through and through', he wrote.[38] The colo-nial order knew of no universal values other than those of force and subordi-nation (as Fanon claimed, the native 'laughs in mockery when Western values are mentioned in front of him') and hence the colonised only had themselves to rely upon; liberation could not be begged for – *it had to be taken.*

The Fanonian remedy to such end was violence; the very ontology of the prevailing order. Notoriously, Fanon saw violence as a 'cleansing force' since it 'frees the native from its inferiority complex . . . it makes him fearless and restores his self-respect'.[39] Significantly, there was a *dual logic* in this perspective: not only was armed struggle the only alternative with which to liberate the land; the very act of doing so would break down those assumptions of weakness and incapacity that the colonial order had fostered among the colonised; it was a question of consciousness, to be aware, not only of prevailing injustices, but also of the *ability* to alter one's grim condition. Since the colonial order would not yield by negotiations, it would significantly crumble once such consciousness took hold of the minds of the oppressed.

While this outlook might appear as mere hyperbole to some, it is absolutely central for Fadlallah's Islamic liberation philosophy and Hizbollah's doctrines of Islamic resistance and martyrdom. As with Fanon, these grow out of the realities of the Shi'as in Lebanon: political and social marginalisation, the years of civil war, the range of Israeli incursions, invasions and occupations, and decades of the Palestinian trauma so closely entangled with the Lebanese strife. 'As for the state of violence we live in today', Fadlallah wrote in 1986, 'the reality [is] that violence is the current condition in the Middle East' which has been 'forced upon the peoples in the region' and it escalates 'as the people feeling themselves bound by impotence, [are] stirred to shatter some of that enveloping powerlessness for the sake of liberty'.[40]

Recalling the brutalities and the hopelessness of the Israeli invasion in 1982, Hizbollah notes in its ideological manifesto how '[t]heir bombs fell on our kinsmen like rain during the Zionist [1982] invasion of our country', concluding:

> We appealed to the world's conscience but heard nothing from it and found no trace in it . . . We were horrified and then realized that this world conscience stirs only at the request of the strong and in response to the interests of arrogance.[41]

Embedded in this 'ontology of violence', Hizbollah sees armed struggle as essential for the liberation of south Lebanon from occupation; in a Fanonian sense, Hizbollah writes that 'freedom is not given but regained with the sacrifice of both heart and soul'.[42] In addition, it would forcefully guard its ambition to fight the Israeli troops and their allies in the so-called 'security-zone', even if it implied clashes, or even a 'mini-war' (from 1988 to 1990) with the Amal movement, which had a more cautious position with regard to challenging the Israeli occupation.[43]

However, the dual logic of Fanon is also evident in the way Hizbollah saw its struggle in both tactical and strategic terms. To Hizbollah, the Arab regimes are, since the miserable Arab defeat in 1967, living in a state of defeatism; their willingness to enter peace negotiations and recognise Israel is the outcome and illustration of this despondent condition, and Hizbollah, offers an alternative. As Nasrallah argued in the early 1990s, the party submitted to a theory which challenged that of 'diplomatic chivalry and international forums' by instead opting for a 'war against the enemy':

> They said that those who advocate this are insane; we said in response, let us try – the sane can talk politics and the insane can fight. Be certain that the theory of the sane will not bear fruit, but that of the insane – the *mujahidin*, the martyrs and suicide bombers – has already caused the enemy to bleed and had doubled the number of its dead and wounded. The bleeding within the Zionist entity had added public pressure on the enemy's government and put it in front of two clear options: either it remains in the south and suffers additional human losses, or it withdraws ... Experience and common sense have shown that the theory of resistance is still valid, and that the other logic has failed and should, therefore, not be counted on anymore.[44]

Furthermore, there was also the *strategic* dynamic – grounded in a psychological dimension – that went beyond the battles in the south. In 1995, Nasrallah told an Egyptian weekly that there were no reasons to conceal the objectives of the 'Islamic resistance' which involved some 'intermediate objectives for the near future' (the liberation of the south) as well a more strategic scheme. Hizbollah, he said, would still insist that 'Israel was not legitimate', and, he stressed, 'we have repeated, and still repeat that even if the whole world and all of its governments recognise a state named Israel, we won't'. He added: 'Thus the strategy of the resistance is to be in operation because there will come a day when ... the Arab and the Muslim *umma* can rise and uproot this usurping entity from existence'. He referred to this ambition as *istinhaad* (awakening). 'We believe this *umma* has many strong cadres, abilities to rise, and revolutionary potentials ... [and] our ambition is to turn these potentials into real activity'. While he conceded that some of this awakening could be spirited by words, it could not do without blood and sacrifice. 'We think that our *jihad* (effort, struggle) and our martyrs have made a great impression upon the Lebanese and the Palestinians [and others] ... and we are still projecting these objectives'.[45]

For Hizbollah, the epitome of sacrifice is the Shi'a saga about the Prophet's grandson Imam Hussein's choice to face the Caliph's forces at the outskirts of Karbala, Iraq in AD 680. This is the historical foundation of Hizbollah's Shi'a revolutionary activism and a classical expression of its 'Fanonian logic'. Imam Hussein, it is recalled, knew he was to die, outnumbered as he was by the troops of the 'corrupted' and degenerate Yazid. However, according to Hizbollah's political lexicon, Hussein's example was a deed that spoke larger than words, it established a principle and infused a norm: to refuse injustice and humiliation. '[Karbala] is a symbol for every mistreated person who refuses submission, resists, and fights by offering his blood, sons, properties, and then cries it out to the whole world', Hassan Nasrallah characteristically said in 2002 at the Ashoura gathering, the tenth day of Muharam, a Shi'a time for collective grief over the sacrifice of the Imam Hussein and to cherish and cultivate the religious, political and moral ethos of the events in Karbala.[46]

Yet while the Imam Hussein's stand symbolised a refusal to surrender, it also carried a deeper message since it symbolised how not even death should scare the pious and the righteous. Rather, to die – or become a martyr – while fighting injustice, is an *ambition*, a reward in itself, as the sacrifice will benefit the community's strength on earth and the martyr's fate in the hereafter. As Naim Qassem, Hizbollah's vice-secretary general puts it:

> When a man is cultivated to seek victory, making it the sole purpose of his actions, his quest ceases as soon as the possibility of victory seems vague or difficult to achieve. But when brought to learn of jihad and martyrdom, his sacrifice would be of the highest order, his actions effective, his martyrdom a fulfilment of desire, and thus victory would be but a worldly blessing and reward for his efforts.[47]

In that sense, the struggle and the resistance have a value in itself, even though it does not obtain for the foreseeable future a worldly achievement, other than strengthening the community. As Qassem continues,

> Cultivating victory does not assure it, and may weaken the strengths of a nation, while cultivation of martyrdom invests all resources to achieve either martyrdom of victory or both, opening the horizon to all possibilities and carrying the hope for victory.[48]

Most important, however, death will not scare Hizbollah's school of believers. 'All that the enemy is capable of is implanting the fear of death in us. When we halt this fear, we render the power of death with which he menaces us futile'.[49]

Since the 1980s Hizbollah has carefully cultivated these norms of resistance and sacrifice in what has been referred to as an *hala al Islamiyya* (Islamic sphere) – or what Hizbollah also refers to as the *mujtamma al-Muqawama* (resistance society) – consisting of a devoted community of Islamic NGOs, welfare organs and social institutions (schools, infirmaries, building and engineering etc), cultural clubs, religious centres and media networks (mainly the TV-channel *Al-Manar*, radio station *Al-Nour* and weekly magazine *Al-Intiqad*). Mona Harb and Reinhod Lendeers refer to this community as 'an integrated and holistic network', centred in areas where Hizbollah's core popular constituencies are found (and sustained) in south Beirut (*al-dahiya*), south Lebanon and the Beqaa area.[50]

As this community provides services, they argue thaat it also generates a sense of meaning and belonging by maintaining an identity of social pathos and sharing, informed by Islamic faith in which sacrifice and resistance are cherished ideals. This sense of capability and belonging empowers the Shi'a community, long deprived, and brings it out of its long felt victimhood; Hizbollah can boost 'meaningful values of justice, solidarity, community, sacrifice, progress etc – which, in turn, instigates high self-esteem and a solid sense of national pride'. This is where the party's solid power is entrenched; its authority is generated from this communal support 'among the majority of the Shi'a', and the '*iltizam* [commitment] of *al hala al Islamiyya* has become, in many ways, the norm of the majority of the community'.[51] In addition, the arms of Hizbollah's military wing, *al-Muqawama* – comprises a solid bedrock of identity for this community; as the perseverance of these arms – and the resistance – has long been the objective of Hizbollah, from the early 1980s and onwards.

Defending the dual logic of the resistance

The meaning of Hizbollah's process of 'Lebanonization' that evolved during the course of the 1990s has, therefore, to be understood in the way the movement sought to embed the idea of the resistance within its own core constituencies of an empowered Shi'a community, and, concurrently, by providing the resistance with national legitimacy it also altered the national identity of Lebanon. It validates Jorge Larrain's claim that the meaning of national identities are never static or given, but subjected to competing interests and are 'always, therefore, a terrain of conflict'.[52] True, Hizbollah was always cynical about the idea of 'Lebanonization', preferring instead the notion of *infitah* (opening). In a critical reading, the conception of 'Lebanonization' suggested that Hizbollah had entered a national community to which it did not really belong. But, Nasrallah demanded rhetorically given the critical allegations over Hizbollah's ties to the religious authorities in Tehran, what of the Lebanese Christians' affiliation with the Vatican in Rome, does that make them 'Vaticanese'?

> We do not speak Persian . . . [but] there are a lot of Lebanese Christians who speak French. Then why are they Lebanese and not French? If the criterion is language, we speak Arabic with [a] Lebanese accent. So what is meant by 'Lebanonization'?[53]

To Hizbollah, the Lebanese identity remained an open field of contest, ready for change. As Nasrallah claimed, 'the man who [offers] his blood [for the] homeland . . . is the most patriotic'. Nasrallah would rather speak of the *infitah* as accommodation and cooperation, or as he put it in 1997:

> What concerns the *infitah*, we are open to everybody and we have relations with personalities and parties and forces which involves different religious communities, and different ideologies and political currents. I

think that Hizbollah was the first Islamist movement, a pioneer, in reaching out to the Arab world on this level of openness, either in Muslim–Christian relations, or in the relation with nationalist parties, or any party which we may agree with on [certain] ideological principles.[54]

However, Hizbollah's logic of resistance did not emerge in a vacuum as, needless to say, the very nature of resistance is contingent upon an adversary; and Israel did not deny the party a reason to convey its Fanonian perspective of the 'ontology of violence'. Indeed, it may be argued that the Israelis squandered an opportunity to relieve itself from its Lebanese miseries by withdrawing from Lebanon in the early 1990s as the Taif Accord was being implemented. After all, at that time the war-weary Lebanese were longing for the state authority of Lebanon to be restored, and Syrian troops were present to supervise the process of national reconciliation. Moreover, Hizbollah, who swore to fight the Israeli occupation as long as it remained in Lebanon, was of a relatively small number (compared to today).

But in the absence of any security agreement worked out with Damascus, it decided to remain loyal to its Lebanese proxy, the South Lebanese Army (SLA). As one prominent observer remarked, Israel might be excused for 'belittling' the Islamic resistance at the time, since the south was relatively calm and the 'security zone' was 'widely viewed as a success within Israel'.[55] Yet, the watershed event was the killing of Sayyed Abbas Musawi and along with his wife and three-year-old son in February 1992. Uri Lubrani, the Israeli government's coordination officer on Lebanon at the time, commented of the operation: 'I see [Abbas Musawi's] demise as a severe blow to the *Hizbullah* and something which might accelerate a process by which the organization comes to realize that militancy is no way to act in Lebanon'.[56]

Sayyed Abbas Musawi's successor would be Hassan Nasrallah, who would lead Hizbollah into the process of 'Lebanonization', to take part in elections and bridge differences both within the Shi'a community and between the confessional divides of Lebanon, while popularising the idea of *al-Muqawama* – resistance. Ironically, the confessional system and the sectarian politics it fostered that were intrinsic to the Taif agreement (accepted, however grudgingly by Hizbollah because of the national legitimacy its implementation provided the resistance), enabled the party to cultivate the *hala al Islamiyya*, alongside its resistance campaign.

Indeed, the neo-liberal reconstruction process of the Lebanese regime in Beirut also benefited the movement because of its widespread corruption and neglect of the already destitute areas, where Hizbollah would deliver its services, gaining popular support. In all this, a rather rough modus operandi was at work. Rafiq Hariri, the Lebanese Prime Minister leading these reconstruction efforts, was never at ease with Hizbollah's resistance campaign; yet he would acknowledge how the movement actually kept a large Shi'a underclass in check. While champions of social pathos, Hizbollah would scorn the thievery and corruption of the regime and its ignorance of social delivery policies, but hardly mobilised any effective opposition against it, for the sake of protecting the rights of the resistance.

Domestic stability became a top priority for the movement. This stability was ensured by the presence of Syrian troops and security services, who also saw to it that the precarious balance was kept in check between resistance and reconstruction. By supporting Hizbollah's guerrillas, Damascus could sustain its self-proclaimed image as a champion of 'Arab nationalism', and bleed the Israelis in the south while equally deriving economic benefit from Lebanese reconstruction efforts through corruption and trade agreements that employed surplus Syrian labour. Indeed, Hizbollah's Shi'a constituency – the natural constituency for such work – suffered in this regard. This was another 'compromise' Hizbollah had to accept for the sake of its continued resistance.[57]

After the Syrian withdrawal in 2005, and as the Lebanese entities in the 14 March group increasingly lambasted Hizbollah for its refusal to disarm, one Lebanese leftist observer critically underlined this irony by suggesting that the harsh policies of reconstruction in the 1990s would naturally 'have provoked violent social insurrections', but these grievances were in large absorbed by Hizbollah's 'social safety net for large sectors of the Lebanese population. However, while the governing elites "should have thanked Hizbollah" they have 'continued to attack it'.[58] Indeed, despite its support, even Damascus remained uncomfortable with Hizbollah's increasing popularity and political stature, and the movement had to contend with 'having its wings clipped' in the parliamentary elections of 1996 and 2000 by sharing lists with its rival, the Amal movement.[59] The former Telecommunications Minister, Asaam Namaan, told this author that the Syrians were consistently afraid that the resistance's operations would get out of hand in the south and that relations with Israel would be 'embarrassing' since 'the Syrians were here and they were not capable of defending Lebanon, they were not even capable of defending themselves'.[60]

Yet Hizbollah's increasing popularity throughout the 1990s, leading to the Israeli withdrawal in May 2000, implied that few Lebanese elites could argue that the armed resistance's activities had been futile. The modus operandi between Hizbollah and the regime, mediated (or imposed) by the Syrians, implied that Israeli efforts to sow division between the resistance and the Lebanese population, or the regime in Beirut (especially during the large-scale bombing campaign of Lebanon in May 1996, the so-called Operation 'Grapes of Wrath') were absorbed and largely neutralised.[61] However, things were to alter drastically after the Israeli withdrawal in May 2000. As noted, many hoped that Hizbollah now would invest their efforts in another kind of battle. As one Lebanese editorial argued some six weeks after the Israeli withdrawal:

> *Hizbullah* understands what most individuals – and a very few politi-
> cians – all over this country do, namely that the status quo, like the occu-

pation before it, is unacceptable . . . people driven by a genuine desire to bring about a far-reaching change in this country have heretofore operated singly in twos or threes, but now they are being presented with an opportunity to ally themselves with a powerful movement whose aims largely coincide with theirs, whose supporters are numerous and enthusiastic, and whose respect abroad grows with each passing day. Since no one doubts *Hizbullah*'s commitment to achieving its goals, and no serious-minded person would argue that Lebanon's political system needs anything short of a drastic overhaul, those who have looted our founding ship of state have been served notice that they will no longer be allowed to do so with impunity. The determined people of *Hizbullah* who dared to take on the Merkava tanks will not be intimidated into silence by a few detestable power-brokers whose bad suits, fat cigars, and loathsome amorality would have made them fit nicely with the mobsters of 1950s Havana.[62]

Nothing like this happened, however, and Hizbollah would, claiming that the Shebaa farms were still under occupation, persist in its path of Islamic resistance, with the (grudging) compliance of Beirut and wary supervision of Damascus. The capture of three Israeli soldiers in the vicinity of the Shebaa farms on 9 October 2000, and a later kidnapping of an Israeli citizen Elhanan Tannenbaum also displayed that the movement had made its choice to continue to challenge Israel, keeping its pledge to Palestine. Of course, despite the lingering Israeli occupation of the Shebaa farms, the outbreak of the Palestinian *al-Aqsa Intifada* quickly dominated the regional agenda and drew immediate support from Hizbollah, not least from the party's own TV-channel *Al-Manar*, but also by keeping the situation tense – albeit controlled – in the south. The movement let tensions in the south mirror the scale of events in Palestine.

In the spring of 2002, for instance, when Israel invaded the Jenin refugee camp to the outrage of much of the Arab world, Hizbollah escalated attacks in the Shebaa farms and admitted, proudly, to being responsible for an arms smuggling operation, uncovered in Jordan, aimed to assist the besieged Palestinians. As Nasrallah told an Arab weekly:

> The Palestinians did not ask for fighting forces. All they ask for is arms . . . So we not only consider it our duty but also the duty of everyone to deliver weapons to the Palestinians. Whoever does not should be condemned, while those who deliver weapons to Palestinians should not be. If smuggling and delivering weapons to the Palestinians is a crime, then we are ready to be punished, or to be called names of any kind, since this is not a problem for us.[63]

As crowds across the Arab and Muslim world demonstrated their solidarity with the Palestinians, Nasrallah chastised their rulers for doing nothing for the Palestinian cause. For Hizbollah, the ongoing struggle demanded sacrifices and courage, not the diplomatic overtures continuously called for by Arab governments. Negotiations from a weak position could only spell defeat. 'They are positioning us before two choices', Nasrallah declared in a commemoration of Ayatollah Khomeini in early June 2003.[64]

> Either we surrender and accept the governments, systems, projects and administrations they want to impose on us, in addition to the solutions and reconciliations [with Israel] [the US] want to achieve in this region. Or we maintain our steadfastness and resist . . . At this stage of the nation's history, if there is any leader, president, thinker, scientist or cleric who is responsible of any position and feel[s] within himself the feebleness, cowardice, and the inability to confront, challenge and defy . . . Let him go and sit at home. Then God will bring to this nation and this people someone who is worthy of leading and continuing the road towards the inevitable victory.[65]

While garnering a consistent regional posture and popularity, however, Hizbollah was increasingly criticised at home for its position in the south and in the region. As the party condemned the Arab initiative for peace in the spring of 2002, the fervent critic of Syria, Gebran Tueni lamented Hizbollah's assumed recklessness and its choice to abide by the Iranian policy of advocating the elimination of Israel. 'Have not we played enough with fire on the Lebanese-Israeli border or through the smuggling of arms to the Palestinians via Jordan? These are the kind of flames that can destroy Lebanon'.[66] At the same time, domestic opposition increased to the Syrian conduct of corruption and repression, and it also started to wear down on the popularity of Hizbollah, even among its own supporters. While officials of Hizbollah declined to speak out against Syrian misconduct, they were frustrated, too, by the alarming growth of corruption within the regime. This was Hizbollah's dilemma: it enjoyed the protection of the Syrian–Lebanese security regime to conduct its cause of resistance, yet, by doing so, it would also be sullied by its malfeasance. To resolve its dilemma, Hizbollah chose to remain aloof, being present in parliament, yet taking no responsibilities of the government. In an interview in 2003, Nasrallah acknowledged the bargain with the government: 'as long as the resistance enjoyed state recognition, the party would accept this system and conduct its role as a loyal, but critical, opposition in parliament. Hard sectarian calculations are ruling the set-up of this system', he said, 'and we are bound by this set-up'.[67]

However, at a nationalist conference in Beirut, only months after the US invasion had consolidated its grip on Iraq, Sayyed Ibrahim al-Amin al Sayyed, a Hizbollah veteran from the top echelon of the party, lashed out at those Lebanese officials who claimed to toe the Arab nationalist line, but yet had their feet so deep into the mud of theft and stealing that ordinary people in the end, he warned, would find it hard to take them seriously, and instead go looking for 'international saviours' and solutions. He argued:

> Today, we must see the domestic situation in Lebanon, from the angle of the [US] aggression the region is facing, and we are afraid that the domestic political and financial crises will pave the way for the American political project, which is creeping towards Lebanon.[68]

With reference to Iraq (and perhaps Syria), he said,

> [J]ust like with the repression and corruption in the Arab world, what happens in Lebanon will force the Lebanese to be snatched by the American calls, even if these calls are lies and deception, and there will be no popular confidence in the nationalist alternative.[69]

Still, Hizbollah would stay committed to the Syrian presence, as evidenced in the controversial decision by the Syrian regime to advocate the extension of the Lebanese President Emile Lahoud's mandate, a decision that provoked the UNSC drafting of resolution 1559. Amid the international and domestic Lebanese condemnation of the extension (even Nasrallah is said to have argued against it in talks with Bashar al-Assad), Nasrallah declared that the Syrian presence in Lebanon, first of all, was a question for the Lebanese to decide; it was not even a Syrian decision.

Indirectly challenging the confessional formula ruling the country, Nasrallah proposed that the Lebanese would decide on all 'important issues concerning the destiny of the country in a national referendum', and 'what would be accepted by the majority should also be accepted by the minority'.[70] This was Hizbollah's way of reminding the other communities of the bargain that the party – holding sway over the large Shi'a community – originally had entered into with the confessional system: it would accept it so long as its resistance was recognised.

Daring the national division

Following the Syrian withdrawal from Lebanon the country entered a new uncertain chapter in its history. Hizbollah remained wedded to its position of resistance, unwilling to disarm and remaining steadfast in its support for the Palestinians. For Hizbollah, 1559 was a mere scheme dreamt up in Washington, another strategic step in its 'war on terror' to weaken the resolve of the various currents of resistance to its hegemony across the region. At a rally in May 2000, Nasrallah wondered where on earth the international community was when the Israelis occupied the south for 22 years in a flagrant violation of UNSC Resolution 425. In contrast, he pointed out, it took the international community only 7 months to apply UN Resolution 1559 which targeted Syria. 'Why?' he asked. 'Because 425 targeted Israel whereas 1559 is in the service of Israel'. Today, he continued, Lebanon is rife with foreign interferences, especially by the United States, who wants to disarm the resistance in a common interest with Israel. Yet, he added:

> Anyone who thinks of disarming the resistance is crazy. In Lebanon, we want the people to live in peace and stability, and in national unity, and we will not be hostile to anyone. But listen carefully: if anybody thinks of removing the weapons from the resistance, anybody, we will fight him in the spirit of *Karbala* and martyrdom, because we know that any step or action in this direction is an Israeli act, and an Israeli decision ... Any arm to reach for our guns we will consider an Israeli arm, and we will cut it off.[71]

In a comment on the speech, one Hizbollah official argued that the Lebanese army would never be able to move against the resistance because 'half of the army', he claimed, 'support us, they are with our cause'. Should any decision be taken to move against the resistance, the official argued, the Lebanese army would probably break apart, with chaotic consequences, as happened during the civil war. Hence, the party felt confident that it is supported (at least indirectly) by one of the country's most vital centres of power.[72] However, the party feared the 'opening floodgates' of Western interference as the Syrians left Lebanon. When this author proposed to the chief editor of Hizbollah's weekly *al-Intiqad*, Hussein Rahal, that the party may be relieved from the troubles instigated by the Syrian–Lebanese security regime, he retorted with a short, 'maybe'. Yet he went on to complain how 'many Western embassies now are increasingly dabbling in Lebanese domestic politics'.[73] The party's back, especially with regard to the resistance, was now exposed to an extent hitherto unknown.

In this context, there was a rising debate on nationalism and identity, and the 14 March camp started to float the discourse of 'Lebanon first', meaning that the Lebanese commitment to Palestine and 'Arabness' was becoming obsolete, again evoking the same old query over the identity of the Lebanese nation. In response, Nasrallah ridiculed such Lebanese discourses by addressing the believers on the issues of responsibility and obligations of solidarity that 'know of no borders at all', especially for those who feared the hereafter:

> What will I say on Judgement Day when I will face the great Lord and he will ask me of my efforts for the oppressed and deprived in Palestine and Iraq? ... Shall I tell him, 'Well, that is not of my concern because I am *Lebanese*?'[74]

The efforts of the party, from its tactical electoral alliance in the parliamentary elections in the summer 2005, its decision to enter government, its 18-month-long boycott of the government, its alliance with Michel Aouns' Free Patriotic Movement, its insistence upon a government of 'national unity' in which the various confessions would have the right to veto any decision, to the decision to abduct Israeli soldiers on that fateful morning in July 2006, to its mass mobilisation of support for Syria in the Lebanese capital and the ensuing formation under the Doha agreement of a new government in May 2008 have all been subservient to maintain one goal: the continued commitment to protect the resistance.

As argued in this chapter, the safeguarding of the resistance has a dualist 'Fanonian' logic of being part of the party's effort to promote *al-istinhaad*, the awakening, since the Lebanese problem, as Nasrallah claimed in 1985, cannot be solved in Lebanon, but only on a regional level. For Hizbollah, Israel remains the main problem and the region will persist in despotism, regime corruption, conspiracies and instabilities as long as Israel is present since this presence expresses, and is conditioned by, a prevailing United States hegemony. In Hizbollah's lexicon, however, this order is very much sustained by the weakness of the Arab regimes.

By challenging this order, especially in Palestine, a larger regional change might be in the offing as a new generation are alerted by the movement's *istinhaad*. In the late 1990s, Mohammed Muslih offered an outline of the various Arab camps and their positions to the ongoing 'peace process'. The camp favouring negotiations relied upon an assumption of realpolitik; any negotiation over Palestine would be promoted with the motto 'salvaging whatever could be salvaged' (*inqadh ma mumkin inqadahuhu*). Yet the Arab camp opposing negotiations were of two different strands: the *idealists* who saw Israel as the ultimate injustice and who would never come to terms with it under any circumstances; and the *pragmatists* who would accept a negotiated solution, but from a position of strength and not under the prevailing weakness and Arab division.[75]

It is easy to situate Hizbollah in the idealist camp of 'rejectionists'. Yet, the movement may also indirectly be placed in the camps of the 'pragmatists' since Hizbollah has hinted several times that it ultimately will have to accept disarmament within the framework of a larger peace agreement. In that sense, the party is conveying the impression to the Arab pragmatists that the movement's arms and principles are in fact assets in the negotiations over Palestine. Still, as the eloquent Azmi Bishara noted with regard to Hizbollah's war effort against Israel in the summer of 2006: '*Hizbullah* isn't looking for peace with Israel', and '[n]or is it interested in receiving brownie points for being "enlightened" or "moderate"'.[76]

> It sees its own enlightenment, as Israel sees hers, in its rationalisation and organisational strength. Ideologically, morally and in its origins, *Hizbullah* is founded within the Palestinian historical narrative, related by Palestinian refugees to the farmers and poets of Lebanon ever since catastrophe brought the poor of the Lebanese south and Palestinian refugees together in the same saga. *Hizbullah* will not lend itself as fodder to the 'dialogue and coexistence industry'. It is too deep for that.

It is too busy writing a hands-on theology for the wretched of the Arab earth. This leaves very little opening for opportunist intellectuals to sell *Hizbullah* to the West. *Hizbullah* is not concerned with 'the recognition of Israel' and, unlike the PLO and others, it refuses to engage in a discourse that involves using basic principles as bargaining chips. *Hizbullah* thrives on fighting as an equal, not on being compensated for its absence in the field by a false equality around the negotiating table.[77]

As Hizbollah probably is banking on its own ideological assumption of the 'ontology of violence', it is confident that Israel never will offer the necessary conditions to please the more demanding pragmatists. Therefore, resistance will continue; Hizbollah will be promoting the *istinhaad*, persistently weakening the clout of those regimes that have opted to move into the orbit of US hegemony, and just as clearly, it will invest every effort in making sure that Lebanon will not.

10 The hubris of initial victory

The IDF and the Second Lebanon War

Uri Bar-Joseph *

Introduction

The Second Lebanon War, as the Israeli Parliament decided in March 2007 to officially name the 12 July–14 August 2006 conflict between Hizbollah and Israel, has attracted an impressive body of academic literature. Among the aspects of the war that have been explored so far are the following: causes of the failures of the Israel Defence Forces (IDF),[1] operational aspects,[2] Hizbollah's method of making war,[3] its short-range rocket arsenal as a new type of challenge for the Israeli Air Force (IAF),[4] Israel's intelligence during the war,[5] the war as a test of Israel's deterrence capability,[6] and the implications of this conflict for US military strategy.[7] In addition, a number of Israeli students used the war in order to shed light on the way democracies fight an asymmetric conflict,[8] the way a civil society functions during a military conflict,[9] and civil–military relations in Israel.[10]

The starting point of this chapter is that the Second Lebanon War constituted a unique event in the history of the IDF. For the first time since its establishment in 1948, the IDF failed to achieve one of its most fundamental goals – the defence of Israel's hinterland from enemy attacks. During the 34 days of the war, almost 4,000 rockets hit northern Israel. Despite extensive IDF efforts to thwart their launching, the largest number of Hizbollah Katyusha rockets, about 250, hit Israel during the war's last 24 hours. This outcome gives weight to the claims made by Hizbollah's leader, Hassan Nasrallah, that his organization held the upper hand in this war despite the IDF's vast military superiority.

The chapter aims at explaining this outcome through an analysis of Israel's war performance at four levels: the political, strategic, operational and tactical. To do so, use will be made in the main of four excellent Israeli reports of the war. The first report comprises the two volumes of the official Winograd Commission Report on the conduct of the war.[11] The three other reports are books by Israeli journalists who had very good access to Israel's civilian and military policymakers, as well as a first-rate grasp of Israel's strategic culture and the IDF's *esprit de corps*.[12] Following the discussion of these reports, a summary section will address two questions. First, which level of analysis provides the best explanation of the Israeli failure? Second, was this failure an idiosyncratic event that is not likely to return in the future or the manifestation of a radical shift in military balance between Israel and her neighbours that will leave Israel exposed to massive rocket and missile attacks in the foreseeable future?

The political level

Rarely, if ever, in its history had Israel enjoyed a more convenient political setting for the initiation of large-scale military action as it did in July 2006. Domestically, the IDF's unilateral withdrawal from southern Lebanon in May 2000 had created a consensus that any violation of the international border should be met with a strong Israeli reaction. This consensus, the broadest since the 1967 war, reached its apex in the aftermath of the 12 July incident, when eight Israeli soldiers were killed and two were kidnapped in a Hizbollah raid along the border. The consensus may be best expressed by the fact that the most left-wing journalist writing for the Israeli press, Gideon Levy of *Ha'aretz*, noted that Israel could not avoid a reaction to this provocation,[13] and that Meretz, the leftist opposition party, supported the government's decision to respond with force.[14]

The international support for the Israeli reaction was even more unprecedented. Motivated by apprehension at rising radical Islam and at Iran's increasing regional power, Washington and Western European capitals considered a blow to Hizbollah, Teheran's closest Arab ally, to be an effective means of slowing down these processes. This view was apparently shared in private by many Arab states.

The combination of internal and external support gave Israel, for the first time in its history, a convenient time frame to reach its strategic goals. In this sense, the mere decision to react massively to the Hizbollah provocation was correct. Paradoxically, however, the open check that the international community gave Israel proved to be a major source of the failure to secure its military and political goals. The reason was that the Israeli leadership continued to think and act according to a traditional and invalid concept. Since the war of 1948, in which American and British pressure had prevented the IDF from reaching a decisive victory over the Egyptian army towards the end of the war, the Israelis had always sensed that external pressure, and not Arab military power, was the barrier to their achieving complete victory. This was the case in 1956, in 1967 (on the Syrian front), in 1973 (on the Egyptian front) and, to some extent, in the First Lebanese War of 1982.

This historical experience created a form of conditioned political–military reflex according to which once Israel seized the military initiative, the hourglass was turned upside down and external pressure started to mount to prevent a complete defeat of the Arab opponent. The fact that Israel's strategic environment had changed dramatically since the end of the Cold War bore little importance for the country's leaders. Thus, hours after the Hizbollah provocation of July 12, Defence Minister Amir Peretz made the assessment that 'international pressure [to end the Israeli reaction] will arrive, and will arrive faster than what we think'. Foreign Minister Tzipi Livni thought that there was 'a very fast point' at which the international community will start 'acting against us'.[15] And Prime Minister Ehud Olmert estimated that 'we enter a situation [i.e., hostilities] that will last days'.[16]

The mistake of misreading international reaction to an Israeli response was enhanced by a lack of experience at the top. In July 2006, Israel's national security apparatus was headed by Ehud Olmert, who had become prime minister following Ariel Sharon's stroke seven months earlier, and Defence Minister Amir Peretz and Foreign Minister Tzipi Livni, who had entered office following the March 2006 elections, or two months before the war started. None of them, and glaringly the new Defence Minister, Peretz, had any significant experience in national security affairs. Consequently, unlike former prime ministers, such as Ehud Barak and Ariel Sharon, and their defence ministers, who could count on their own vast security experience, the trio heading Israel's national security in July 2006 had to rely far more on military advice. In this case, as we will see, the generals' professional advice was of low quality.

From the military perspective, once the IDF carried out its opening gambit in the form of a well-planned air strike against Hizbollah's heavy-rocket installations (operation 'Specific Gravity'), two courses of action were possible. The first option was to use the Israeli Air Force (IAF) to destroy Lebanese infrastructure (e.g. the Beirut airport, power stations, bridges) as a means of exerting pressure on the Lebanese government to take action against Hizbollah. This course was advocated primarily by the IDF Chief of Staff, Maj. Gen. Dan Halutz, a former commander of the IAF. The second was a massive ground offensive to take over southern Lebanon and destroy Hizbollah's short-range rocket launchers. This course of action was advocated by the IDF's Northern Command but opposed by the Chief of Staff. Within hours of the border incident on 12 July, the White House made it clear that strikes against Lebanese installations should be ruled out. Thus, the first course of action became invalid. At the same time, the Chief of Staff did not advocate any ground option for the war's first stage. The result, simply put, was that the IDF had no feasible course of action for the continuation of the war. Unfortunately, in his discussions with the political echelon, the Chief of Staff had avoided making this lacuna clear. The same gap held true with regard to the intelligence input made available to Olmert and Peretz on 12 July.[17]

The combination of political misconception in regard to the international reaction, an inexperienced political leadership, over-dependence on military advice and the poor quality of this advice combined to lead to two major political mistakes. The first was the lack of a clear definition of the war's political and military goals. Olmert, Peretz and Halutz agreed, within two hours of the Hizbollah attack, that the magnitude of the provocation made a massive Israeli response unavoidable. From that stage on, the main dimension of the political discussion involved operational issues. Discussions at the level of prime minister and defence minister focused primarily on the type of targets that should be attacked. The same question was at the centre of the government meeting that convened about 11 hours after the incident. Under pressure of time because of the need to begin execution of Operation 'Specific Gravity', the ministers were requested to authorize the planned operation. There was no substantial discussion of the ramifications of the operation or of Israel's political goals in escalating the conflict. The only one to clearly raise this issue was Foreign Minister Livni, who suggested that the Israeli demand should be the implementation of UN Security Council Resolution 1559, which called, inter alia, for the establishment of Lebanon's sovereignty over all Lebanese territory and the dismantling of all Lebanese and non-Lebanese militias. Livni's suggestion was ignored throughout most of the discussion although this demand was mentioned in the government's resolution. The focus of the cabinet discussion was on the need to react massively in order to restore 'the deterrence balance' in Israel's favour.[18] A smaller political forum of senior cabinet ministers ('the forum of the seven') authorized the operation, which was carried out shortly afterwards. This forum hardly touched upon the aims of the war.[19]

The lack of a clear definition of the political goals of a war initiated by Israel was not unique to this case. In 1956, Israel had avoided defining specific war goals beyond the destruction of the Egyptian army and the reopening of the Tiran Straits. In 1967, Israel's war initiative did not include the occupation of the West Bank or the Golan Heights, and the Israelis themselves were surprised by the way the war developed. And in 1982, the declared definition of the war goals contradicted the more ambitious but latent goals of Defence Minister Sharon – a fact that contributed significantly to the limited achievements of this war. In 2006, however, the situation was different. The pressure of time and the availability of UN Resolution 1559, which reflected the international consensus and suited Israel's security interests, created a convenient setting for a discussion that could lead to the definition of a feasible war goal. This did not take place, once again because of the poor, inexperienced political leadership, the dominance of the IDF in these discussions and the low quality of the advice given by the generals.

The second major mistake at the political level derived from the first. Since no clear definition of war goals took place, none of the ministers, including the prime minister himself, had any well-defined strategy for the war's next stages, in particular how to bring it to an end. The gravity of this mistake becomes clearer when one takes into account that the Director of Military Intelligence Maj. Gen. Amos Yadlin, who served *ex officio* as the government intelligence officer, warned that Hizbollah was likely to start launching rockets at Israel's hinterland in reaction to 'Specific Gravity'. The *Mossad* chief, Meir Dagan, concurred.[20] On the other hand, Chief of Staff Halutz gave the ministers the impression that the IDF had operational plans for the continuation of hostilities. In response to a remark by the experienced Vice Prime Minister, Shimon Peres, that there was need to think two steps ahead, Halutz said:

> I think two steps ahead and I also think four steps ahead . . . [B]ut I do not know [how] to give a scenario of four steps ahead, and whoever thinks that he knows should put it on the table and I am ready to dispute it.[21]

It is clear *post factum* that the impression created by Halutz was at least partially wrong. At this point, he knew that the course of action that he wanted to take, the destruction of Lebanese infrastructure as a means of pressuring Lebanese Prime Minister Fouad Siniora's government to act against Hizbollah, had been vetoed by Washington. Olmert had repeatedly said so and made it clear that he would not allow this action. Halutz wanted to avoid a large-scale ground operation for fear of heavy IDF casualties. As an experienced IAF officer, he knew that the air force lacked the capability to locate and destroy the hundreds of rocket launchers deployed in southern Lebanon. He must also have known that the number of Hizbollah targets that could be destroyed from the air was limited although the IAF could knock out most of them within a day or two. What remains unclear is why he did not report this to the cabinet and why Olmert and his ministers did not ask him the right questions during this discussion.

Psychological explanations (primarily a certain dynamic associated with groupthink), reasons of bureaucratic politics (mainly the interest of the IDF and its chief in controlling as much of the war policymaking process as possible) and security concerns (Israeli ministers are notorious for leaking sensitive information) can partially account for the two principal mistakes. But the most viable explanation is the belief, which was shared by most policymakers, that international pressures will compel Israel to cease the firing within two or three days. In Clausewitzian terms, Israel's 'culmination of victory' was on the second or the third day of the war, following the successful destruction of most of Hizbollah's known targets and before Hizbollah had accumulated any significant success. But the international pressure did not come, and, thus, Israel found itself extending a conflict that under the circumstances was unwinnable.

The military/strategic level

The professional advice that the military echelon gave its political consumers, as well as certain elements of the IDF's performance in the conflict, reflects a number of fundamental shortcomings in Israel's military preparations for the confrontation. It is important to note, however, that in contrast to past practice, the strategic intelligence estimate was not the source of the problem this time. Prior to the war, *Agaf Modi'in* (*AMAN* – Military Intelligence) warned that Hizbollah was planning to kidnap IDF soldiers near the border, that a massive Israeli reaction would lead to large-scale rocket attacks against northern Israel and that an escalation would involve rocket attacks against the city of Haifa and even the coastal plane up to Tel Aviv. Moreover, this agency estimated that the Hizbollah short-range rocket arsenal numbered more than 10,000 rockets, and it also made it clear that it could not provide operational intelligence concerning the location of the short-range rocket launchers. Consequently, the only way to stop the likely massive bombardment of northern Israel would be the occupation of southern Lebanon.[22]

In reality, therefore, the source of the IDF's poor preparations for the war was insufficient attention to the northern front. Since the beginning of the *al-Aqsa Intifada* in September 2000, Israel's security apparatus had turned its attention, almost entirely, to the conflict with the Palestinians. Consequently, despite being aware of the estimate that a large-scale provocation by Hizbollah was highly likely and despite a growing resolve to react massively, preparations to respond to such an act were insufficient.

In the summer of 2006, the IDF was in the midst of overhauling its war plans for confronting Hizbollah. One plan, '*Mei Marom*' ('Water from Above'), was played out by Staff Officers of Northern Command in June 2006. It called for an extensive ground operation to occupy southern Lebanon in order to achieve a decisive victory. A second plan, more limited in scope and entitled 'Icebreaker', was under preparation when war broke out. It called for a massive use of stand-off fire, mostly by the IAF, as a means of changing the situation in southern Lebanon without the use of ground forces. A second draft of this plan, completed in mid-March 2006, regarded it as the initial stage of a future conflict with Hizbollah, with '*Mei Marom*' to be employed in case of escalation.[23]

Having no approved war plan when the confrontation started, the Chief of Staff opted for 'Icebreaker' although he did not officially call it as such.[24] This preference was probably motivated by four considerations. First, 'Icebreaker' was planned as a response to the circumstances that existed on 12 July. Second, it was to be carried out almost solely by the IAF; Halutz, having been a career pilot and former IAF commander, was an expert in this field and had confidence in the IAF's ability to successfully carry out its missions. Third, Halutz was aware of the fact that the IDF ground forces were not prepared for the occupation of southern Lebanon, since, for almost six years, they had been policing the occupied territories rather than training for war. Finally, and probably most importantly, Israeli society in the summer of 2006 was highly sensitive to the loss of soldiers, and the military, like the political echelon, was acutely aware of this. Under these circumstances, a ground operation that would likely cost the lives of 100 to 200 soldiers had become unacceptable.

Intolerance of military losses is not unique to Israel. Edward Luttwak regards this sensitivity, combined with the need to avoid enemy non-combatant losses, as a feature of post-heroic conflicts – the way of war of modern industrialized countries.[25] In the Israeli case, this was evident in the first

Lebanon war, in the conflict with Hizbollah in southern Lebanon until 2000, during the *al-Aqsa Intifada* and in Prime Minister Ariel Sharon's decision to unilaterally disengage from the Gaza Strip in 2005. But in the Second Lebanon War, this factor had become the most important consideration. As Maj. Gen. (Res.) Giora Romm, formerly deputy commander of the IAF, put it, 'The IDF's reluctance to conduct ground operations in southern Lebanon . . . reflects a belief that the threat (Katyusha fire against civilians) does not justify the price (the lives of combat soldiers)'.[26] The political echelon expressed a similar thinking.[27] Consequently, during the Second Lebanon War, avoiding IDF losses had covertly become a more important mission than securing war goals.[28]

Under these circumstances, the preference for 'Icebreaker' made sense in many respects, except for two: First, the plan gave no answer to Hizbollah's ability to launch short-range rockets against northern Israel. This was well known in July 2006. During a military exercise that simulated a confrontation with Hizbollah about a month earlier, the IAF commander, Maj. Gen. Eliezer Shkedy, made it clear that his pilots could not prevent massive short-range rocket attacks. He estimated that the IAF's success rate in destroying these launchers was likely to be no more than 1 per cent to 3 per cent.[29] Second, the number of Hizbollah targets that could be hit by the IAF was rather limited. The northern command had prepared 83 such targets before the war, and additional objectives were located at the GHQ level under the unofficial title of 'target bank'. By the fourth day of the war, however, all the targets had been attacked and destroyed.[30]

Indeed on 16 July, the IDF Chief of Staff faced a rather simple situation: The IAF had destroyed all or almost all of Hizbollah's known targets. At the same time, it could not stop the massive rocket fire that Hizbollah had started on 13 July and that had already caused ten civilian losses, including eight in the city of Haifa. In order to put an end to these attacks, three courses of action were possible: to bomb Lebanese infrastructure facilities as a means of pressuring the Lebanese Government and the international community to take control of southern Lebanon; to occupy southern Lebanon and then to accept a political settlement, in the framework of which the IDF would be replaced by the Lebanese army and/or an international force; or to accept a ceasefire in accordance with the principles that had been set, for example, by the G8 at its St. Petersburg summit on the same day calling for the return of the kidnapped IDF soldiers and the implementation of UN Resolution 1559.[31]

Given these options, the first two courses of action, as noted above, were regarded as unfeasible, and the third option as the most viable choice. The transcripts of political and military discussions that day, however, show that, with the exception of Foreign Minister Livni, none of Israel's top decision makers really suggested adopting this third option. Since the inexperienced Olmert and Peretz both expressed their willingness to allow the army maximal freedom of action,[32] the Chief of Staff had in effect become the prime policymaker at this stage of the war. Consequently, his perception of the situation seems to provide the best explanation for Israel's policy during this critical stage.

Halutz, at least from the second day of the conflict, was thinking in terms of war rather than the more traditional confrontations with Hizbollah, such as 'Accountability' (1993) or 'Grapes of Wrath' (1996). Following the success of operation 'Specific Gravity', he explained in a meeting of the Minister of Defence forum that the operation's main achievement so far had been to change the mode of thinking from that of 'targeted killings' to a mode of war. The main implication of this change was the understanding that the conflict would last more than a few days. On 13 July, he started expressing his opinion that the IDF would need about two more weeks in order to weaken Hizbollah and to radically change the status at Israel's border with Lebanon. For this reason, he rejected voices at GHQ that suggested preparing for the ending of the conflict. In the days that followed, Halutz continued to advocate his initial opinion.[33]

There is no clear evidence of the achievements Halutz had in mind when pursuing two more weeks of fighting. It is quite obvious that his frame of mind was the traditional one, in which the main barrier to a decisive Israeli victory was international intervention aimed at rescuing the Arabs from a dire situation. Like others, he did not realize that this time the international community wanted to see just the opposite. Operationally, despite the political veto, Halutz was still thinking about the destruction of Lebanese infrastructure facilities as leverage on Siniora's government to take control of southern Lebanon. On the night of 12–13 July, he estimated that this political barrier would be removed following the launching of rockets against Israel,[34] and on 13 July he repeatedly raised this option in various forms.[35] It remained his *idée fixe* throughout the war.[36]

As time passed with no additional military achievements, he started pressuring the IDF to produce an 'image of victory' aimed at 'shaping consciousness' – an Israeli version of the American 'effects-based operations' (EBO).[37] Thus, the IDF was instructed to take the town of Bint Jbeil, which bore no military significance but was the place where Nasrallah had delivered his 'spider web' speech following the IDF pullout from southern Lebanon in May 2000. This speech, in which Israel was likened to a spider web that can be destroyed, was perceived by many Israelis, including the IDF officer corps, as a grave humiliation. The occupation of the town was to avenge that humiliation. However, capturing Bint Jbeil could have cost the lives of many soldiers, and the lower echelon commanders were reluctant to pay this price for a target that bore no military value.[38] In the face of unexpectedly stiff resistance, Halutz then demanded the killing of Hizbollah fighters or, even better, their capture. And the best 'spectacle of victory' could be the targeted killing of a senior Hizbollah leader, preferably Nasrallah or Imad Mugniyeh, the organization's head of security.[39] These attempts ended in failure, as well. Whatever Halutz's mode of thinking, it is obvious that it did not fit Israel's strategic environment at this stage of the war.

The positions that Halutz presented to Olmert and Peretz did not reflect the professional disagreements within the army. This was evident, for example, in the first meeting between Olmert and Maj. Gen. Ehud Adam, the Commander of the Northern Command, which took place almost four weeks after the war started. It was then that Olmert heard about the difficulties that the Command faced when conducting small operations rather than the large-scale operation to occupy southern Lebanon. He told Adam: 'I'd like you to know that today was the first time . . . that we received for approval an operational plan for the occupation of the Litany area'.[40] Halutz's behaviour in this regard was not always the rule: in the far-more stressful days of the 1973 Yom Kippur War, the Chief of Staff at the time used to bring along his deputy to critical discussions so that Prime Minister Golda Meir and her aides would be able to receive a different opinion.

The significance of Halutz's professional judgment was increased by the fact that it was not challenged by most senior IDF officers during the discussions he held in Tel Aviv. This, again, was not a typical situation. The General Staff under Ehud Barak and Amnon Lipkin-Shahak in the 1990s included a large number of opinionated officers who were not afraid to voice their opposition even when it contradicted the Chief of Staff's position. The result was a pluralist forum in which more refined and better decisions could be made.[41] In the summer of 2006, the General Staff was far more conformist, and Halutz acted as soloist. During the war, the forum of the General Staff, the highest, most experienced and most professional forum for military decision-making, was not convened at all. Instead, Halutz's discussions were made in small groups of officers, many of whom were former IAF pilots who tended to conform to the Chief of Staff's estimates. Thus, for example, on 15 July he convened the 'model battling forum', a group of four or five officers who served during the war as his 'mini' General Staff. Their discussion focused on how long the hostilities should continue. According to the minutes of the meeting, 'the head of the Operation Branch estimated 14 days, the Chief of Staff 14–16 days, and the head of the Modelling Division, 14 days'.[42] Other General Staff officers believed at the time that either a ground offensive should be launched or that fighting should be brought to an end. But most of these officers did not participate in these discussions; and when they did, they did not present their alternative positions firmly enough.[43]

All in all, at the most critical stage of the war, after Israel had maximized her military achievements and before the IDF's futility in trying to stop the bombardment of northern Israel was fully revealed, Israel's inexperienced political leadership was ill advised by a Chief of Staff who understood too little of ground warfare and believed too much in air power. He was assisted by a group of conformist officers who seem to have told him precisely what he wanted to hear. The result was the mistaken decision to continue the fighting. This led to a rather static war, in which northern Israel suffered heavy rocket shelling for another four weeks without major Hizbollah losses. Ultimately the strategic deadlock ended in a failed ground operation that the Chief of

Staff and his political superiors had wanted to avoid from the start. Had they ended the war in its first days, the outcome for Israel in general, and for them personally, would have been far better.

The operational level

The Chief of Staff's poor leadership during the war, as well as various defects in the IDF's level of professionalism, led to a number of shortcomings at the operational level, as well. With the exception of operation 'Specific Gravity' – its only major success – the IDF performance at this level was a far cry from its past performances.

The success of operation 'Specific Gravity' was first and foremost an intelligence achievement. Prior to the war, *AMAN* and the *Mossad* succeeded in precisely locating the Hizbollah's long-range rocket arsenal. In most cases, the information was accurate enough to point out not only the house where the rockets or launchers were stored, but also the specific room.[44] This critical information enabled the IAF to destroy most of the 150-km-range Zelzal 1 launchers and missiles, as well as about 500 Fajr 3 and Fajr 5 shorter-range rockets. But even here, the intelligence picture was far from perfect. Prior to the war, *AMAN* did not know that some of the 122mm rockets were upgraded and now had a range of 42 km instead of 20 km and that Syria had supplied Hizbollah with 220mm rockets with a range of 50 km to 70 km. The Syrian rockets that were targeted at Haifa caused considerable damage.[45]

The rest of the IDF's performance at the operational level was far less impressive. As already noted, it was caught in the midst of preparations for a confrontation with Hizbollah. In the past, insufficient planning by itself had not been a major cause of an Israeli military failure. As an army whose unofficial motto was 'every plan is a basis for changes', the IDF's ability to improvise, not only at the tactical but also at the operational level, was in many cases one of the sources of its strength; this was clearly evident in the 1967 war, especially on the Jordanian and Syrian fronts. It was not the situation in the summer of 2006.

One major problem was the lack of coordination between the General Head Quarters – *Kiryah* – in Tel Aviv and the Northern Command. During the first two weeks of the war, the Commander of the Northern Command, Maj. Gen. Ehud Adam, and his deputy, Maj. Gen. Eyal Ben-Reuven, continued preparing operation '*Mei Marom*' for the occupation of southern Lebanon. At the same time, the Chief of Staff ruled out any large-scale ground operation; at most, he was willing to authorize limited raids, aimed at creating a 'spectacle of victory'.

The result was a conceptual gap between Adam and Ben-Reuven, two traditional armoured corps officers who termed a victory the removal of the Katyusha threat through Israel's occupation of southern Lebanon, and Halutz and his staff, who looked for a substitute for such an operation by way of a 'spectacle of victory' rather than a real victory. From Halutz's perspective, as he noted on 18 July, even the detailed planning of an operation to occupy southern Lebanon was a waste of time.[46] The gap was deepened, furthermore, by the fact that the dialogue between Adam and Halutz was minimal. Adam visited Tel Aviv only once, when Halutz was away. Halutz, on his behalf, distanced Adam from participation in central discussions. In other talks, in which he participated by means of video conference, Adam's microphone was turned to a mute condition so he could not express his opinion. The result was that Adam learned more than a week after war started that the occupation of southern Lebanon was highly unlikely.[47] And it took Halutz close to an additional two weeks (August 3) to reach the conclusion that operation '*Mei Marom*' was the only viable solution for ending the Hizbollah rocket bombardment.

Halutz's objection to a ground operation was the major factor that delayed, by more than two weeks, the mobilization of reserve forces. On 26 July, a military consensus had been reached that a partial or a complete occupation of southern Lebanon might be necessary in light of the continued failure to stop the rocket bombardment. A day later, the cabinet approved the mobilization of two to three reserve divisions. On 28 July, the mobilization process of one division started, but it was completed only on August 5.[48] It is important to note that it was known that the reserve forces were not ready for war; '*Mei Marom*' called for an early mobilization in order to enable the time span needed to prepare the forces for combat. This was hardly done at all, and the result was a poor level of combat performance, as well as command and control among reserve officers and soldiers once they entered battle.

The tactical level

At least once in its history, the IDF experienced a situation in which failures at the political, strategic and operational levels left the fighting forces in a very difficult situation. This was the 1973 War of Yom Kippur, but then the Israeli soldiers, primarily the armoured corps, showed a very high level of professionalism and motivation, a combination that enabled Israel to move from a near defeat at the initial stage of the war to a victory at its end. The Second Lebanon War saw a similar failure at the higher levels of war management. Unfortunately, the IDF soldiers of the summer of 2006 lacked, in most cases, the high standards of training and preparation of those in 1973. For this reason, they could not save Israel from the mistakes that were conducted at the upper levels.

This problem did not involve the IAF – Israel's most professional arm. Paraphrasing Winston Churchill's promise in 1941, the IAF's motto in 2006 could have been, 'Give us the coordinates, and we will finish the job'. Being highly professional, technologically advanced and operationally flexible, the IAF proved to be the most effective arm of the Israeli military during the war and the only force that completely met its professional duties. Its only problem was an insufficient number of operational targets.

The IAF had prepared operation 'Specific Gravity' for six years and carried it out efficiently on the night of 12–13 July. Altogether, 278 targets, mostly in densely populated areas, were attacked within 34 minutes by 40 aircraft. Between 40 and 44 of the 150–200-km-range Zelzal 1 and 2 rocket launchers were destroyed as were most of the missiles. In addition, about half of the launchers of the medium-range (45–75 km) Fajr 3 and Fajr 5 rockets were destroyed. Collateral damage was less than expected – about 20 civilians were killed in contrast to the hundreds that had been anticipated. It is still unclear whether the IAF completely destroyed Hizbollah's arsenal of Iranian-made rocket launchers or just crippled it considerably. Israel made no claim of total destruction, but the fact is that, with one exception, no Iranian-made Fajr rockets reached Israeli territory during the war. An alternative explanation is political: Teheran decided to veto their use to avoid the sight of Israeli cities being hit by Iranian-supplied rockets at a time when the international community was considering a menu of sanctions against Iran over its ongoing nuclear program.[49]

The IAF, however, was less effective in carrying out the rest of its missions. Shortly after the strike against the heavy-rocket arsenal, it carried out a massive bombing of Beirut's Dahia quarter, the Shi'a political and cultural centre where Hizbollah housed its main command posts. The strike focused on two buildings in which Nasrallah maintained his private residence, as well as many of his offices and staff. Although all these targets were completely destroyed, none of the Hizbollah leaders was hit. By this stage, they had all gone underground and Israeli intelligence failed to provide timely information about their whereabouts. No senior members of the Hizbollah were killed by Israel during the war.[50]

The lack of high-quality target intelligence was the sole cause of the IAF's failure to put an end to the launching of short-range rockets against Israel. Throughout the war, the air force carried out 11,897 sorties, of which 6,900 were attack sorties, and dropped 13,916 bombs, of which 7,732 were smart munitions. A total of 3,100 sorties directly targeted Hizbollah's short-range rocket launching capabilities, and a large proportion of the rest of the sorties aimed at limiting the organization's freedom of operations in this domain.[51] However, the results were poor because of the lack of intelligence. The Hizbollah carried out about 475 rocket attacks during the war, with an average of eight to nine rockets per salvo. A total of 3,970 rockets hit Israel. The estimated number of rocket launchers destroyed by the IAF is, about, 15.[52] This outcome is slightly better than the IAF's pessimistic estimate prior to the war, which forecasted a 1 per cent to 3 per cent rate of success.[53] The IAF was far more successful in hunting down medium-range rocket launchers. Following the destruction of half of them in its opening strike, the air force attacked and destroyed most of the rest during the war.[54]

The IDF's military superiority enabled it to destroy almost every Hizbollah target as is usually the case in this type of asymmetric conflict. However, this capability is the function of the intelligence system's ability to distinguish the targets that needed to be hit. *AMAN*'s balance sheet in this respect was mixed. As noted already, *AMAN*, in cooperation with the *Mossad*, was highly successful in precisely locating the long-range rocket arsenal of the Hizbollah.[55] But even here the intelligence picture was far from perfect. Prior to the war *AMAN* did not know that some of the 122 mm rockets were upgraded and that now their range was 42 km instead of 20 km and that Syria supplied the Hizbollah with 220 mm rockets with a range of 50–70 km. The Syrian rockets, which hit Haifa, caused considerable material damage and disruption to the civilian population.[56]

Therefore, in the provision of accurate information about the Hizbollah command and control system, the location of its leaders and the location of hundreds of short-range Katyusha rocket launchers *AMAN* was found wanting. Despite extensive efforts throughout the war, the IDF failed to disrupt the organization's rather simple but highly secretive communication system or to hit any of its senior leaders. The intelligence that enabled effective targeted killing operations in the West Bank and Gaza during the *Intifada* was not available in Lebanon in 2006. Israel's sole chance to hit Hassan Nasrallah during the war took place on 12 July, when he made his last public appearance. Following operation 'Specific Gravity', Nasrallah went underground, and throughout the war neither he nor any other senior leader of the Hizbollah was located by *AMAN*.

Even more disturbing, as previously noted, was *AMAN*'s failure to provide any accurate information about the location of the short-range rocket launchers. Prior to the war, the agency had estimated correctly that any significant military conflict with Hizbollah would involve the massive use of this arsenal against Israeli civilian targets. Nevertheless, *AMAN* assigned a relatively low ranking to the targeting of these launchers, with the result that during the war it could not provide information that would enable their destruction. As mentioned previously, Hizbollah's short-range rocket-launcher deployment remained almost intact, and northern Israel was subject to continuous rocket attacks right up to the last day of the war when it suffered its heaviest bombardment of the conflict.

Before the war, *AMAN* had succeeded in collecting only partial information about the underground layout that the Hizbollah had built in southern Lebanon since the Israeli withdrawal of May 2000. When war started, the agency could provide very partial information about these bunker sets, known in IDF jargon as 'nature reserves'. Even worse, owing to a cumbersome and highly compartmented distribution system, most of the available information did not reach the fighting forces. As the commander of a regular paratrooper brigade said after the war, his biggest surprise was the Hizbollah's impressive bunkers. When he sent his troops to occupy them at the beginning of the war, he had understood that they were 'merely a number of small tents, sleeping bags and conserve cans'.[57] The provision of elementary intelligence to the ground forces did not improve during the war. In some cases, for example, the troops had to use aerial photographs that were years old despite the fact that same-day air photographs were available in central command posts, as well as in Tel Aviv.[58]

The IDF ground forces proved to be highly motivated but, in many cases, poorly trained for their missions. Moreover, and in contrast to its past history, the command, especially at the regimental and divisional levels, was of low professional quality. When that deficiency is added to the problems at the operational and strategic levels, the result was near chaos. A typical example was the series of battles conducted by the regular Golani and paratrooper brigades to occupy the town of Bint Jbeil. In three consecutive battles (23–29 July, 1–3 August and 6–9 August) against this target, 11 Israeli soldiers were killed and 23 were wounded. Despite massive artillery and air support Bint Jbeil was not occupied. The Winograd Commission concluded:

> It seems that the failure in Bint Jbeil was the product of a combination of improper planning and the setting of unsuitable targets, a complete blurring of the operation's goals and ends, lack of harmony between the operational targets and the OB [Order of Battle] that was allocated to reach them, a search for intangible and semi-solid 'conscious effects', hesitancy in the use of forces, rapid changes in orders, fear of IDF losses, imperfect communications between commanders at senior level, inadequate tactical activation of the forces and faults in SOP [Standard Operating Procedure] and in the management of the battle.[59]

While the IDF employed its best trained forces in the battle of Bint Jbeil, the army used less capable soldiers in other confrontations, and the outcome was even worse. Many of the tank teams had not practised for long periods of time because they had been used for policing missions in the occupied territories during the Second *Intifada* years. Some reserve tank drivers had not driven a tank for six years, the gunners had shot their last round in the twentieth century and the commanders had no experience in operating more than three tanks simultaneously.[60] One of the reserve division commanders, Brig. Gen. Erez Zukerman, had no experience at all in commanding armoured units. He was a naval commando officer who later became the commander of a regular infantry brigade and reached the command post of the division without going through a divisional command course or any professional course in armoured warfare. His division had conducted no divisional exercise for years, and the soldiers, as well as the commanders at all levels, were poorly trained for their mission. Zukerman's first test as a division commander under fire was also the first time he commanded his division. The result was one of the most humiliating defeats in Israel's military history:

> An IDF divisional attack in close and almost complete eyesight range from Israeli territory against a small-size enemy that took no initiatives, faded away within less than a day and turned into a humiliating retreat back into Israeli territory. . . . Three IDF soldiers were killed during this

move. There is no way to summarize it other than by saying that the 'Pillar of Fire' Division defeated itself.[61]

The performance of regular tank units was not much better. Battalion 9 of Armoured Brigade 401, equipped with Israel's most modern tank, the Merkava Mk4, lost 11 of 24 tanks in the Saluki battle, in which 11 soldiers were killed and more than 50 wounded. The tanks were hit by Russian-made AT-14 Kornet missiles, which were operated by about 20 teams from a range of up to 5 km. As far as is known, Hizbollah suffered no losses. As a post-battle investigation concluded, the main causes of the Israeli failure were a fundamental mistake in the selection of the axis of advance, flawed coordination between the infantry forces that were supposed to provide cover to the crossing tanks and the tank brigade, lack of command resolve in a number of cases and a poor level of professionalism of the tank teams, which had not practised for months prior to the war. Among others, they failed to operate the tanks' smoke canisters properly, they did not know how to advance in the dark and they failed to use a rear slope in order to find protection from the anti-tank fire.[62]

Conclusion

Three critical factors account for Israel's failure to defend itself against the massive rocket attack launched by Hizbollah that lasted for more than a month. The first, at the political level, was a lack of understanding of Israel's room for manoeuvre in the post-9/11 system. The belief that there was only a narrow window of opportunity to punish Hizbollah facilitated and dominated an impulsive and hasty decision-making process, leaving the option chosen – a massive military reaction – with no apparent political goal. The second factor was personal, the dominance of the Chief of Staff, Lt. Gen. Dan Halutz, in the policymaking process and his tendency to ignore the Procrustean bed in which the war took place: the American veto of the destruction of Lebanese infrastructure, on the one hand, and the inability to put an end to the short-range rocket bombardment without the occupation of southern Lebanon, on the other. The third critical factor was at the tactical level – the poor level of readiness of the IDF ground forces, especially the tank units, which made the occupation of southern Lebanon, when this was finally attempted, so difficult.

In light of the problems that were revealed during the war, IDF generals started warning in the fall of 2008 that any new Hizbollah provocation should be met by massive retaliation. The commander of the Northern Command, Maj. Gen. Gadi Eizenkott, said in an interview that Israel would act in the next confrontation according to the 'Dahia doctrine', meaning the disproportional destruction of any village from which rockets were launched.[63] Retired senior IDF officers backed this threat.[64] Such threats, however, seem to be hasty and, in light of the change of guard in the White

House, also politically unrealistic. To a large extent, Israel's poor perform-ance in the Second Lebanon War was an idiosyncratic event, the product of a combination of circumstances that are not likely to be repeated in the same manner in the foreseeable future. Certainly, poor political leadership and low-quality military advice can recur.

However, in light of the IDF's flawed performance in that war, significant measures have since been taken to train the army for large-scale conflict rather than for policing missions in the territories. To a large extent, it may be said that the IDF lost the Second Lebanon War in the West Bank and Gaza. The fading of the Second *Intifada* enabled Israel's armed forces to invest their main effort in preparations for a confrontation in Lebanon or with Syria. And since Hizbollah leaders had learned a lesson from the 2006 war, as well, it is also possible that no such confrontation will ever take place at all.

11 Conclusion

Sergio Catignani

This study set out to analyse the causes, conduct and outcomes of Israel's protracted and asymmetric conflict with terrorist/insurgent groups that have operated out of south Lebanon since the late 1960s. Whilst the motivations and actions of various actors involved in this conflict arena were examined, particular attention was given to the two principal belligerents of this enduring low-intensity asymmetric conflict: Israel and Hizbollah.

It is, therefore, perhaps somewhat ironic that Israel's northern neighbour, Lebanon, was perceived as the least threatening Arab state from Israel's pre-state era up until the first two decades of its existence. Yet, its weak state structure – due to its internally destabilizing ethno-nationalist and religious cleavages – proved an increasing cause for concern on the part of Israel. As Laurie Zittrain Eisenberg examined in Chapter 2, Lebanon's weak state apparatus and the enduring rivalries within Lebanese society and polity between Sunni, Shi'a, Christian, Druze and, since the late 1960s, Palestinian factions, turned the country into a battleground in which these ethnic and religious groups vied for power and influence often by attracting or recruiting more powerful external actors to their particular cause. Syria's historical links with and claims over Lebanon as well as its direct involvement in Lebanese society following the outbreak of the Lebanon Civil War, Iran's religious affinity with Lebanon's growing, but politically and economically disenfranchised Shi'a population and Israel's proxy relationship with local Christian Maronite factions based on a tenuous Judeo-Christian heritage as well as on their mutually perceived minority status within the greater Middle East, encouraged and facilitated the involvement of these states in Lebanon's conflict arena in order to pursue their own strategic interests.

As seen throughout this book, Israel's longstanding strategic interest in and preoccupation with Lebanon has been predicated on its need to significantly curtail, if not eliminate totally, cross-border terrorist (and insurgent) activity originating from southern Lebanon in order to secure its northern communities, particularly those situated in the Galilee panhandle. Whereas during the 1970s Jerusalem was chiefly preoccupied with Palestine Liberation Organization (PLO) terrorist actions, Israel's 1982 invasion of Lebanon set the conditions for the emergence and establishment of the Shi'a militant group, Hizbollah, a much more ideologically inspired and organizationally compact insurgent group that proved to be a more significant and resilient challenge to Israeli interests in Lebanon as well as to its national security.

In Chapter 3, when examining the after-effects of Israel's invasion of Lebanon, Asher Kaufman noted pointedly that 'if revolutionary Iran was the ideological mother of Hizbollah and Syria was the instrumental father, then the Israeli invasion of Lebanon could be considered . . . the midwife that brought the Shi'a organization to life'. Indeed, these three actors played a crucial part in facilitating the ideological, organizational and, eventually, military development of Hizbollah. Nonetheless, as Hassan Barari and Hani A. M. Akho-Rashida, Hussain Sirriyeh and Mats Wärn have argued in their respective chapters, the Shi'as' socio-economic deprivation and lack of political clout in Lebanon's confessionalist political system also galvanized Shi'a political and militant activism initially via Amal and subsequently via Hizbollah. So, whilst Shi'a activism and militancy was bound to occur in order to redress the domestic inequalities that the Shi'a population had endured as a result of the 1943 'National Pact', it did not have to necessarily turn against Israeli forces present in Lebanon since the 1982 invasion.

Despite the fact that many among the southern Shi'a population had at first welcomed the Israeli invasion – given indigenous hostility towards the PLO – Israel, in fact, failed to capitalize on such hostility by alienating rather than co-opting Shi'a collaboration in its fight against the PLO. As argued in Chapter 6, this lost window of opportunity, together with the Israeli forces' subsequent failure to implement a more refined and hearts-and-minds-based counter-terrorism/counter-insurgency approach against Hizbollah, forced Israel to conduct a protracted, bloody and asymmetric war of attrition with the highly ductile and effective *al-Muqawama* in south Lebanon until its unilateral withdrawal in May 2000.

Although Asher Kaufman argued that Israel's invasion of Lebanon was an 'aberration of previously held policies' vis-à-vis Lebanon and more a manifestation of the specific 'ideological worldview of a few politicians and military officials' that attempted to realise their hegemonic ambitions by trying to stamp out the PLO and socio-politically engineer Lebanon into a Zionist-friendly state, such an 'aberration' does not account for the fact that Israel maintained its occupation of south Lebanon for a further 15 years following the Israel Defence Forces' (IDF) initial redeployment in 1985. Israel's continued and costly presence in south Lebanon during the 18-year occupation was, in fact, the product of Israel's inability to come up with an alternative political-strategic solution to the Israeli–Lebanese conflict. This book has argued that Israel's inability to find a solution to its security concerns vis-à-vis Lebanese-based terrorist and guerrilla threats exposes the limits of undue reliance on military means alone to secure the borders of the state, not least in its failure to cohere an effective counter-insurgency, as opposed to counter-terrorist strategy that acknowledged the quantitative and qualitative difference between the PLO and Hizbollah. This and the ability of Damascus and

Tehran to both undermine Israeli diplomatic efforts at trying to reach a separate peace agreement with Lebanon as well as the training, arming and support given to Hizbollah's insurgency over the last two decades largely accounts for the failure of Israel to secure a regional dispensation attuned to its own strategic interests, mainly peace on its northern border.

Although Iran and Syria provided Hizbollah with the ideological, logistical and organizational wherewithal to fight the Israeli occupation, the occupation itself, as asserted by Mats Wärn in Chapter 9, contributed to the development of Hizbollah's 'ontology of violence' and resistance, which also enabled it to justify the preservation of its military capabilities and activities despite the disbanding of other Lebanon-based militias following the 1989 Taif Agreement. With Hizbollah's growing success at targeting Israeli and South Lebanon Army (SLA) forces in Lebanon and at frustrating Israel's attempts at deterring further attacks against its land and its population, Hizbollah's popularity and support for *al-Muqawama*'s resistance campaign increased during the 1990s. This alone, however, could not justify the maintenance of its military capabilities and militant stance, particularly after Israel's redeployment from south Lebanon in accordance with UN Security Resolution 425 in May 2000.

Hizbollah's ability to maintain its military capabilities as well as its reputation as the only organization able to frustrate what it perceived as Israel's, and by extension its allies', hegemonic aspirations over Lebanon and the Middle East in general was in a sense posited in such a way that it has been able to moderate and integrate its Iranian-inspired Islamist revolutionary programme by opening up to other players in Lebanon's political scene. As seen in Wärn's and Sobelman's chapters, by postponing its radical domestic agenda through the process of *Infitah* and participation in the confessionalist political system and by portraying itself as the only effective deterrent vis-à-vis Israel, Hizbollah hoped to convince Lebanese society that it would have to continue accepting its resistance agenda and by extension, its controversial monopoly over the maintenance and use of armed force.

However, as seen in Sobelman's chapter, following the assassination of Prime Minister Rafiq Hariri and Syria's subsequent withdrawal from Lebanon amid accusations of its complicity in the attack – Hizbollah no longer enjoyed the 'near-untouchable status' it had enjoyed since its perceived victory over Israel in 2000. Despite Hizbollah's claim that Israel was still occupying the disputed Shebaa Farms, its rhetoric and actions of resistance as well as the continuing flexing of its military muscle came to be seen within increasing segments of Lebanese society as a challenge to the state's post-Taif Agreement and efforts at reconstruction. Some quarters within Lebanese society began to seriously question Hizbollah's fidelity to the existing order due to its ongoing relationship with its Syrian and Iranian patrons. And whilst Barari and Akho-Rashida offer a strong critique of the characterization of the Hizbollah–Syrian and the Hizbollah–Iranian relationships as proxy alliances, one cannot discount the fact, as argued by Sirriyeh, that

Hizbollah has often taken, and will continue to take, its ideological and strategic cue from Tehran and the *ayatollahs*.

Thus, whilst internal factors – mainly domestic negotiations between Lebanese factions and Hizbollah over, amongst other things, the future status of its military wing – played a significant factor in Hizbollah's decision to initiate another (limited) round of confrontation with Israel in July 2006, one cannot discount the possibility that Hizbollah's provocative abduction of IDF troops in northern Israel was employed as a diversionary tactic used to distract the world from Iran's uranium enrichment and alleged nuclear weapons development programmes.[1] Such a diversion did, in fact, occur, but this had more to do with Israel's disproportionate response to the abduction. Israel's frustrations with previous Lebanon and Gaza-based abductions together with the belief that its deterrent stance vis-à-vis Hizbollah, Hamas and other terrorist-insurgent organizations had been seriously undermined, led Jerusalem to respond aggressively, yet rather ineffectively, to the Hizbollah abduction and subsequent rocket campaign.

The resultant 2006 Lebanon War brought, in effect, Israel back full circle to confront similar weaknesses it had encountered during the 1982 Lebanon War invasion. In 1982 the Israeli leadership's ambitious, if not far-fetched strategic aims, led to the creation of a botched strategy that neglected to correctly account for the very complex realities of the Lebanese conflict arena. By contrast, Uri Bar-Joseph demonstrated in Chapter 10 how the Israeli civilian leadership failed in 2006 to generate a clear strategy, which the IDF could operate on. Israel's failure to defend itself against Hizbollah's rocket campaign was due not only to poor strategy, but also a result of the IDF's lack of preparedness caused by the IDF's continuous constabulary operations carried out in the Occupied Territories of the West Bank and Gaza Strip since the outbreak of the *Al-Aqsa Intifada* in September 2000.

Furthermore, in both conflicts the lack of clear strategic and, consequently, operational goals as well as their manipulation by certain security actors during hostilities – for example, Ariel Sharon and IDF Chief of Staff Rafael Eitan in 1982 and Chief of Staff Dan Halutz and his 'model battling forum' of like-minded officers – were the product of the peculiar nature of Israeli civil–military relations. Israeli civil–military relations, in fact, have never been clearly delineated and have often enabled the security services to have greater decision-making influence than their uniformed counterparts in comparable liberal democracies.[2] This has been due to the fact that, even though the Israeli political leadership has played a crucial role in watching over and adjudicating on security issues, their reliance on the IDF's strategic and intelligence assessments and reports – given the lack of an equivalent civilian agency able to provide such security estimates – has frequently led the political echelons to defer to the IDF's advice. This advice has proven invaluable in many instances, but with specific reference to the Israeli–Hizbollah conflict, Clive Jones clearly argued in Chapter 7 how IDF intelligence estimates have frequently proved erroneous, perceiving 'Hizbollah as anything more than terrorists' and failing consistently to appreciate the 'wider political context in which the conflict was being played out'.

It has been this inability to effectively grasp the wider political context of the Israeli– Hizbollah conflict that has undeniably led Israel to often employ force without necessarily understanding how such force could achieve clear political ends or, even worse, without fully thinking through the strategic repercussions that IDF operations could have on Israel's insurgent/terrorist foes, their regional supporters and – most importantly – on the local popula- tion, the traditional centre of gravity when fighting an insurgency. Thus, as seen throughout this book, IDF actions often led to an escalation rather than reduction in violence between Lebanese-based insurgent groups and Israel.

Even following Israel's massive bombardment campaigns during Operations 'Accountability' and 'Grapes of Wrath', Israel was unable to defeat or, at least, re-establish a clear deterrent posture vis-à-vis Hizbollah. This was clearly apparent by Hizbollah's growing ability to inflict significant damage and havoc on the Israeli civilian population, whenever Israel caused collateral damage, killed Lebanese civilians or assassinated high-ranking Hizbollah officials during the numerous pre-emptive (or retaliatory) opera- tions carried out throughout the conflict's history. Sobelman, in fact, showed how Hizbollah was able to turn the tables by establishing a balance of deter- rence that forced Israel to follow the 'rules of the game' in which IDF/SLA counter-insurgency operations came to be circumscribed when operating against Hizbollah units in the South Lebanon Security Zone. Operating out- side these 'understandings' led to certain Hizbollah retaliation against the Israeli civilian population, something the establishment of the Security Zone was paradoxically intended to safeguard against in the first place.

However, with the 2006 Summer Lebanon War, the Israeli– Hizbollah bal- ance of deterrence has to some extent changed. Despite the IDF's overall lack- lustre performance (particularly that of its ground units) and Hizbollah's declarations that it had won the war, the extent of Israel's disproportionate retaliation did lead Sheikh Sayyed Nasrallah to seriously reconsider the degree to which Hizbollah can continue to pursue its resistance campaign against Israel without suffering major political setbacks at home and military losses on the ground. This reconsideration has become particularly critical since the end of the war, given that Israel has set out to improve its opera- tional and tactical preparedness and readiness in order to avoid a similarly woeful military performance in the future.

Yet, as this book has argued throughout, many internal as well as external factors could easily affect the current delicate balance of deterrence between Israel and Hizbollah as has been the case in the past. As Lebanon attempts to reconstruct itself as well as continue the 'National Dialogue' between the var- ious parties representing their particular 'confessions', Hizbollah's special status may come to be increasingly questioned by those elements of Lebanese society, both Christian and Muslim that support the 'Cedar Revolution'. Syrian attempts at pushing the Israeli occupation of the Golan Heights back onto the international agenda or Iranian efforts at diverting international attention from its ongoing nuclear acquisition programme may lead these states to provide further military and economic assistance to Hizbollah or to support further Hizbollah attacks on Israeli targets within the disputed Shebaa Farms area and beyond. This is but one of the many scenarios that threaten to ignite violence between Israel and its nemesis in Lebanon once again.

As Clive Jones stated in his introductory chapter, 'there can be no guarantee that future conflict between Israel and Hizbollah can remain limited in scope' let alone avoided. This will indeed be the case as long as the complex and intertwining domestic and regional factors that have influenced the intensity and longevity of this protracted conflict continue to remain unresolved. Much will depend on the extent to which diplomats in Tel Aviv and Washington believe that given the appropriate incentive, the secular regime in Damascus can be separated from its strategic tryst with Tehran. To date, there is little evidence that such a realignment is forthcoming, despite Ankara acting as an intermediary in exploratory talks between Israel and Syria in 2008. Indeed, given the fractured nature of Lebanese sovereignty and the legitimacy Hizbollah derives from both the Shi'a community as well as the wider Muslim world as a consequence of its 'resistance' to Israel, the most optimistic scenario would suggest that containment of violence, rather than resolution will define the future along the Israel–Lebanon border.

Even so, it is unlikely that any Israeli government would ever embark on a military adventure so Clausewitzian in its logic, yet so disastrous in its outcome as the 1982 invasion of Lebanon. For, as it states in the Torah, 'The violence done to Lebanon will overwhelm you'.[3]

Glossary

Term Translation

Afwaj Al-Muqawamah Al-Lubnaniyyah (Amal)	Lebanese Resistance Detachments
Agaf Modi'in (AMAN)	IDF Military Intelligence
Al-Muqawama al-Islamiyya	The Islamic Resistance
Arba Imahud	The Four Mothers Movement
Bitachon Shotef	Current Security
Dar al-Harb	House of War
Dar al-Islam	House of Islam
Da'wah	Call
Hala al Islamiyya	Islamic space
Harakat al-Muqawamat al-Islamiyya (Hamas)	Islamic Resistance Movement
Harb al-Tammuz	The July War
Hizb'allah	Party of God
Istinhaad	Awakening
Jihad al-Bina	Holy Struggle for Reconstruction
Ma'arakh	Labour Alignment
Mangenon ha'Bitachon (Mabat)	South Lebanon Army Intelligence
Mossad	Israeli Secret Services
Mujtahid	Islamic scholar
Mukhabarati	Intelligence agent
Mustafadin	Downtrodden
Sayeret Egoz	*Egoz* Reconnaissance Unit
Shayetet 13	Flotilla 13 (Naval Special Forces)
Shin Bet	Israeli General Security Service
Umma	Islamic community
Va'ad Rashei Sherutim (Varash)	Committee of the Chiefs of the Services
Wadis	Dry riverbeds
Waqf	Inalienable religious endowment
Yakal	South Lebanon Liaison Unit
Yesh Gvul	There is a Limit/Border
Yishuv	Jewish settlement
Zu'ama	Feudal forces

Notes

1 Introduction

1 For a theoretical discussion of asymmetric warfare see: Ivan Arreguín-Toft, *How the Weak Win Wars: a theory of asymmetric conflict* (Cambridge: Cambridge University Press, 2005), p. 250.

2 From benign to malign: Israeli–Lebanese relations, 1948–78

1 Walid Khalidi, *Conflict and Violence in Lebanon* (Harvard College: Center for International Affairs, 1979), note 27, p. 162.
2 For treatment of the Zionist inclination to ally with the Maronites, see: Laura Zittrain Eisenberg, *My Enemy's Enemy: Lebanon in the early Zionist imagination, 1900–1948* (Detroit: Wayne State University Press, 1994); for the Lebanese Christian perspective see: Walid Phares, *Lebanese Christian Nationalism: the rise and fall of an ethnic resistance* (Boulder, CO: Lynne Rienner, 1995).
3 Laura Zittrain Eisenberg, 'Desperate Diplomacy: the Zionist-Maronite treaty of 1946', *Studies in Zionism*, 13/2 (Autumn 1992), pp. 147–63.
4 Eisenberg, *My Enemy's Enemy*, pp. 32–33, 65–66, 110–11, 136–41, 163–69; Eisenberg, 'Desperate Diplomacy', pp. 147–63; Yoav Gelber, 'Antecedents of the Jewish-Druze Alliance in Palestine', *Middle Eastern Studies*, 28/2 (April 1992), pp. 352–73.
5 The Israeli campaign to rescue the Jewish settlements was called 'Operation Hiram'. Not coincidentally, Hiram was the Phoenician King of Tyre who enjoyed a close alliance with Kings David and Solomon. In the pre-state period the romantic wing of the minority alliance school cited the biblical pact between the Hebrews and the Phoenicians, from whom some Maronites claimed descent, as a precedent for a modern Zionist–Maronite partnership.
6 Eisenberg, *My Enemy's Enemy*, p. 159; Kirsten E. Schulze, *Israel's Covert Diplomacy in Lebanon*, St. Antony's Series (Houndmills, Basingstoke, and London: Macmillan Press, 1998), pp. 33–36; Benny Morris, 'Israel and the Lebanese Phalange: the birth of a relationship, 1948–51', *Studies in Zionism*, 5/1 (Spring 1984), pp. 125–44.
7 Itamar Rabinovich, *The War for Lebanon, 1970–1983* (Ithaca, NY: Cornell University Press, 1984), p. 105.
8 David Ben-Gurion, 24 May 1948 and 18 June 1948, *Yoman Hamilchama*, vol. 2 (Tel Aviv: Misrad Habitachon, 1982), pp. 454, 533 and 19 December 1948, vol. 3, p. 887 [in Hebrew].
9 David Ben-Gurion to Moshe Sharett, 27 February 1954 and Moshe Sharett to David Ben-Gurion, 18 March 1954, in Moshe Sharett, *Yoman Ishi*, vol. 8

(Tel Aviv: Am Oved, 1978), p. 2397–400 [in Hebrew]. See also: Eliahu Sasson to Moshe Sharett, 25 March 1954, reprinted in *Davar*, 29 October 1971 [in Hebrew].

10 Sharett, 16 and 28 May 1955, vol. 4, pp. 996, 1024.
11 Chief among Chamoun's offending pro-West positions were not cutting ties with Britain and France after their 1956 attack (with Israel) on Egypt, and his apparent endorsement of the Baghdad Pact and acceptance of the Eisenhower Doctrine.
12 Yair Evron, *War and Intervention in Lebanon: the Israeli-Syrian deterrence dialogue* (Baltimore, MD: The Johns Hopkins University Press, 1987), p. 26.
13 Ibid., pp. 26–28; Irene L. Gendzier, *Notes from the Minefield: United States Intervention in Lebanon and the Middle East, 1945–1958* (Boulder, CO: Westview, 1999), pp. 256–57, 291; Schulze, *Israel's Covert Diplomacy*, pp. 61–62.
14 For a particularly cogent treatment see: Rashid Khalidi, 'Problems of Foreign Intervention in Lebanon', *American Arab Affairs*, 7 (Winter 1983–84), pp. 24–30.
15 Benny Morris, *Israel's Border Wars, 1949–1956* (Oxford: Clarendon Press, 1993), pp. 92–95.
16 Ghada Hashem Talhami, *Palestinian Refugees: from pawns to political actors* (Hauppauge, NY: Nova, 2003), pp. 92–93.
17 Evron, *War and Intervention in Lebanon*, p. 30.
18 Ibid., pp. 45–47.
19 Ze'ev Schiff and Ehud Ya'ari, *Israel's Lebanon War* (New York: Simon & Schuster, 1984), chap. 1; Evron, *War and Intervention in Lebanon*, pp. 42–45.
20 Evron, *War and Intervention in Lebanon*, pp. 45, 69.
21 An excellent introduction is Glenn E. Perry, 'Israeli Involvement in Inter-Arab Politics', *International Journal of Islamic and Arabic Studies*, 1/1 (1984), pp. 11–31.

3 From the Litani to Beirut – Israel's invasions of Lebanon, 1978–85: Causes and consequences

1 Kirsten E. Schulze, *Israel's Covert Diplomacy in Lebanon*, St. Antony's Series (Houndmills, Basingstoke, and London: Macmillan Press, 1998).
2 Avner Yaniv, *Dilemmas of Security: Politics, Strategy and the Israeli Experience in Lebanon* (New York: Oxford University Press, 1987).
3 Shai Feldman, 'Israel's involvement in Lebanon: 1975–85', in Ariel E. Levite, Bruce W. Jentleson and Larry Berman (eds), *Foreign Military Intervention* (New York: Columbia University Press, 1992), p. 131.
4 Oren Barak, book review of Kirsten E. Schulze, *Israel's Covert Diplomacy in Lebanon* in *International Journal of Middle East Studies*, 32/3 (August 2000), pp. 436–38.
5 For more on this see: Farid al-Khazen, *The Breakdown of the State in Lebanon 1967–1976* (London: I. B. Tauris, 2000), pp. 361–78.
6 Ze'ev Maoz, *Defending the Holy Land* (Ann Arbor, MI: The University of Michigan Press, 2006), p. 177.
7 Beate Hamizrachi, *The Emergence of the South Lebanon Security Belt* (New York: Praeger, 1988), pp. 45–75.
8 Arie Naor, *Begin ba-Shilton: 'Edut Ishit* (Tel-Aviv: Yediot Aharonot, 1993).
9 Yair Evron, *War and Intervention in Lebanon: The Israeli-Syrian Deterrence Dialogue* (Baltimore, MD: The Johns Hopkins University Press, 1987), pp. 60–104.
10 Baruch Kimmerling, *Politicide: Ariel Sharon's Wars against the Palestinians* (New York: Verso, 2003).

11 Ze'ev Schiff and Ehud Ya'ari, *Milhemet Sholal* (Jerusalem: Shoken, 1984), pp. 32–38.
12 Irit Gal and Ilana Hamerman, *Mi-Beirut le-Jenin, Milhemet Levanon 1982/2002* (Tel-Aviv: 'Am 'Oved, 2002); Yesh Gvul, *Gevul ha-Tsiyut u-Zekhut ha-Seruv* (Tel-Aviv: Tenuat Yesh Gevul, 1983).
13 A reference to 'war is peace', the first of the three slogans of the Party in George Orwell's, *Nineteen Eighty-Four* (New York: Chelsea House, 1987), p. 6; (The other two slogans are 'freedom is slavery' and 'ignorance is strength').
14 *Mivtza Shelom Ha-Galil* (Merkaz ha-Hasbara, March 1983), p. 3.
15 See particularly: Shai Feldman and Heda Rechnitz-Kijner, *Deception, Consensus and War: Israel in Lebanon* (Tel-Aviv: Jaffee Center for Strategic Studies, 1983); and Schiff and Yaari, *Milhemet Sholal.*
16 See: Schiff and Yaari, *Milhemet Sholal.*
17 Yair Evron, *War and Intervention in Lebanon*, p. 117.
18 *Al-Nahar*, 2 September 1982.
19 'Lebanese add 1,200 to Beirut Seige Death Toll', [no author mentioned] *The Washington Post*, 2 December 1982; *Israel in Lebanon: the report of the International Commission* (London: Ithaca Press, 1983), pp. 18–19.
20 Numbers of casualties vary from 700, according to Israeli sources, to 2,000, according to Palestinian sources. Lebanese authorities put the death toll at 1,200 fatalities.
21 For more on the question of the morality of this war and the way it is remembered in Israel see: Asher Kaufman, 'Forgetting the Lebanon War? On Silence, Denial and Selective Remembrance of the First Lebanon War', in Jay Winter, Efrat Ben Ze'ev and Ruth Ginio (eds), *Shadows of War: the social history of silence in the Twentieth Century* (Cambridge: Cambridge University Press, 2009).
22 Arie Naor, *Begin ba-Shilton*, pp. 317–48.
23 Gil Merom, *How Democracies Lose Small Wars?* (New York: Cambridge University Press, 2003), pp. 177–226.
24 Magnus Ranstorp, *Hizb'allah in Lebanon: the politics of the western hostage crisis* (New York: St. Martin's Press, 1997), pp. 33–40; Yitzhak Nakash, *Reaching for Power: the Shi'a in the modern Arab world* (Princeton: Princeton University Press, 2006), p. 121.
25 'Cabinet Communique on the Withdrawal from Lebanon, 14 January 1985', available at: http://www.mfa.gov.il/MFA/Foreign%20Relations/Israels%20 Foreign%20Relations%20since%201947/1984–88/36%20Cabinet%20Comm unique%20on%20the%20Withdrawal%20from%20Lebanon (accessed on 17 July 2009).
26 S. N. Eisenstadt, *The Internal Repercussions of the Lebanon War* (Jerusalem: The Leonard Davis Institute for International Relations, August 1986).
27 Avraham Sela, 'Civil Society, the Military, and National Security: the case of Israel's security zone in south Lebanon', *Israel Studies*, 12/1, (Spring 2007), p. 63.

4 The emergence of Hizbollah and the beginnings of resistance, 1982–85

1 See: *Mawsu'at Hizb'allah* (*The Encyclopaedia of Hizb'allah*), vol. 1, Series on the Senior Lebanese Personalities (Beirut: Hanah International Institution, n.d.), pp. 17–19. The same point was reiterated in Sheikh Naim Qassem, Deputy Secretary-General of *Hizb'allah* in *Hizb'allah: Al-Manhij, Al-Tajribah, Al-Mustaqbal* (*Hizb'allah: the method, the experiment, the future*), 2nd Edition (Beirut: Dar Al-Hadi, 2002), pp. 15–16.
2 See: Augustus Richard Norton, *Amal and the Shi'a: Struggle for the Soul of Lebanon* (Austin, TX: The University of Texas Press, 1987), pp. 13–14 and 19.

3 See, for example: Riad Tabbarah, 'Background to the Lebanese Conflict', *International Journal of Comparative Sociology*, 20/1–2 (March 1979), p. 112. This article indicates that in 1971 the Lebanese Christian community was estimated at 43 per cent, whereas the Muslims were estimated at 57 per cent. The Shi'a constituted 28 per cent, i.e. larger than either the Maronites or the Sunnis.

4 Marius Deeb, '*Shia* Movements in Lebanon: their formation, ideology, social basis and links with Iran and Syria', *Third World Quarterly*, 10/2 (April 1988), p. 685.

5 Norton, *Amal and the Shi'a*, p. 56. On Imam Al-Sadr's disappearance and its implications, the best work is that of Fouad Ajami, *The Vanished Imam: Musa Al-Sadr and the Shia of Lebanon* (London: I. B. Tauris, 1986).

6 See: *The Encyclopaedia of Hizb'allah*, vol. 1, pp. 19–24; and Qassem, *Hizb'allah*, pp. 16–20.

7 See: Martin Kramer, 'The Oracle of *Hizbullah*', in R. Scott Appleby (ed.), *Spokesmen for the Despised: fundamentalist leaders in the Middle East* (Chicago, IL: The University of Chicago Press, 1997), pp. 106 and 114; Marius Deeb, '*Shia* Movements', p. 693; 'Abd al-'Aziz Belqziz, *Hizb'allah: min Al-Tahrir ila Al-Rad'* (*Hizb'allah: From Liberation to Deterrence, 1982–2006*), An Expanded Edition of the Book on Resistance and the Liberation of South Lebanon (Beirut: Centre for Arab Unity Studies, 2006), p. 35; and John Obert Voll, *Islam: continuity and change in the modern world*, 2nd Ed. (Syracuse, NY: Syracuse University Press, 1994), p. 371.

8 Joseph Alagha, *The Shifts in Hizbullah's Ideology: religious ideology, political ideology and political program* (Amsterdam: Amsterdam University Press, 2006), p. 33.

9 On indicators for state failure see: Robert I. Rotberg (ed.), *State Failure and State Weakness in a Time of Terror* (Washington DC: Brookings Institution Press, 2003), pp. 1–10 and, on Lebanon, pp. 305–39; and Robert I. Rotberg (ed.), *When States Fail: causes and consequences* (Princeton and Oxford: Princeton University Press, 2004), pp. 1–10.

10 See: Simon Shapira, 'The Origins of *Hizbollah*', *The Jerusalem Quarterly*, 46 (Spring 1988), pp. 121–22; Marius Deeb, *Militant Islamic Movements in Lebanon: origins, social basis and ideology*', Occasional Paper Series (Washington DC: Center for Contemporary Arab Studies, Georgetown University, November 1986), pp. 12–13, available at: http://ccas.georgetown. edu/research-papers.cfm?id = 444 (accessed on 25 November 2008); and Alagha, *The Shifts in Hizbullah's Ideology*, p. 32.

11 *The Encyclopaedia of Hizb'allah*, vol. 1, pp. 26–27; and Qassem, *Hizb'allah*, pp. 23–24.

12 See: Ronen Bergman, *The Secret War with Iran: the 30 year covert struggle for control of a 'rogue' state* (Oxford: Oneworld Publications, 2008), pp. 58–59 and 86–87.

13 English text of the letter in: Norton, *Amal and the Shi'a*, pp. 167–87. The present writer is in possession of the Arabic text, but no source is indicated for this text. The Arabic text was published in the weekly magazine (*Al-ahd*) issued by *Hizb'allah* on 22 February 1985.

14 As'ad Abu Khalil, 'Ideology and Practice of *Hizbollah* in Lebanon: Islamization of Leninist organizational principles', *Middle Eastern Studies*, 27/3 (July 1991), p. 393.

15 Qassem, *Hizb'allah*, pp. 85–87; 'Abd al-Ghani Imad, *Al-Harakat Al-Islamiyyah fi Lubnan: Ishkaliyyat Al-Din wa Al-Siyasah fi Mujtam' Mutanawwi'* (*The Islamic Movements in Lebanon: the problem of religion and politics in a variegated society*), (Beirut: Dar Al-Tali'ah for Printing and Publications, 2006), pp. 167–69. On the internal structure of *Hizb'allah*, see: Ahmad Nizar Hamzeh,

'Lebanon's *Hizbullah*: from Islamic revolutionary to parliamentary accommodation', *Third World Quarterly*, 14/2 (1993), pp. 325–29.

16 On these institutions see: Belqziz, *Hizbullah*, pp. 38–45; Qassem, *Hizb'allah*, pp. 104–7; Imad, *The Islamic Movements*, pp. 167–75; and Lara Deeb, '*Hizbollah* and Its Civilian Constituencies in Lebanon', in Nubar Hovsepian (ed.), *The War on Lebanon: a reader* (Moreton in Marsh, UK: Arris Books, 2007), pp. 67–68.

17 Lara Deeb, '*Hizbollah*', pp. 69–70.

18 See: Open Letter in Norton, *Amal and the Shi'a*, pp. 172–73; *The Encyclopaedia of Hizb'allah*, pp. 71–72; and Hamzeh, 'Lebanon's *Hizbullah*', p. 324.

19 For evidence on this see: Qassem, *Hizb'allah*, pp. 26–34, 40–43 and 68–78.

20 See: text of Open Letter in Norton, *Amal and the Shi'a*, pp. 173 and 179. For an elaboration on *Hizb'allah*'s policy regarding the Arab–Israeli conflict, see: Amal Saad-Ghorayeb, *Hizbu'llah: politics and religion* (London: Pluto Press, 2002), pp. 134–67, especially pp. 161–67.

21 See: text of Open Letter in Norton, *Amal and the Shi'a*, pp. 169–71 and 178–79.

22 Augustus Norton, *Hizbollah: a short history* (Princeton and Oxford: Princeton University Press, 2007), pp. 35–36; and Augustus Norton, *Hizbullah of Lebanon: extremist ideals vs. mundane politics* (New York: Council on Foreign Relations, 1999), pp. 11–14.

23 Norton, *Hizbollah*, pp. 37–38.

24 See: Qasim, *Hizb'allah*, pages 77, 99–102 and 110–14.

25 See: Qasim, *Hizb'allah*, pp. 133–36.

26 For details on this issue, see: Bergman, *The Secret War*, pp. 110–30.

27 See: Matthew Levitt, *Hizbollah: A Case Study of Global Reach*, available at http://www.washingtoninstitute.org/print.php?template = CO7&CID = 132, 8 September 2003, (accessed on 25 November 2008).

28 See: The *Encyclopaedia of Hizb'allah*, vol. 1, pp. 122–23.

29 Alagha, *The Shifts in Hizbullah's Ideology*, p. 192.

30 *The Encyclopaedia of Hizb'allah*, vol. 1, pp. 95–104, and 141; and Qasim, *Hizb'allah*, pp. 68–78.

5 Hizbollah – from terror to resistance: Towards a national defence strategy

1 In his public address on International Jerusalem Day, which was broadcast on *Al-Manar* television on 26 November 2008, Hizbollah Secretary General Hassan Nasrallah admitted that 'even with regard to the liberation of Palestine we are clear: We say that our duty as Lebanese is to support the Palestinian people's resistance'.

2 Nasir al-Assad, 'Amid Information on Wide-Scale Israeli Military Operation Against the Palestinian Territories and Warning to Damascus not to "Intervene", Lebanon's Interest is to Protect itself from the Dangerous Implications', *Al-Mustaqbal*, 7 July 2006, p. 2.

3 'Al-Hariri: Priority Goes to Rendering the Tourist Season a Success, Concentrating on the People's Needs and on the Economy', *Al-Mustaqbal*, 30 June 2006.

4 Nasir al-Assad, 'Amid Information on Wide-Scale Israeli Military Operation Against the Palestinian Territories and Warning to Damascus not to "Intervene", Lebanon's Interest is to Protect itself from the Dangerous Implications', *Al-Mustaqbal*, 7 July 2006, p. 2.

5 'Al-Hariri and Nasrallah Stress Need for Cooperation Among Parties Within the Government', *Al-Mustaqbal*, 9 July 2006.

6 Nasir al-Assad, 'The Dialogue in the Wake of the Summit: Advance Declaration

of Intent, International Tribunal Issue Removed from the Agenda', *Al-Mustaqbal*, 25 March 2007.

7 *New TV*, 27 August 2006.

8 Talal Salman, 'Comprehensive Political Discussion With *Hizb'allah* Secretary General on the Impact of the July War; Nasrallah Tells *Al-Safir*: the Resistance has no Problem With the National Army or UNIFIL', *Al-Safir*, 5 September 2006.

9 '*Hizb'allah* Admits Misevaluating the Retaliation for Faithful Pledge Operation, Naim Qassem Decries the Government's Flawed Political Vision', *Al-Mustaqbal*, 29 October 2006.

10 Anthony Shadid, 'Inside Hezbollah, Big Miscalculations', *The Washington Post*, 8 October 2006.

11 *Al-Manar*, 14 July 2006.

12 *Al-Safir*, 15 June 1982.

13 Shimon Shapira, *Hizbullah: between Iran and Lebanon* (Tel Aviv: Hakibbutz Hameuchad, 2000), pp. 97–98, 113–14.

14 Augustus Richard Norton, *Hezbollah: a short history* (Princeton: Princeton University Press, 2007), pp. 32–33.

15 *Ha'aretz*, 17 January 1985.

16 Thus, for example, in September 1981 the French ambassador to Beirut was assassinated. Three months later the Iraqi embassy was devastated by a suicide bomber. In March of 1982 an explosion at the French embassy in Beirut killed nine people and wounded 27 others.

17 Hala Jaber, *Hezbollah: born with a vengeance* (New York: Columbia University Press, 1996), pp. 111–12; Norton, *Hezbollah*, pp. 71–72.

18 Although Hizbollah's founding had yet to be formally declared, three years later the organisation claimed responsibility for the attack.

19 *Al-Safir*, 27 September 2004.

20 'Fathi Mahmoud, Sheikh Naim Qassem, Hizbollah Deputy Secretary General Tells *Al-Ahram*: We Will Not Act as Syria's Arm Against the Lebanese Opposition, Our Street Activities are a Message to Whoever is Concerned', *Al-Ahram*, 10 March 2005.

21 See, for example: Amal Saad-Ghorayeb, *Hizb'ullah: politics and religion* (London: Pluto Press, 2002).

22 Ahmad Nizar Hamzeh, *In the Path of Hizbullah* (New York: Syracuse University Press, 2004), pp. 88–89.

23 Amos Har'el, 'Chief of Staff: Last Year Was IDF's Best Year in Lebanon', *Ha'aretz*, 4 January 2000.

24 It was during 2002 that Syria began supplying Hizbollah with Katyusha rockets and other military equipment, which were eventually put to intensive use in the Second Lebanon War.

25 Fares Khashan, 'Suleiman Tells Nasrallah: the Resistance is Our Smart Weapon', *Al-Mustaqbal*, 30 July 2004.

26 Naim Qassem, *Hizbullah: the story from within* (London: Saqi Books), p. 158.

27 *Al-Manar*, 16 February 2002.

28 *Agence France Presse* (AFP), 31 July 1993.

29 Nicholas Noe, *Voice of Hezbollah: the statements of Hassan Nasrallah* (London: Verso, 2007), pp. 104–05.

30 Ibid., p. 107.

31 *Ha'aretz*, 8 July 1994.

32 Eitan Rabin and Aluf Benn, '*Katyusha* Salvos Hit Galilee in Retaliation for Killing of two Lebanese by IDF Artillery', *Ha'aretz*, 31 March 1996.

33 In an interview with the author, 30 August 2003.

34 'Shahak Tells Foreign Affairs and Security Committee: *Hizb'allah* Endangering Life of Thousands of Residents in South Lebanon', *Ha'aretz*, 29 November 1995.

35 Eitan Rabin and Guy Bechor, 'Fearing *Katyushas*, IDF Orders Northern Residents Into the Shelters', *Yedi'ot Aharonot* and *Ha'aretz*, 9 April 1996.
36 Eitan Rabin, 'For the First Time Since the Lebanon War, IAF Strikes Southern Beirut', *Ha'aretz*, 12 April 1996.
37 Gid'on Alon, 'Peres: We Will Not Agree to Go Back to the Situation that existed on the eve of the military operation', *Ha'aretz*, 24 April 1996.
38 For the official version of the understanding, see: http://www.mfa.gov.il/MFA/ Peace%20Process/Guide%20to%20the%20Peace%20Process/Israel-Lebanon% 20Ceasefire%20Understanding (accessed on 17 July 2009).
39 AFP, 16 April 1996.
40 Noe, *Voice of Hezbollah*, p. 148.
41 Eitan Rabin, 'Military Intelligence Chief: *Hizb'allah* will try to wear out the understandings', *Ha'aretz*, 28 April 1996.
42 Qassem, *Hizbullah*, p. 158.
43 Ze'ev Schiff, 'How Iran Decided on the Attack in Argentina', *Ha'aretz*, 18 March 2003.
44 *Voice of the Oppressed* radio station, Ba'albek, 12 April 1996.
45 *Al-Manar*, 14 February 2008.
46 Daniel Sobelman, 'Hizbullah Lends Its Services to the Palestinian Intifada', *Jane's Intelligence Review*, 13/ 11 (2001), pp. 12–15.
47 *Al-Manar*, 8 April 2002 and *Al-Hayat*, 10 April 2002.
48 See: Nasrallah's comments in the National Dialogue, *Al-Safir*, 16 March 2006. Also his remarks in an interview to *Al-Safir*, 5 September 2006. See: Qassem in an interview to *A-Sharq al-Awsat*, 11 September 2006.
49 Hamzeh, *In the Path of Hizbullah*, p. 90.
50 *Al-Manar*, 16 March 2005.
51 Daniel Sobelman, '*Hizbollah* after the Syrian Withdrawal', *Strategic Assessment*, 8/1(June 2005), available at: http://www.inss.org.il/publications.php?cat=25& incat=&read=20 (accessed on 17 July 2009).
52 Lebanese Broadcasting Corporation, 5 September 2006.
53 *Al-Manar*, 24 April 2006.
54 After the IDF withdrawal, the UN found the international border ran through the village. Israel accepted the residents' request to refrain from dividing the village. In reality, this resulted in a breach exploited for years by Hizbollah as well as Lebanese drug runners using the village to make drug deals in Israel.
55 Ze'ev Schiff, 'Kidnapping was *Hizb'allah*'s fifth attempt', *Ha'aretz*, 19 September 2006.
56 Amos Har'el and Avi Issacharoff, *Spider Webs* (Tel Aviv: Yedi'ot Aharonot Books, 2008), pp. 142–43. It is noteworthy that *Al-Manar* even aired footage showing Israeli tanks being targeted by the organisation.
57 Yosi Yehoshu'a, Eitan Glikman, Go'el Beno, and Eran Navon, 'North comes under fire', *Yedi'ot Aharonot*, 22 November 2005.
58 'Fierce clashes along the border', *Al-Mustaqbal*, 22 November 2005.
59 *Al-Mustaqbal*, 28–29 March 2006.
60 For the full text of UN Resolution 1701, see: http://daccessdds.un.org/ doc/UNDOC/GEN/N06/465/03/PDF/N0646503.pdf?OpenElement (accessed on 17 July 2009).
61 Tha'ir Abbas, 'Naim Qassem: The Rockets we fired account for possibly 10% of our arsenal', *A-Sharq al-Awsat*, 10 September 2006.
62 See, for example: Nasrallah's speech on *Al-Manar*, 11 November 2008.
63 *Al-Akhbar*, 30 May 2008.
64 *Al-Manar*, 26 September 2008.
65 *Al-Manar*, 11 November 2008.
66 *Al-Akhbar*, 7 November 2008.

67 Ibid.
68 'Ja'ja proposes "strong neutrality" option', *Al-Mustaqbal*, 23 December 2008.

6 Israeli counter-insurgency strategy and the quest for security in the Israeli–Lebanese conflict arena

1 David Rodman, 'Israel's National Security Doctrine: an introductory overview', *Middle East Review of International Affairs*, 5/3 (September 2001), p. 77.
2 Sergio Catignani, *Israeli Counter-insurgency and the Intifadas: dilemmas of a conventional army* (London: Routledge, 2008), pp. 48–49.
3 David Rodman, 'Combined Arms Warfare in the Israel Defence Forces: an historical overview', *Defence Studies*, 2/1 (Spring 2002), p. 123.
4 Yoram Peri, 'Co-existence or Hegemony? Shifts in the Israeli Security Concept', in D. Caspi (ed.), *The Roots of Begin's Success: the 1981 Israeli elections* (London: Croom Helm, 1984), p. 206.
5 Catignani, *Israeli Counter-insurgency and the Intifadas*, p. 62.
6 Peri, 'Co-existence or Hegemony?', p. 203.
7 Dan Horowitz, 'Israel's War in Lebanon: new patterns of strategic thinking and civilian-military relations', *Journal of Strategic Studies*, 6/3 (1983), p. 95.
8 Robert Fisk, *Pity the Nation: the abduction of Lebanon* (New York: Nation Books, 2002) and Avner Yaniv, *Dilemmas of Security: politics, strategy and the Israeli experience in Lebanon* (Oxford: Oxford University Press, 1987), p. 72.
9 See: *United Nations Interim Forces in Lebanon*, available at: http://www.un.org/Depts/dpko/missions/unifil/index.html (accessed on 3 February 2009).
10 Ruth Linn, 'Terrorism, Morality and Soldier's Motivation to Fight: an example from the Israeli experience in Lebanon', *Studies in Conflict and Terrorism*, 11/2 (1988), p. 143.
11 See: Martin Van Creveld, *The Sword and the Olive: a critical history of the Israel Defence Force* (New York, NY: Public Affairs, 1998), pp. 291–96.
12 Zvi Lanir, 'Political Aims and Military Objectives – some observations on the Israeli experience', in Zvi Lanir (ed.), *Israeli Security Planning in the 1980s: its politics and economics* (Eastbourne: Praeger, 1984), p. 12. See also: Ze'ev Schiff and Ehud Ya'ari, *Israel's Lebanon War* (New York, NY: Simon & Schuster, 1984).
13 Ariel Sharon, *Warrior: an autobiography* (London: Simon & Schuster, 2001), p. 456.
14 Peri, 'Co-existence or Hegemony?', p. 203.
15 On Israeli strategic calculations that led to the 1982 Lebanon War see: Avner Yaniv and Robert J. Lieber, 'Personal Whim or Strategic Imperative? The Israeli Invasion of Lebanon', *International Security*, 8/2 (Autumn 1983), pp. 117–42.
16 Ruth Linn, 'Terrorism, Morality and Soldier's Motivation to Fight', p. 144. On the implications of Israel's decision to conduct a 'war of choice', see: A. Mack, 'Israel's Lebanon War', *Australian Journal of International Affairs*, 37/1 (April 1983), pp. 1–9.
17 Edward Walsh, 'Lebanon has Sapped Israel's Army; Now it is Smaller, Less Well-Trained, More Dependent on U.S.', *The Washington Post*, 20 April 1985.
18 Moshe Maoz, *Defending the Holy Land: a critical analysis of Israel's security and foreign policy* (Ann Arbor, MI: University of Michigan Press, 2006), p. 251.
19 On initial Syrian attempts at curbing Iran's and Hizbollah's influence in Lebanese politics, see: Ali Hillal, *Security in a Fractured State: the conflict over Lebanon*, Adelphi Paper, 28/230 (1988), pp. 17–18.
20 Magnus Ranstorp, '*Hezbollah*'s Future? -Part 1', *Jane's Intelligence Review*, 7/1 (January 1995), p. 35.

21 Laura Zittrain Eisenberg, 'Israel's Lebanon Policy', *Middle East Review of International Affairs*, 1/3 (September 1997), available at: http://meria.idc.ac.il/journal/1997/issue3/jv1n3a3.html (accessed on 3 February 2009).

22 Clive Jones, 'Israeli Counter-Insurgency Strategy and the War in South Lebanon, 1985–97', *Small Wars and Insurgencies*, 8/3 (Winter 1997), pp. 87–88.

23 Chris Mowles, 'The Israeli Occupation of South Lebanon', *Third World Quarterly* 8/4 (October 1986), p. 1352.

24 On Israeli security and administrative measures and their radicalizing effect on the local south Lebanese population, see: Chris Mowles, Ibid., pp. 1361–63.

25 Thomas H. Henriksen, 'Security Lessons from The Israeli Trenches', *Policy Review* (February-March 2007), available at: http://www.hoover.org/publications/policyreview/5516341.html (accessed on 3 February 2009).

26 Trevor N. Dupuy and Paul Martell, *The Arab-Israeli Conflict and the 1982 War in Lebanon* (Fairfax, VA: Hero Books, 1986), p. 207.

27 Between September 1982, when the IDF redeployed from Beirut, and mid-January 1983, guerrilla groups had 'killed 17 Israeli soldiers and wounded more than 70 in grenade, mine and shooting attacks'. Cited in: Robert Fisk, *Pity the Nation*, p. 537.

28 An Israeli fact-finding commission led by Israeli Supreme Court President, Yitzhak Kahan, determined that Ariel Sharon bore personal responsibility 'for ignoring the danger of bloodshed and revenge' and 'not taking appropriate measures to prevent bloodshed'. Whilst the Kahan Commission also condemned Prime Minister Begin, IDF Chief of Staff Rafael Eitan and other senior IDF officers, only Defence Minister Sharon was required to resign. Quoted in: Ze'ev Schiff and Ehud Ya'ari, *Israel's Lebanon War*, p. 284.

29 Gal Luft, 'Israel's "Security Zone" in Lebanon – A Tragedy?', *The Middle East Quarterly*, 7/3 (September 2000), available at: http://www.meforum.org/article/70 (accessed on 5 February 2009).

30 Cited in: Michael Jansen, *The Battle for Beirut: why Israel invaded Lebanon* (London: Zed Press, 1982), p. 120.

31 Andrew Rathmell, 'The War in South Lebanon', *Jane's Intelligence Review*, 6/4 (April 1994), p. 179.

32 David Rudge, 'Lubrani: no change likely in Lebanon security zone deployment', *The Jerusalem Post*, 10 November 1991.

33 Frederic M. Wehrey, 'A Clash of Wills: *Hizbollah*'s psychological campaign against Israel in South Lebanon', *Small Wars and Insurgencies*, 13/3 (Autumn 2002), p. 57.

34 Al J. Venter, 'Lebanon: A pawn in the power struggle', *Jane's Intelligence Review*, 10/6 (June 1998), p. 22.

35 By the mid-1990s, Hizbollah also became very adept at psychologically targeting IDF and SLA units as well as Israel's domestic constituencies by filming and airing its successful attacks carried out against forces stationed in the security zone. Such propaganda had a clear demoralizing effect on Israel's counter-insurgency campaign in Lebanon. See, for example: David Rudge, 'Hizbullah Shows Video of Attack on Soujud', *The Jerusalem Post*, 29 April 1999.

36 Magnus Ranstorp, '*Hezbollah*'s Future? – Part 2', *Jane's Intelligence Review*, 7/2 (February 1995), p. 81.

37 By the late 1990s Israel was spending $32 million a year in south Lebanon, most of it going to pay the salaries of SLA members and for infrastructure there. See: Arieh O'Sullivan and David Rudge, 'Fighting Against Time', *The Jerusalem Post*, 31 July 1998.

38 On the domestic political developments prior and particularly after the attainment of the Taif Agreement as well as on the reconstruction difficulties the Lebanese government faced following the civil war, see: Augustus Richard

Norton, 'Lebanon After Ta'if: is the civil war over?', *Middle East Journal*, 45/3 (Summer 1991), pp. 457–73; Charles Winslow, *Lebanon: war and politics in a fragmented society* (London: Routledge, 1996), pp. 276–97.

39 On Israel's security requirements vis-à-vis Syria, see: Ze'ev Schiff, *Peace with Security: Israel's minimal security requirements in negotiations with Syria, Policy Paper No. 34* (Washington DC: Washington Institute for Near East Policy, 1994).

40 The following account, which will focus on the first three central features of Israel's counter-guerrilla/counter-terrorist strategy and operational doctrine in south Lebanon, is based on: Shmuel Gordon, *The Vulture and The Snake. Counter-Guerrilla Air Warfare: the war in southern Lebanon, Security policy studies 39* (Ramat Gan: Begin-Sadat Centre for Strategic Studies, July 1998), available at: http://www.biu.ac.il/SOC/besa/books/39pub.html (accessed on 7 February 2009).

41 Mary Curtius, 'Israel Tough in S. Lebanon', *The Christian Science Monitor*, 13 January 1987, p. 1.

42 Nicholas Blanford, '*Hizbullah* Attacks Force Israel to Take a Hard Look at Lebanon', *Jane's Intelligence Review*, 11/4 (April 1999), p. 33.

43 Amir Oren, 'The Price of Restraint, the Price of Response', *Ha'aretz*, 1 February 2000.

44 See: David Rudge, 'Life Under the Katyushas', *The Jerusalem Post*, 21 February 1992.

45 Ranstorp, '*Hezbollah*'s Future? – Part 2', (February 1995), p. 82.

46 Simon Murden, 'Understanding Israel's Long Conflict in Lebanon: the search for an alternative approach to security during the peace process', *British Journal of Middle Eastern Studies*, 27/1 (May 2000), p. 35.

47 Jones, 'Israeli Counter-Insurgency Strategy', p. 94.

48 Jones, Ibid., p. 95.

49 David Rudge, '*Hizbullah* Moves in to Repair Homes Damaged in IDF Operation', *The Jerusalem Post*, 31 August 1993.

50 Murden, 'Understanding Israel's Long Conflict in Lebanon', p. 35.

51 Ariel Sharon, 'A real war in S. Lebanon', *The Jerusalem Post*, 16 December 1994.

52 'Army Fiasco in Lebanon', *The Jerusalem Post*, 1 November 1994.

53 Figures taken from: 'Israel/Lebanon: "Operation Grapes of Wrath"', *Human Rights Watch Report*, 9/8 (September 1997), *Human Rights Watch*, http://hrw.org/reports/1997/isrleb/Isrleb.htm (accessed 20 November 2009).

54 'Most of the Electorate is Against a Unilateral Exit from Lebanon', *Mideast Mirror*, 3/44, 5 March 1999.

55 Catignani, *Israeli Counter-Insurgency and the Intifadas*, p. 70.

56 Ed Blanche, 'Latest Attack in Lebanon May Dash Hope for Peace', *Jane's Defence Weekly*, 28/9 (3 September 1997), p. 34.

57 Wehrey, 'A Clash of Wills', p. 57.

58 See: Yigal Levy, 'Military Doctrine and Political Participation: toward a sociology of strategy', January 1996, available at: www.ciaonet.org/wps/ley02/index.html (accessed on 1 February 2009).

59 Jeffrey Record, 'Force-Protection Fetishism: sources, consequences, and (?) solutions', *Air and Space Power Journal*, 14/2 (Summer 2000), pp. 4–11.

60 See: James Bruce, 'Israel Breaks Cover to Reveal Its Commando Tactics in Lebanon', *Jane's Defence Weekly*, 26/24 (11 December 1996), p. 17.

61 See: Ed Blanche, 'Israel Has 2,000 Troops in South Lebanon Zone', *Jane's Defence Weekly*, 27/9 (5 March 1997), p. 15.

62 Ed Blanche, 'A Bizarre yet Bloody Conflict Drags on in South Lebanon', *Jane's Intelligence Review*, 9/9 (September 1997), p. 414.

63 Arieh O'Sullivan, 'Not all quiet on the northern front', *The Jerusalem Post*, 22 November 1996.

64 This number excludes the 73 IDF personnel tragically killed in a mid-air collision between two IDF CH-53 transport helicopters during their deployment flight to Lebanon on 4 February 1997. See: 'Risks and responsibility', *The Jerusalem Post*, 17 February 1997.

65 Nicholas Blanford, '*Hizbullah* Attacks', p. 34.

66 Ed Blanche, 'Israel Signals Conditions for Lebanon Withdrawal', *Jane's Defence Weekly*, 29/11 (18 March 1998), p. 21.

67 Ed Blanche, 'Lebanon Disaster Has Deeper Consequences for Israeli Policy', *Jane's Defence Weekly*, 28/11 (17 September 1997), p. 21.

68 According to then head of the Northern Command, Maj.-Gen. Gabi Ashkenazi, during 1998 there had been over 1,000 incidents of attacks on Israeli and SLA targets in south Lebanon. Figure quoted in: 'Israel to Review Lebanon Withdrawal', *The Jerusalem Post*, 27 November 1998.

69 Ed Blanche, 'Israel's "Human Sandbags" Set to Collapse in South Lebanon', *Jane's Intelligence Review*, 11/8 (August 1999), p. 24.

70 For a cross-party overview of the policy debates regarding the peace process with Syria and the future of Lebanon, see: 'Lebanon/Syria Debate Rages On', *Mideast Mirror*, 12/232, 1 December 1998.

71 Maoz, *Defending the Holy Land*, p. 215.

72 Nicholas Blanford, 'Israeli Cabinet Endorses Strikes on Lebanon', *Jane's Defence Weekly*, 31/2 (13 January 1999), p. 20.

73 In 1997, 59 per cent of the Israeli population surveyed were against unilateral withdrawal from Lebanon. By 2000, however, 62 percent had stated a preference for unilateral withdrawal. See: Asher Arian, *Israeli Public Opinion on National Security 2000, Memorandum No. 56* (Tel Aviv: Jaffee Center for Strategic Studies, 2000).

74 See, for example: Gideon Alon and Amos Harel, 'Mofaz Warns Withdrawal Won't End Conflict', *Ha'aretz*, 8 March 2000.

75 See: David Eshel, 'The Leaving of Lebanon . . .', *Jane's Defence Weekly*, 33/23 (7 June 2000), p. 20.

76 Nicholas Blanford, 'Post-Israel Stability in South Lebanon', *Jane's Intelligence Review*, 12/10 (October 2000), p. 25.

77 Stuart Cohen and Efraim Inbar, 'Varieties of Counter-Insurgency Activities: Israel's military operations against the Palestinians, 1948–90', *Small Wars and Insurgencies*, 2/1 (1991), p. 44.

78 Uri Dromi, 'When Restraint is Strength', *The Jerusalem Post*, 16 March 1999.

7 'A reach greater than the grasp': Israeli intelligence and the conflict in south Lebanon 1990–2000

* This chapter is a shortened version of an article by the same name which appeared in *Intelligence and National Security* 16/3 (September 2001) pp. 1–25.

1 Ronen Bergman, 'Fighting Blind', *Ha'aretz*, 14 May 1999.

2 See, for example: Hala Jaber, *Hezbollah: born with a vengeance* (London: Fourth Estate, 1997).

3 One study by Reuven Erlich has traced the historic relationship between Israel and the Shi'as of south Lebanon. As early as 1948, cordial relations that had existed previously between the pre-state Jewish community in mandate Palestine and the Shi'a community were shattered by the IDF raids on villages in south Lebanon. According to Erlich, these traumatic events were the first steps in the radicalization of the Shi'a of south Lebanon. For a summary of Erlich's argument see: Amir Oren, 'A war waged by the ignorant', *Ha'aretz*, 24 July 1998.

4 For Israel's historic relations with the Maronite community of south Lebanon see:
   Kirsten Schulze, *Israel's Covert Diplomacy in Lebanon* (London: Macmillan
   1998). For a detailed account of Israel's invasion of Lebanon in 1982 that led to
   18 years of occupation see: Ze'ev Schiff and Ehud Ya'ari, *Israel's Lebanon War*
   (London: Allen and Unwin, 1986). Accounts of the rise and development of
   Hizbollah are as numerous as they are varied in quality. Among the best are James
   Piscatori, 'The Shi'a of south Lebanon and Hizbollah, the Party of God', in
   Christine Jennett and Randal G. Stewart (eds), *Politics of the Future* (Melbourne:
   Macmillan 1989), pp. 292–320. See also: Martin Kramer, 'The Oracle of
   Hizbullah', in R. Scott Appleby (ed.), *Spokesman for the Despised* (Chicago, IL:
   University of Chicago Press, 1997), pp. 83–181.
5 Norvell de Atkine, 'Why Arab Armies lose Wars', *Middle East Review of
   International Affairs*, 1/4 (2000), available at: http://www.biu..ac.il/
   SOC/besa/meria/index/html (accessed on 17 April 2001).
6 Stuart A. Cohen, 'Changing emphases in Israel's military commitments, 1981–91:
   causes and consequences', *The Journal of Strategic Studies*, 15/3 (September
   1992), pp. 341–42.
7 Stuart A. Cohen and Efraim Inbar, 'Varieties of counter-insurgency activities:
   Israel's military operations against the Palestinians, 1948–90', *Small Wars and
   Insurgencies*, 2/1 (April 1991), pp. 41–60.
8 See: David Rodman, 'Regime-Targeting: a strategy for Israel', *Israel Affairs*, 2/1
   (Autumn 1995), pp. 153–67. For the origins of regime-targeting, located in the
   wider strategic studies literature of the Cold War, see: Desmond Ball and Jefferson
   Richardson (eds), *Strategic Nuclear Targeting* (London: Cornell University
   Press/Ithaca, 1986); Robert Aldridge, *First Strike* (London: Pluto Press, 1983).
9 Ian Black and Benny Morris, *Israel's Secret Wars* (New York: Grove Weidenfeld
   1991), pp. 469–72.
10 Keith Jeffrey, 'Intelligence and Counter-Insurgency Operations: some reflections
   on the British experience', *Intelligence and National Security*, 2/1 (1987), p. 119.
   Jeffrey notes that '[T]he exemplary use of violence – common in wartime – may
   only serve to exacerbate a problem and alienate the community in general'.
11 'The Good Fence in 1981: The other side of Israel-Lebanon Relations', *Briefing
   document 125/24.1.82/2.04.045*, Israel Ministry of Foreign Affairs, Information
   Division, Jerusalem.
12 Schulze, *Israel's Covert Diplomacy*, p. 158.
13 Schiff and Ya'ari, *Israel's Lebanon War*, pp. 240–42.
14 Ibid., p. 239; Helena Cobban, *The Making of Modern Lebanon* (London:
   Hutchinson 1985), p. 184.
15 Augustus Norton, '(In)Security Zones in Southern Lebanon', *Journal of Palestine
   Studies*, 23/1 (August 1993), pp. 68–69.
16 'Israeli General says Iran and Syria behind Hizbollah actions', *British
   Broadcasting Corporation Summary of World Broadcasts* (BBC-SWB), ME/2438
   MED/15, 19 October 1995.
17 Michael Herman, *Intelligence Power in Peace and War* (Cambridge: Cambridge
   University Press/Royal Institute for International Affairs, 1999), p. 247.
18 Gideon Doron and Reuven Pedatzur, 'Israeli Intelligence: utility and cost-effec-
   tiveness in policy formation', *International Journal of Intelligence and
   Counterintelligence* 3/3 (1989), pp. 357–58.
19 This point was made forcefully by Yossi Melman, a noted commentator on
   Israel's intelligence community. See: Yossi Melman, 'Where's the Brain',
   Ha'aretz, 9 September 1997. See also the commentary by Ron Ben-Yishai, 'What
   is this war about?' *Yediot Aharonot*, 2 March 1999.
20 Zvi Bar'el, 'How the IDF kept itself in Lebanon', *Ha'aretz*, 12 June 2000.
21 Ibid.

22 Black and Morris, *Israel's Secret Wars*, p. 395.
23 Ronen Bergman, 'Fighting Blind', *Ha'aretz Magazine Supplement* (in English) 14 May 1999.
24 Ibid.
25 Ronen Bergman, 'Thanks for your cooperation', *Ha'aretz*, 29 October 1999.
26 *Shabbak* is the alternative Hebrew acronym for the General Security Service or *Shin Bet*. Robert Fisk, 'Israeli spies betrayed for sake of love', *The Independent*, 28 August 1998.
27 David Hirst, 'South Lebanon: the war that never ends', *Journal of Palestine Studies*, 28/3 (1999), p. 15.
28 Frank Kitson, *Low Intensity Operations: subversion, insurgency and peacekeeping* (London: Faber, 1971), pp. 96–97.
29 Eitan Rabin, 'IDF trying to track down infiltrators from Lebanon', *Ha'aretz*, 13 October 1997. The former head of Israel's Northern Command who bore operational responsibility for south Lebanon, Major-General Amiram Levine believed that training and funding from Tehran had resulted in the qualitative transformation of the Islamic Resistance. See: 'Israeli army commander on unprecedented Iran involvement in Lebanon', *BBC-SWB*, ME/2685 MED/8, 8 August 1996.
30 Brendan O'Shea, 'Israel's Vietnam', *Studies in Conflict and Terrorism*, 21/3 (1998), pp. 315–16.
31 Eitan Rabin, '*Hizbollah* reportedly executes SLA figure', *Ha'aretz*, 21 October 1997.
32 Ze'ev Schiff, 'Only a Stone's throw away', *Ha'aretz*, 1 August 1990.
33 Robert Fisk, 'Israeli spies betrayed for the sake of love', *The Independent*, 28 August 1998; Guy Brechor, 'Lebanon charges 77 for spying for Israel', *Ha'aretz*, 10 July 1998.
34 Zvi Barel, 'Imposible Loyalties', *Ha'aretz*, 20 May 1999.
35 Eitan Rabin and David Makovsky, 'Eleven IDF soldiers killed in ambush', *Ha'aretz*, 7 September 1997.
36 'In Long Fight with Israel, *Hizbullah* Tactics Evolved', *New York Times*, 19 July 2000.
37 Peter Hirschberg, 'Lebanon: Israel's Vietnam', *The Jerusalem Report*, 8/16 (11 December 1997), pp. 8–13.
38 Robert Fisk, 'Why Israel didn't avenge its general', *The Independent*, 10 March 1999.
39 Patrick Cockburn, '*Hizbollah* kills Israeli general', *The Independent*, 1 March 1999.
40 Amos Harel, 'Time to go', *Ha'aretz*, 5 March 1999.
41 Ze'ev Schiff, 'The Ambushed Ambush', *Ha'aretz*, 26 February 1999.
42 Patrick Cockburn, 'General's call for Lebanon pull-out now', *The Independent*, 20 May 1999.
43 Amnon Barzilai, 'Tzahal's History Division distributes pamphlet differentiating between guerrilla warfare and terrorist activity', *Ha'aretz*, 4 August 1997.
44 Sharon Gal, 'IDF officers fingered in drug smuggling', *Ha'aretz*, 9 November 1999.
45 Yossi Melman, 'Those were the days, my friend', *Ha'aretz*, 10 December 2000.
46 Ibid.
47 'Israel/South Lebanon: Israel's Forgotten Hostages – Lebanese Detainees in Israel and Khiam Detention Centre', *Amnesty International Report*, July 1997.
48 Zvi Bar'el, 'Obeid plus 12 years of interest', *Ha'aretz*, 13 October 2000.
49 Zvi Bar'el, '*Hezbollah*'s private war', *Ha'aretz*, 8 October 2000.
50 'Israeli officials interviewed on Musawi killing: "Critical blow to *Hizbollah*"', *BBC-SWB*, ME/1307, A/2–3, 18 February 1992.
51 Yossi Melman, 'Still shrouded in mystery', *Ha'aretz*, 26 January 2001.

52 The destruction of homes elicited a sharp rebuke from Musawi's successor, Sheikh Hussein Nasrallah who threatened increased rocket attacks on Israel in retribution. See the commentary by Alex Fishmann, *Yediot Aharonot*, 29 November 1995.

53 Saguy's comments were made during the course of the documentary, 'Israel 50: the spy machine', *Open Media/Channel Four*, May 1998.

54 David Hirst, 'Israelis shocked by video shocker', *The Guardian*, 10 November 1994.

55 'Tzahal sets up guerrilla warfare school to deal with Lebanon's *Hizbollah*', *Yediot Aharonot*, 16 September 1997; Amir Rappaport, 'The IDF's secret weapon against *Hizbollah*, *Yediot Aharonot*, 5 December 1996.

56 One commentator also noted that the Islamic Resistance had in its possession both Israeli and US Army manuals dealing with RMA (Revolution in Military Affairs) that allowed it to develop suitable counter measures. See: Anthony Cordesman, *Israel and Lebanon: the new strategic and military realities* (Washington DC: Center for Strategic and International Studies 2000), p. 32.

57 Jeffrey, 'Intelligence and Counter-Insurgency Operations', p. 138.

58 See, for example: Ronen Bergman, 'A painful lesson in guerrilla warfare', *Ha'aretz*, 5 March 1999.

59 'Israel Air Force Chief confirms political goals of Lebanon operation', *BBC-SWB* ME/2494 MED/11, 24 April 1996.

60 Eitan Rabin, 'Israel's Northern Command officers cited on "intelligence failure"', *Ha'aretz*, 21 April 1996.

61 David Hirst, 'We are all *Hizbollah* here: our boys are defending our land', *The Guardian*, 15 April 1996.

62 Shmuel Gordon, '*The Vulture and the Snake' Counter-Guerrilla Air Warfare: the war in southern Lebanon*, Mideast Security Policy Studies 39 (Ramat Gan: Begin-Sadat Centre for Strategic Studies, July 1998).

63 Leslie Silver, 'IDF plans to beef up Lebanon intelligence', *The Jerusalem Report*, 14 September 1998, p. 6; 'The IDF's Technological War against *Hizbollah* through the eyes of the Lebanese media', *ICT Consultants*, 28 January 1999, available at: http://www.ict.org.il/articles (accessed on 2 April 2001).

64 Dani Reshef, 'Lebanon: the rise and fall of the security zone'. Posted on: http://www.angelfire.com/il2/redline (accessed on 28 May 2001).

65 Uzi Benziman, 'A guide to local conflicts', *Ha'aretz*, 8 October 1999.

66 Zvi Bar'el, 'Who owns the northern border?', *Ha'aretz*, 21 November 1999.

8 The pragmatic and the radical: Syria and Iran and war by proxy

1 The American administration refused to support a ceasefire in the hope that Israeli forces would be able to crush Hizbollah. The administration was not happy with the outcome of the war, especially since the Israeli government had committed ground forces toward the end of the war in a failed bid to break Hizbollah. The Israeli public was also shocked by the outcome of the war when Israel failed to restore its deterrent power. Israeli Prime Minister Ehud Olmert had to bow down to pressure and set up a committee to investigate the conduct of the war. Furthermore, Olmert himself never recovered from the war and his popularity remained within the margin of error.

2 Khairallah Khairallah, a leading Lebanese columnist, maintains that Hizbollah is simply an Iranian tool rented to Syria to avoid the international tribunal. In his writings and many media appearances, he has stressed the point that Hizbollah is a mere proxy for Iran and Syria. Although the columnist is widely seen in the Arab world as biased and prejudiced in his pronouncements, he represents a trend within Lebanon that considers Hizbollah a proxy.

3 Radwan al-Sayyed, a well-known academic and politician, wrote intensively on this issue. In many articles in *al-Sharq al-Awsat*, he maintained this line of thought and bid to build support for the anti-Hizbollah forces in Lebanon and the wider Middle East.

4 Egyptian president Hosni Mubarak told *al-Arabiya* the satellite channel that most Shi'as across the Arab world are loyal to Iran first, rather than the countries where they live, AFP reported. 'There are Shiites in all these countries [of the region], significant percentages, and Shiites are mostly always loyal to Iran and not the countries where they live'. He singled out Iraq for special attention. 'Naturally Iran has an influence over Shiites who make up 65 per cent of Iraq's population', Mubarak said when asked about Iran's role in neighbouring Iraq.

5 Augustus Richard Norton, *Hezbollah* (Princeton and Oxford: Princeton University Press, 2007), p. 15.

6 For an in-depth discussion of the origins of *Hizb'allah*, see: Magnus Ranstorp, *Hizb'allah in Lebanon: the politics of the western hostage crisis* (New York: St. Martin's Press, 1997), pp. 25–38.

7 For a full account of the life of Musa al-Sadr, see: Fouad Ajami, *The Vanished Imam: Musa al-Sadr and the Shia of Lebanon* (London: I. B. Tauris, 1986).

8 James Piscatori, 'The *Shi'a* of Lebanon and *Hizbullah*, the Party of God', in C. Jennett and R. G. Stewart (eds), *Politics of the Future* (Melbourne: Macmillan, 1989), p. 298.

9 See: Kirsten E. Schulze, *Israel's Covert Diplomacy in Lebanon*, St. Antony's Series (Houndmills, Basingstoke, and London: Macmillan Press, 1998), pp. 113–36.

10 Robert Fisk, *Pity the Nation: Lebanon at war* (Oxford: Oxford University Press, 1991), pp. 359–400.

11 For an overview of *Hizb'allah*'s aims and objectives, see: Martin Kramer, 'Redeeming Jerusalem: The Pan-Islamic Premise of *Hizb'allah*', in D. Menashri (ed.), *The Iranian Revolution and the Muslim World* (Boulder, CO: Westview Press, 1990), p. 108.

12 On this point, see: Gary C. Gambill and Ziad K. Abdelnour, '*Hezbollah*: between Tehran and Damascus', *Middle East Intelligence Bulletin*, 4/2 (February 2002).

13 Under heavy pressure from Hizbollah, and with the Israeli death toll rising, the Israeli National Unity Government, led by Shimon Peres, decided to withdraw from central Lebanon in 1985. That withdrawal was a victory for the resistance, which later became the hallmark of Hizbollah. Indeed, one of the complaints of moderate Arab forces is that Israel always gives victory to the radical forces, consequently empowering them.

14 The 'war of the camps' was when the Shi'a Amal movement attacked and besieged Palestinian refugee camps in a series of battles that lasted for two years (ending in 1987) during the Lebanese Civil War. In 1987, it came to an end, costing 2,500 lives.

15 For an interesting analysis of their relationship, see: Emile El-Hokayem, '*Hizbollah* and Syria: outgrowing the proxy relationship', *The Washington Quarterly*, 30/2 (Spring 2007), pp. 35–52.

16 Nizar Hamzeh, 'Lebanon's *Hizbollah*: from revolution to parliamentary accommodation', *Third World Quarterly*, 14/2 (1993), pp. 321–37.

17 The Taif Accord (the National Reconciliation Accord) was signed in Saudi Arabia to end the civil war in Lebanon, and to provide a basis for a return to political normalcy. It apportioned the same numbers of seats in parliament to Christian and Muslim sects, but barred the Shi'a community from the office of either the presidency or the premiership. This accord was opposed by Hizbollah from the beginning.

18 The *Jerusalem Post*, 3 April 1996. In early 1996, Hizbollah escalated its attacks against the Israel Defence Forces (IDF) in the southern Lebanon security zone

(a no-go zone determined by an earlier US-mediated ceasefire). When the IDF tried to respond to these attacks, Hizbollah fired Katyusha rockets at Israel's northern communities. In one such Katyusha attack, 38 Israeli civilians were wounded. This, in effect, was the last straw, setting the stage for Operation 'Grapes of Wrath'. On April 18, the Israeli army hit a UN post in Kfar Qana, where dozens of villagers were being sheltered. Approximately a hundred Lebanese civilians were killed, and dozens were wounded. International condemnation swiftly followed. Images of the dead and wounded were broadcast around the world, and Israel was placed under intense pressure to end the operation, although its objectives had not yet been achieved. Shortly after the Kfar Qana incident, the Americans mediated negotiations between Israel and Syria/Lebanon.

19 For more details, see: Dennis Ross, *The Missing Peace: the inside story of the fight for Middle East peace* (New York: Farrar, Straus and Giroux, 2004).

20 The Four Mothers group, from 1997, contested national security officials' assertions of the war's existential importance. The movement was founded and led by the family members of Israeli combat soldiers, and turned domestic opinion against the war in Lebanon, thus, precipitating the unilateral withdrawal of forces in 2000.

21 Emile El-Hokayem, '*Hizbollah* and Syria', p. 39.

22 Ibid., p. 42.

23 See: Nicholas Blandford, *The Death of Mr Lebanon* (London: I. B. Tauris, 2007).

24 Emile El-Hokayem, '*Hizbollah* and Syria', p. 43.

25 Graham E. Fuller, 'The *Hizballah*-Iran Connection: model for Sunni resistance', *The Washington Quarterly*, 30/1 (Winter 2006–7), pp. 139–50.

26 Graham E. Fuller, Ibid., p. 140.

27 For more details on the alliance, see: Fred H. Lawson, 'Syria's Relations with Iran: managing the dilemmas of alliance', *Middle East Journal*, 61/1 (Winter 2007), pp. 29–47.

28 For a detailed account of this vexed relationship, see: Eberhard Kienle, *Ba'th Versus Ba'th: the conflict between Syria and Iraq, 1968–1989* (London: I. B. Tauris, 1990).

29 Ze'ev Schiff, 'Israel's War with Iran', *Foreign Affairs* 85/6 (November/December 2006), pp. 23–31.

30 The Israeli government kept changing the objectives of the war, and it was reluctant to commit its ground forces until almost the end. When Tel Aviv finally did, the operation failed and the war ended with a general feeling in Israel that Hizbollah had not been defeated.

31 The poll was conducted in both rural and urban areas. Respondents were asked to rank 30 prominent Middle Eastern politicians from 1 to 20 in order of significance. The pollster then counted the total number of times that each figure was chosen. Nasrallah appears on 82 per cent of responses, followed by Iranian president Mahmoud Ahmadinejad (73 per cent), Khaled Mashal of Hamas (60 per cent), and Osama bin Laden (52 per cent).

32 In most of his speeches, Hassan Nasrallah emphasizes that resistance is not something that is subject to internal politics. To him, fighting Israel to realize the total liberation of occupied Lebanese land is a sacred mission that no government in Lebanon can impede.

33 Prime Minister Rafiq Hariri opposed the Syrian desire to extend the term of the former Lebanese President Emile Lahoud for another year. To the chagrin of Hariri, the Lebanese Parliament voted for the extension, a move that created a rift between Syria and Hariri. The disagreement between Syria and Hariri extended to other issues as well. While Hariri believed that Hizbollah should not provoke Israel after driving Israel from the South in 2000, Syria sought to keep resistance as a card in dealing with Israel in Syria's bid to recover the Golan Heights.

34 In May 2008, the Lebanese government made two decisions: to fire a security officer working at the airport who was seen as working for Hizbollah; and to target
the party's communication system. These two decisions provoked a political crisis and Hizbollah occupied Beirut, forcing the government to cave in.
35 Avi Shlaim, *The Iron Wall: Israel and the Arab world* (New York: Norton, 2000).
36 The May 2008 Doha agreement, following the violent armed altercations between
Sunni and Shi'a forces, defused tensions between these two major Muslim religious factions, thus, creating a new climate that in Lebanese terms can even be
described as calm and promising. Although some experts have interpreted the
results of the negotiations as a victory for Hizbollah, the big picture that emerges
from the success of the negotiations is an encouragement for Lebanon as a whole
and for the Lebanese people given that the country was able to avoid sliding back
into a state of civil war.

9 Forever at the crossroads: Hizbollah's combined strategies of accommodation and resistance

1 For a full text of UN Security Council Resolution 1559, see: http://
daccessdds.un.org/doc/UNDOC/GEN/N04/498/92/PDF/N0449892.pdf?OpenE
lement (accessed on 23 July 2009).
2 *Assafir*, 9 March 2005
3 Ibid.
4 Michael Young, 'Must Lebanon pay for *Hizbullah*'s pride?', *Daily Star*, 10 March
2005.
5 David Ignatius, 'Lebanon's next steps', *The Washington Post*, 11 March 2005.
6 Cécile Hennion, 'Le Hezbollah démontre qu'il est un force political majeur au
Liban', *Le Monde*, 10 March 2005.
7 For example, Thomas J. Butko, 'Revelation or Revolution: a Gramscian approach
to the rise of political Islam', *British Journal of Middle Eastern Studies*, 31/1 (May
2004), pp. 141–62.
8 Sheri Berman, 'Islamism, Revolution, and Civil Society', *Perspective on Politics*,
1/2 (2003) pp. 257–72.
9 Nizar Hamzeh, *In the Path of Hizbollah* (New York: Syracuse University Press),
p. 145.
10 Olivier Roy, *The Failure of Political Islam* (Cambridge, MA: Harvard University
Press, 1994) and *Globalised Islam* (New York: Columbia University Press, 2003).
11 See, for instance: Larbi Sadiki, *The Search for Arab Democracy* (New York:
Columbia University Press, 2002), pp. 111–31.
12 See: Roxanne L. Euben, *Enemy in the Mirror: Islamic Fundamentalism and the
Limits of Modern Rationalism* (Princeton, NJ: Princeton University Press, 1999).
13 See, for instance: Augustus R. Norton, *Hizballah of Lebanon: extremist ideals vs.
mundane politics* (New York: Council on Foreign Relations, 1999).
14 Fawaz A. Gerges, 'Introduction: understanding the phenomenon of *Hizbullah*', in
Dima Danawi, *Hizbullah's Pulse Into the dilemma of Al-Shahid and Jihad Al-
Bina Foundations* (Berlin: Friedrich Ebert Stiftung, 2002).
15 For a description of this particular period of time, see: Hala Jaber, *Hezbollah:
born with a vengeance* (New York: Columbia University Press, 1996), pp. 29–30.
16 See, for instance: 'An interview with the secretary-general of *Hizbollah* Sheikh
Hassan Nasrallah', *Middle East Insight* (May–August 1996).
17 Augustus R. Norton, *Amal and the Shi'a: Struggle for the soul of Lebanon*
(Austin, TX: University of Texas Press, 1987), p. 179.
18 As quoted in: Walid Charara and Fréderic Domont, *Le Hizbollah: un movement
Islamo-nationaliste* (Paris: Librarie Arthème Fayard, 2004), pp. 99–100.

19 *Al-Ahd*, 26 June 1985.
20 Augustus R. Norton, *Amal and the Shi'a*, p. 175.
21 Ibid., p. 175.
22 Mahmoud Soueid, 'Islamic Unity and Political Change. Interview with Shaykh Muhammad Hussayn Fadlallah', *Journal of Palestine Studies*, 25/1 (Autumn 1995), pp. 61–75.
23 Joseph Alagha, '*Hizbullah*'s Conception of the Islamic State', in Sabrina Mervin (ed.), *Les mondes chiites et L'Iran* (Paris: Karthala et IFPO, 2007), p. 109.
24 Jacob Hoigilt, 'Islamism, Pluralism, and the Palestine Question: the case of *Hizbullah*', *British Journal of Middle Eastern Studies*, 34/2 (August 2007), pp. 123–36. His argument is directly related to Nizar Hamzeh's conclusion in: *In the Path of Hizbollah*, p. 108 ff.
25 Hoigilt, 'Islamism, Pluralism, and the Palestine Question', p. 130.
26 Ibid., p. 131.
27 Ibid., pp. 132–33.
28 Ibid.
29 Tabitha Petran, *The Struggle over Lebanon* (New York: Monthly Review Press, 1987), p. 15.
30 See, for instance: Dilal al-Bizri, 'L'Islamisme Libanais et Palestinien, rupture dans la continuité', *Peuples Mediterraneens*, 64 (July 1993), pp. 265–76.
31 See: Immanuel Wallerstein, 'Islam, the West, and the world', *Journal of Islamic Studies*, 10/2, (1999), pp. 109–25.
32 *Al-Ahd*, 12 July 1985.
33 See: *Al-Ahd*, 12 July 1985.
34 For a discussion, see: Roxanne L. Euben, *Enemy in the Mirror*.
35 Nikki Keddie, 'Islamic Revival as Third Worldism', in Jean-Pierre Digard (ed.), *Le Cuisinier et le philosophie: hommage à Maxime Rodinson* (Paris: Maisonneuve et Larose, 1982), pp. 275–77.
36 Jamal Sankari, *Fadlallah: the making of a radical Shi'ite leader* (London: Saqi Books), pp. 181.
37 Ibid.
38 As cited in: Paul Nursery-Bray, 'Race and Nation: ideology in the thought of Frantz Fanon', *The Journal of Modern African Studies*, 18/1 (March 1980) pp. 135–42.
39 Frantz Fanon, *The Wretched of the Earth* (New York: Grove Press, 1963), p. 94.
40 Sayyed Muhammad Husayn Fadlallah, 'Islam and Violence in Political reality', *Middle East Insight*, 4/4–5, (1986).
41 Augustus R. Norton, *Amal and the Shi'a*, p. 171.
42 Ibid., p. 170.
43 For the *Hizbollah–Amal* conflict, see: Jubin M. Goodarzi, *Syria and Iran: diplomatic alliance and power politics in the Middle East* (London: I. B. Tauris, 2006).
44 As quoted in: Nicholas Noe, *Voice of Hizbollah: the statements of Hassan Nasrallah* (London: Verso, 2007), p. 94.
45 Quoted in: *Kitab Senoi, Hizbollah's Year Book 1995–1996* (in Arabic), p. 629.
46 Speech by Hassan Nasrallah, 23 March 2002, available at: www.nasrollah.net.
47 Naim Qassem, *Hizbullah: the story from within* (London: Saqi Books, 2005), pp. 44–45.
48 Ibid.
49 Ibid., p. 48.
50 Mona Harb and Reinoud Leenders, 'Know thy enemy: *Hizbullah*, "terrorism" and the politics of perception', *Third World Quarterly* 26/1 (February 2005), pp. 173–97.
51 Ibid., p. 192.

52 Jorge Larrain, *Identity and Modernity in Latin America* (London: Polity Press, 2000), p. 35.
53 Quoted in an undated leaflet *Al Maokif (The Standpoint)*, Hizb'allah's Foreign Relations Department, 1996.
54 *Al Bayrak*, 19 February 1997.
55 Augustus R. Norton, 'Lebanon after Ta'if: is the civil war over?', *Middle East Journal*, 45/3 (Summer 1991), pp. 456–73.
56 *Jerusalem Post*, 18 February 1992.
57 Cambill, Gary C. 'Hizbollah and the Political Ecology of Postwar Lebanon', *Mideast Monitor*, September (2006).
58 As cited in: Gilbert Achcar with Michel Warschawski, *The 33-Day War: Israel's war on Hezbollah in Lebanon and its consequences* (London: Paradigm Publishers, 2007), p. 31.
59 Graham Usher, 'Hizbollah, Syria, and the Lebanese Elections', *Journal of Palestine Studies*, 27/2 (Winter 1997) pp. 59–67; Hamzeh, *In the Path of Hizbullah*, pp. 108–22.
60 Interview, Beirut, 11 January 2007.
61 See: Judith Harik-Palmer, *Hizbollah: the changing face of terrorism* (London: I. B. Tauris, 2004), pp. 111–24.
62 Editorial in: *The Daily Star*, 'Here comes Hizbullah', 5 July 2000.
63 *Al Majallah*, 30 March 2002.
64 Speech by Hassan Nasrallah 4 June 2003, available at: www.nasrollah.net.
65 Ibid.
66 *An-Nahar*, 26 March 2002.
67 *Al-Arabi*, 24 March 2003.
68 *Al Mustaqbal*, 20 October 2003.
69 Ibid.
70 Speech by Hassan Nasrallah, 4 September 2004, available at: www.moqawama.org (accessed on 23 July 2009).
71 *Assafir*, 26 May 2005.
72 Conversation with Ali Fayyad, Beirut, 7 June 2005.
73 Conversation with the author, Beirut, 8 June 2005.
74 Speech, 24 May 2005, available at: www.moqawama.org (accessed on 23 July 2009).
75 Muhammed Muslih, 'Palestinian and Other Arab Perspectives on the Peace Process', in Robert O. Freedman (ed.) *The Middle East and the Peace Process: the impact of the Oslo Accords* (Gainesville, FL: University of Florida Press,1998), pp. 81–100.
76 Azmi Bishara, 'Self-fulfilling Prophecy', *Al-Ahram Weekly*, 10–16 August 2006.
77 Ibid.

10 The hubris of initial victory: The IDF and the Second Lebanon War

* The author would like to thank Dr Dima Adamsky for his excellent comments on this chapter.
1 Avi Kober, 'The Israel Defense Forces and the Second Lebanon War: why the poor performance?', *Journal of Strategic Studies* 31/1 (February 2008) pp. 3–40; Avi Kober, 'The Second Lebanon War', *Begin-Sadat Center for Strategic Studies Perspectives*, Paper No. 22 (September 2006); Matt M. Matthews, *We Were Caught Unprepared: the 2006 Hizbollah-Israeli war* (Ft. Leavenworth, KS: US Army Combat Studies Institute 2008); Sarah E. Kreps, 'The 2006 Lebanon War: lessons learned', *Parameters*, 37/1 (Spring 2007), pp. 72–83; Brig. Gen. Itai Bron, 'Where Did the Ground Manoeuvre Disappear?', *Maarachot* 420–21 (2008) pp. 4–15.

2 Amir Kulick, '*Hizbollah* vs. the IDF: the operational dimension', *Strategic Assessment* 9/3 (Tel Aviv: Institute for National Security Studies, November 2006); Alon Ben-David, 'Israel Reflects – New Model Army?', *Jane's Defence Weekly* 43/42 (11 October 2006); Alon Ben-David, 'Debriefing Teams Brand IDF Doctrine "Completely Wrong"', *Jane's Defence Weekly* 44/1 (3 January 2007); Gabriel Siboni, 'The Military Campaign in Lebanon', in Shlomo Brom and Meir Elran (eds), *The Second Lebanon War: strategic perspectives* (Tel Aviv: Institute for National Security Studies, 2007), pp. 61–76.

3 Ralph Peters, 'Lessons from Lebanon: the new model terrorist army', *Armed Forces Journal*, 144/3 (October 2006); Reuven Erlich and Yoram Kahati, *Hizbollah as a Case Study of the Battle for Hearts and Minds* (Gelilot: Center for Special Studies/Intelligence and Terrorism Information Center 2007); Reuven Erlich, *The Use of Lebanese Civilians as Human Shields* (Gelilot: Center for Special Studies/Intelligence and Terrorism Information Center, 2006); David Makovsky and Jeffrey White, *Lessons and Implications of the Israel-Hizbollah War: a preliminary assessment* (Washington, DC: Washington Institute for Near East Policy, 2006).

4 Uzi Rubin, *The Rocket Campaign against Israel during the 2006 Lebanon War* (Ramat Gan: Begin-Sadat Center for Strategic Studies, 2007); William M. Arkin, *Divining Victory: airpower in the 2006 Israel-Hizbollah War* (Maxwell Air Force Base, AL: Air University Press, 2007); Noam Ophir, 'Back to Ground Rules: some limitations of airpower in the Lebanon war', *Strategic Assessment*, 9/2 (Tel Aviv: Institute for National Security Studies, August 2006).

5 Uri Bar-Joseph, 'Israel's Military Intelligence Performance in the Second Lebanon War', *International Journal of Intelligence and Counter-Intelligence*, 20/4 (December 2007) pp. 583–601; Aharon Ze'evi Farkash, 'Intelligence in the War: observations and insights', in Brom and Elran (eds), *The Second Lebanon War*, pp. 76–86; Nicholas Blanford, 'Deconstructing *Hizbullah*'s Surprise Military Prowess', *Jane's Intelligence Review* 18/11 (1 November 2006); Yoaz Hendel, 'Failed Tactical Intelligence in the Lebanon War', *Strategic Assessment*, 9/3 (Tel Aviv: Institute for National Security Studies, November 2006).

6 Yair Evron, 'Deterrence and Its Limitations', in Brom and Elran (eds), *The Second Lebanon War*, pp. 35–46; Efraim Inbar, 'Strategic Follies: Israel's mistakes in the second Lebanese war', *Begin-Sadat Center for Strategic Studies Perspectives*, Paper No. 21 (September 2006).

7 Stephen Biddle and Jeffrey A. Friedman, *The 2006 Lebanon Campaign and the Future of Warfare* (Carlisle, PA: The Strategic Studies Institute of the U.S. Army War College, 2008); Andrew Exum, *Hizballah at War: a military assessment* (Washington, DC: Washington Institute for Near East Policy, 2006); Makovsky and White, *Lessons and Implications of the Israel-Hizbollah War*; Matthews, *We Were Caught Unprepared*.

8 Gil Merom, 'The Second Lebanon War: democratic lessons imperfectly applied', *Democracy and Security* 4/1 (2008), pp. 5–33.

9 Eran Zaidise, 'The Democratic Role, Function and Effect of Civil Society in Times of War: Learning from the Israeli Experience', *Democracy and Security*, 4/1 (January 2008), pp. 69–85.

10 Yagil Levy, 'The Second Lebanon War: from republican control to market control over the army', *Democracy and Security*, 4/1 (January 2008), pp. 48–68.

11 Justice (ret.) Eliyahu Winograd (Chair), Prof. Ruth Gavison, Prof. Yehezkel Dror, Maj. Gen. (ret.) Menachem Einan, Maj. Gen. (ret.) Chaim Nadel, *The Inquiry Commission to Examine the Events of the Military Campaign in Lebanon 2006. Interim Report* (Tel Aviv: 2007) (hereafter: Winograd, *Interim Report*); Eliyahu Winograd *et al.*, The Inquiry Commission to Examine the Events of the Military Campaign in Lebanon 2006, *Final Report* (Tel Aviv: January 2008) (hereafter: Winograd, *Final Report*).

12 Ofer Shelah and Yoav Limor, *Captives in Lebanon* (Tel Aviv: Yedioth Ahronoth, 2007); Amir Rapoport, *Friendly Fire* (Tel Aviv: Ma'ariv, 2007); Amos Harel and Avi Issacharof, *Spider Webs* (Tel Aviv: Yedioth Ahronoth 2008); Amos Harel and Avi Issacharoff, *34 Days: Israel, Hizbollah, and the War in Lebanon* (New York: Palgrave Macmillan 2008).

13 Gideon Levy, 'The War of "Peace for the IDF"', *Ha'aretz*, 16 July 2006, p. 16.

14 *Ha'aretz*, 13 July 2006.

15 Winograd, *Interim Report*, pp. 77, 80.

16 Ibid., p. 76; Harel and Issacharof, *Spider Webs*, p. 159.

17 Winograd, *Final Report*, p. 261.

18 Winograd, *Interim Report*, pp. 76–83.

19 Ibid., pp. 83–84.

20 Ibid., p. 80.

21 Ibid., p. 78.

22 Bar-Joseph, 'Israel's Military Intelligence Performance in the Second Lebanon War', pp. 584–92.

23 Winograd, *Interim Report*, pp. 55–56.

24 Ibid., pp. 57, 75.

25 Edward N. Lutwak, 'Towards Post-Heroic Warfare', *Foreign Affairs*, 74/3 (1995) pp. 109–22; Edward N. Luttwak, 'A Post-Heroic Military Policy', *Foreign Affairs*, 75/4 (1996, pp. 33–44.

26 Giora Romm, 'The Test of Rival Strategies: Two Ships Passing in the Night', in Brom and Elran, *The Second Lebanon War*, pp. 49–60.

27 For example, during the cabinet meeting of 12 July, a number of ministers expressed concern that any ground warfare might involve a high number of losses among Israeli soldiers. See: Winograd, *Interim Report*, pp. 78–80.

28 For a good discussion of the impact of this factor on the conduct of the war, see: Kober, 'The Israel Defense Forces and the Second Lebanon War: why the Poor Performance?', pp. 10–14.

29 Shelah and Limor, *Captives in Lebanon*, p. 138. Quite surprisingly, the Chief of Staff seemed to have ignored the well-known obstacles to the destruction of the *Katyusha* launchers. Following the success of operation 'Specific Gravity' on 13 July and the bombing of Dahia a day later, he said at a GHQ meeting on 15 July: 'Now the whole IDF should focus on Katyusha hunting. If weather tomorrow allows, we will attack southern Lebanon'. See: Harel and Issacharof, *Spider Webs*, p. 228. Despite the fact that the weather was fine, the IAF rate of success in the destruction of the systems was no better than expected by Shkedy in June.

30 Harel and Issacharof, *Spider Webs*, p. 228.

31 For the G8 statement, see: 'Issue of Mideast Violence Dominates G8 Summit Talks', *The New York Times*, 17 July 2006.

32 On 13 July, Olmert told Halutz and other senior IDF officers: 'You have here a minister of defense and a prime minister who are willing to take responsibility over difficult questions. Use it, don't do our calculus. Think as far as you can and let us make the decision'. Cited in: Winograd, *Interim Report*, p. 89.

33 Ibid., pp. 85, 86, 93, 96.

34 Ibid., p. 84.

35 For example, in a meeting with the Defence Minister. See: Ibid., p. 86.

36 For example, on 4 August he said in a discussion at the GHQ: 'I still think that we should destroy Lebanon, threaten with the destruction of Lebanon and bring it to the dark and stone age – with no water, no electricity, no oil, no roads, no government institutions, nothing'. Cited in: Harel and Issacharoff, *Spider Webs*, p. 263.

37 Halutz's predecessor, Lt. Gen. Moshe Ya'alon, defined the IDF's strategic goal in the Second *Intifada* as 'burning into the consciousness of the Palestinians' that

violence would yield no gains; see: Ari Shavit, 'People from Your Side Come and Really Undermine You', an interview with the IDF Chief of Staff, *Ha'aretz*, 19 August 2002. This, by itself, was a rather infeasible goal. Halutz stretched this concept further. For him, alleged military victories became a means to shape not only the enemy's but also the Israeli public's 'consciousness'. For a good critique of Halutz's 'spectacle of victory' concept, see: Matthews, *We Were Caught Unprepared*.

38   Harel and Issacharof, *Spider Webs*, pp. 259–61.
39   Ibid., pp. 236, 251–61, 327–34. Mugniyeh was finally assassinated in Damascus in February 2008.
40   Winograd, *Final Report*, p. 168.
41   Shelah and Limor, *Captives in Lebanon*, p. 156.
42   Winograd, *Final Report*, p. 93.
43   Shelah and Limor, *Captives in Lebanon*, p. 153–57. Former Chief of Staff. Gen. (Res.) Moshe Ya'alon, while in Washington DC, was shocked to learn on 19 July that Israel had asked the White House for two more months 'to crack down' on the Hizbollah. He could not see any reason for such a demand in a situation in which there was no answer to the *Katyusha* problem and any willingness to carry out a ground offensive. See: Harel and Issacharoff, *Spider Webs*, pp. 237–39.
44   Shelah and Limor, *Captives in Lebanon*, p. 78.
45   Harel and Issacharof, *Spider Webs*, p. 263.
46   Winograd, *Final Report*, p. 82.
47   Shelah and Limor, *Captives in Lebanon*, pp. 225–36; Harel and Issacharoff, *Spider Webs*, pp. 302–06.
48   Winograd, *Final Report*, pp. 117–25, 130, 161.
49   Shelah and Limor, *Captives in Lebanon*, pp. 77–81; Harel and Issacharoff, *Spider Webs*, p. 180; Rapoport, *Friendly Fire*, pp. 143–45; Romm, 'The Test of Rival Strategies', pp. 51–54.
50   Harel and Issacharoff, *Spider Webs*, pp. 200–202; Shelah and Limor, *Captives in Lebanon*, pp. 92–94.
51   Maj. Gen. (res.) Yitzhak Ben-Yisrael, *The First Rocket War: Israel-Hizbollah 2006: a position paper* (Tel-Aviv University, May 2007) p. 40.
52   Rubin, *The Rocket Campaign*, pp. 9, 20.
53   Shelah and Limor, *Captives in Lebanon*, p. 138.
54   Romm, 'The Test of Rival Strategies', p. 53.
55   Shelah and Limor, *Captives in Lebanon*, p. 78.
56   Harel and Issacharof, *Spider Webs*, p. 263.
57   Ibid., p. 241.
58   For an elaborated discussion of this subject, as well as of the causes of *AMAN*'s limited success in providing intelligence at the tactical level, see: Bar-Joseph, 'Israel's Military Intelligence Performance in the Second Lebanon War', p. 590–98.
59   Winograd, *Final Report*, p. 369.
60   Shelah and Limor, *Captives in Lebanon*, p. 356.
61   Ibid., p. 367
62   Harel and Issacharof, *Spider Webs*, p. 425–28.
63   Alex Fishman and Ariella Ringel-Hofman, 'An Interview with the Commander of the Northern Command', *Yedioth Ahronoth*, (weekend supplement), 2 October 2008.
64   Col. (Res.) Siboni Gabriel, 'Disproportionate Force: Israel's Concept of Response in Light of the Second Lebanon War', *The Institute for National Security Studies Insight*, No. 76 (28 October 2008); Maj. Gen. (Res.) Giora Eiland, 'The Third Lebanon War: The Target Lebanon', *Strategic Assessment* 11/2, (Tel Aviv: Institute for National Security Studies, October 2008), pp. 9–16.

11 Conclusion

1 David Makovsky and Jeffrey White, *Lessons and Implications of the Israel-Hizballah War: a preliminary assessment*, *Policy Focus 60* (Washington DC: The Washington Institute for Near East Policy, October 2006), p. 4.
2 See, for example, Eyal Ben-Ari and Uri Ben-Eliezer, *The Making of Israeli Militarism* (Bloomington, IN: Indiana University Press, 1998); and Yoram Peri, *Generals in the Cabinet Room: How the military shapes Israeli Policy* (Washington DC: United States Institute of Peace, 2006).
3 *Book of Habbakuk* 2:17, *The Bible*, (edition and date not specified).

Select bibliography

Achcar, Gilbert with Warschawski, Michel, *The 33-Day War: Israel's war on Hezbollah in Lebanon and its consequences* (London: Paradigm Publishers, 2007).

Ajami, Fouad, *The Vanished Imam: Musa Al-Sadr and the Shia of Lebanon* (London: I. B. Tauris, 1986).

Alagha, Joseph, *The Shifts in Hizbullah's Ideology: religious ideology, political ideology and political program* (Amsterdam: Amsterdam University Press, 2006).

—— 'Hizbullah's Conception of the Islamic State', in Sabrina Mervin (ed.), *Les mondes chiites et L'Iran* (Paris: Karthala et IFPO, 2007).

Aldridge, Robert, *First Strike* (London: Pluto Press, 1983).

Al-Khazen, Farid, *The Breakdown of the State in Lebanon 1967–1976* (London: I. B. Tauris, 2000).

Arian, Asher, *Israeli Public Opinion on National Security 2000*, Memorandum No. 56 (Tel Aviv: Jaffee Center for Strategic Studies, 2000).

Arreguín-Toft, Ivan, *How the Weak Win Wars: a theory of asymmetric conflict* (Cambridge: Cambridge University Press, 2005).

Ball, Desmond and Richardson, Jefferson (eds), *Strategic Nuclear Targeting* (London: Cornell University Press/Ithaca, 1986).

Ben-Ari, Eyal and Ben-Eliezer, Uri, *The Making of Israeli Militarism* (Bloomington, IN: Indiana University Press, 1998).

Bergman, Ronen, *The Secret War with Iran: the 30 year covert struggle for control of a 'rogue' state* (Oxford: Oneworld Publications, 2008).

Biddle, Stephen and Friedman, Jeffrey A., *The 2006 Lebanon Campaign and the Future of Warfare* (Carlisle, PA: The Strategic Studies Institute of the U.S. Army War College, 2008).

Black, Ian and Morris, Benny, *Israel's Secret Wars* (New York: Grove Weidenfeld, 1991).

Blandford, Nicholas, *The Death of Mr Lebanon* (London: I. B. Tauris, 2007).

Catignani, Sergio, *Israeli Counter-insurgency and the Intifadas: dilemmas of a conventional army* (London: Routledge, 2008).

Charara, Walid and Domont, Fréderic, *Le Hizbollah: un movement Islamo-nationaliste* (Paris: Libraire Arthème Fayard, 2004).

Cobban, Helena, *The Making of Modern Lebanon* (London: Hutchinson, 1985).

Cordesman, Anthony, *Israel and Lebanon: the new strategic and military realities* (Washington DC: Center for Strategic and International Studies, 2000).

Deeb, Lara, '*Hizbollah* and Its Civilian Constituencies in Lebanon', in Nubar Hovsepian (ed.), *The War on Lebanon: a reader* (Moreton in Marsh, UK: Arris Books, 2007).

Deeb, Marius, '*Shia* Movements in Lebanon: their formation, ideology, social basis and links with Iran and Syria', *Third World Quarterly*, 10/2 (April 1988), 683–98.

Dupuy, Trevor N. and Martell, Paul, *The Arab-Israeli Conflict and the 1982 War in Lebanon* (Fairfax, VA: Hero Books, 1986).

Eiland, Giora, 'The Third Lebanon War: The Target Lebanon', *Strategic Assessment* 11/2, (Tel Aviv: Institute for National Security Studies, October 2008).

Eisenberg, Laura Zittrain, *My Enemy's Enemy: Lebanon in the early Zionist imagination, 1900–1948* (Detroit: Wayne State University Press, 1994).

Eisenstadt, S. N., *The Internal Repercussions of the Lebanon War* (Jerusalem: The Leonard Davis Institute for International Relations, August 1986).

Erlich, Reuven, *The Use of Lebanese Civilians as Human Shields* (Gelilot: Center for Special Studies/Intelligence and Terrorism Information Center, 2006).

Erlich, Reuven and Kahati, Yoram, *Hizbollah as a Case Study of the Battle for Hearts and Minds* (Gelilot: Center for Special Studies/Intelligence and Terrorism Information Center, 2007).

Euben, Roxanne L., *Enemy in the Mirror: Islamic Fundamentalism and the Limits of Modern Rationalism* (Princeton, NJ: Princeton University Press, 1999).

Evron, Yair, *War and Intervention in Lebanon: the Israeli-Syrian deterrence dialogue* (Baltimore, MD: The Johns Hopkins University Press, 1987).

—— 'Deterrence and Its Limitations', in Shlomo Brom and Meir Elran (eds), *The Second Lebanon War: strategic perspectives* (Tel Aviv: Institute for National Security Studies, 2007).

Exum, Andrew, *Hizballah at War: a military assessment* (Washington DC: Washington Institute for Near East Policy, 2006).

Fanon, Frantz, *The Wretched of the Earth* (New York: Grove Press, 1963).

Farkash, Aharon Ze'evi, 'Intelligence in the War: observations and insights', in Shlomo Brom and Meir Elran (eds), *The Second Lebanon War: strategic perspectives* (Tel Aviv: Institute for National Security Studies, 2007).

Feldman, Shai, 'Israel's involvement in Lebanon: 1975–85', in Ariel E. Levite, Bruce W. Jentleson and Larry Berman (eds), *Foreign Military Intervention* (New York: Columbia University Press, 1992).

Feldman, Shai and Rechnitz-Kijner, Heda, *Deception, Consensus and War: Israel in Lebanon* (Tel-Aviv: Jaffee Center for Strategic Studies, 1983).

Fisk, Robert, *Pity the Nation: Lebanon at war* (Oxford: Oxford University Press, 1991)

—— *Pity the Nation: the abduction of Lebanon* (New York: Nation Books, 2002).

Gal, Irit and Hamerman, Ilana, *Mi-Beirut le-Jenin, Milhemet Levanon 1982/2002* (Tel-Aviv: 'Am 'Oved, 2002).

Gendzier, Irene L., *Notes from the Minefield: United States Intervention in Lebanon and the Middle East, 1945–1958* (Boulder, CO: Westview, 1999).

Gerges, Fawaz A., 'Introduction: understanding the phenomenon of *Hizbullah*', in Dima Danawi, *Hizbullah's Pulse Into the dilemma of Al-Shahid and Jihad Al-Bina Foundations* (Berlin: Friedrich Ebert Stiftung, 2002).

Goodarzi, Jubin M., *Syria and Iran: diplomatic alliance and power politics in the Middle East* (London: I. B. Tauris, 2006).

Gordon, Shmuel, *The Vulture and The Snake. Counter-Guerrilla Air Warfare: the war in southern Lebanon*, Security Policy Studies 39 (Ramat Gan: Begin-Sadat Centre for Strategic Studies, July 1998).

Hamizrachi, Beate, *The Emergence of the South Lebanon Security Belt* (New York: Praeger, 1988).

Hamzeh, Ahmad Nizar, *In the Path of Hizbullah* (New York: Syracuse University Press, 2004).

Har'el, Amos and Issacharoff, Avi, *Spider Webs* (Tel Aviv: Yedi'ot Aharonot Books, 2008).

——*34 Days: Israel, Hizbollah, and the War in Lebanon* (New York: Palgrave Macmillan 2008).

Harik-Palmer, Judith, *Hizbollah: the changing face of terrorism* (London: I. B. Tauris, 2004).

Hendel, Yoaz, 'Failed Tactical Intelligence in the Lebanon War', *Strategic Assessment*, 9/3 (Tel Aviv: Institute for National Security Studies, November 2006).

Herman, Michael, *Intelligence Power in Peace and War* (Cambridge: Cambridge University Press/Royal Institute for International Affairs, 1999).

Hillal, Ali, *Security in a Fractured State: the conflict over Lebanon*, Adelphi Paper, 28/230 (1988).

Inbar, Efraim, 'Strategic Follies: Israel's mistakes in the second Lebanese war', *Begin-Sadat Center for Strategic Studies Perspectives*, Paper No. 21 (September 2006).

Jaber, Hala, *Hezbollah: born with a vengeance* (New York: Columbia University Press, 1996).

Jansen, Michael, *The Battle for Beirut: why Israel invaded Lebanon* (London: Zed Press, 1982)

Kaufman, Asher 'Forgetting the Lebanon War? On Silence, Denial and Selective Remembrance of the First Lebanon War', in Jay Winter, Efrat Ben Ze'ev and Ruth Ginio (eds), *Shadows of War: the social history of silence in the Twentieth Century* (Cambridge: Cambridge University Press, 2009).

Keddie, Nikki, 'Islamic Revival as Third Worldism', in Jean-Pierre Digard (ed.), *Le Cuisinier et le philosophie: hommage à Maxime Rodinson* (Paris: Maisonneuve et Larose, 1982).

Khalidi, Walid, *Conflict and Violence in Lebanon* (Harvard College: Center for International Affairs, 1979).

Kienle, Eberhard, *Ba'th Versus Ba'th: the conflict between Syria and Iraq, 1968–1989* (London: I. B. Tauris, 1990).

Kimmerling, Baruch, *Politicide: Ariel Sharon's wars against the Palestinians* (New York: Verso, 2003).

Kitson, Frank, *Low Intensity Operations: subversion, insurgency and peacekeeping* (London: Faber, 1971).

Kober, Avi, 'The Second Lebanon War', *Begin-Sadat Center for Strategic Studies Perspectives*, Paper No. 22 (September 2006).

Kramer, Martin, 'Redeeming Jerusalem: The Pan-Islamic Premise of *Hizb'allah*', in D. Menashri (ed.), *The Iranian Revolution and the Muslim World* (Boulder, CO: Westview Press, 1990).

—— 'The Oracle of *Hizbullah*', in R. Scott Appleby (ed.), *Spokesmen for the Despised: fundamentalist leaders in the Middle East* (Chicago, IL: The University of Chicago Press, 1997).

Kulick, Amir, '*Hizbollah* vs. the IDF: the operational dimension', *Strategic Assessment* 9/3 (Tel Aviv: Institute for National Security Studies, November 2006).

Lanir, Zvi, 'Political Aims and Military Objectives – some observations on the Israeli experience', in Zvi Lanir (ed.), *Israeli Security Planning in the 1980s: its politics and economics* (Eastbourne: Praeger, 1984).

Larrain, Jorge, *Identity and Modernity in Latin America* (London: Polity Press, 2000).

Makovsky, David and White, Jeffrey, *Lessons and Implications of the Israel-Hizballah War: a preliminary assessment, Policy Focus 60* (Washington DC: Washington Institute for Near East Policy, October 2006).

Maoz, Ze'ev, *Defending the Holy Land* (Ann Arbor, MI: The University of Michigan Press, 2006).

Matthews, Matt M., *We Were Caught Unprepared: the 2006 Hizbollah-Israeli war* (Ft. Leavenworth, KS: US Army Combat Studies Institute 2008).

Merom, Gil, *How Democracies lose Small Wars?* (New York: Cambridge University Press, 2003).

Morris, Benny, *Israel's Border Wars, 1949–1956* (Oxford: Clarendon Press, 1993).

Muslih, Muhammed, 'Palestinian and Other Arab Perspectives on the Peace Process', in Robert O. Freedman (ed.) *The Middle East and the Peace Process: the impact of the Oslo Accords* (Gainesville, FL: University of Florida Press, 1998).

Nakash, Yitzhak, *Reaching for Power: the Shi'a in the modern Arab world* (Princeton: Princeton University Press, 2006).

Naor, Arie, *Begin ba-Shilton: 'Edut Ishit* (Tel-Aviv: Yediot Aharonot, 1993).

Noe, Nicholas, *Voice of Hezbollah: the statements of Hassan Nasrallah* (London: Verso, 2007).

Norton, Augustus Richard, *Amal and the Shi'a: Struggle for the soul of Lebanon* (Austin, TX: The University of Texas Press, 1987).

—— *Hizballah of Lebanon: extremist ideals vs. mundane politics* (New York: Council on Foreign Relations, 1999).

—— *Hezbollah: a short history* (Princeton: Princeton University Press, 2007).

Ophir, Noam, 'Back to Ground Rules: some limitations of airpower in the Lebanon war', *Strategic Assessment*, 9/2 (Tel Aviv: Institute for National Security Studies, August 2006).

Peri, Yoram, *Generals in the Cabinet Room: How the military shapes Israeli Policy* (Washington DC: United States Institute of Peace, 2006).

—— 'Co-existence or Hegemony? Shifts in the Israeli Security Concept', in D. Caspi (ed.), *The Roots of Begin's Success: the 1981 Israeli elections* (London: Croom Helm, 1984).

Petran, Tabitha, *The Struggle over Lebanon* (New York: Monthly Review Press, 1987).

Phares, Walid, *Lebanese Christian Nationalism: the rise and fall of an ethnic resistance* (Boulder, CO: Lynne Rienner, 1995).

Piscatori, James, 'The *Shi'a* of south Lebanon and *Hizbollah*, the Party of God', in Christine Jennett and Randal G. Stewart (eds), *Politics of the Future* (Melbourne: Macmillan 1989).

Qassem, Naim, *Hizbullah: the story from within* (London: Saqi Books, 2005).

Rabinovich, Itamar, *The War for Lebanon, 1970–1983* (Ithaca, NY: Cornell University Press, 1984).

Ranstorp, Magnus, *Hizb'allah in Lebanon: the politics of the western hostage crisis* (New York: St. Martin's Press, 1997).

Rapoport, Amir, *Friendly Fire* (Tel Aviv: Ma'ariv, 2007).

Romm, Giora, 'The Test of Rival Strategies: Two Ships Passing in the Night', in Shlomo Brom and Meir Elran (eds), *The Second Lebanon War: strategic perspectives* (Tel Aviv: Institute for National Security Studies, 2007).

Ross, Dennis, *The Missing Peace: the inside story of the fight for Middle East peace* (New York: Farrar, Straus and Giroux, 2004).

Rotberg, Robert I. (ed.), *State Failure and State Weakness in a Time of Terror* (Washington DC: Brookings Institution Press, 2003).

—— *When States Fail: causes and consequences* (Princeton and Oxford: Princeton University Press, 2004).

Roy, Olivier, *The Failure of Political Islam* (Cambridge, MA: Harvard University Press, 1994).

—— *Globalised Islam* (New York: Columbia University Press, 2003).

Rubin, Uzi, *The Rocket Campaign against Israel during the 2006 Lebanon War* (Ramat Gan: Begin-Sadat Center for Strategic Studies, 2007).

Saad-Ghorayeb, Amal, *Hizbu'llah: politics and religion* (London: Pluto Press, 2002).

Sadiki, Larbi, *The Search for Arab Democracy* (New York: Columbia University Press, 2002).

Sankari, Jamal, *Fadlallah: the making of a radical Shi'ite leader* (London: Saqi Books, 2005).

Schiff, Ze'ev, *Peace with Security: Israel's minimal security requirements in negotiations with Syria*, Policy Paper No. 34 (Washington DC: Washington Institute for Near East Policy, 1994).

Schiff, Ze'ev and Ya'ari, Ehud, *Israel's Lebanon War* (New York: Simon & Schuster, 1984).

—— *Milhemet Sholal* (Jerusalem: Shoken, 1984).

—— *Israel's Lebanon War* (London: Allen and Unwin, 1986).

Schulze, Kirsten E., *Israel's Covert Diplomacy in Lebanon*, St. Antony's Series (Houndmills, Basingstoke, and London: Macmillan Press, 1998).

Shapira, Shimon, *Hizbullah: between Iran and Lebanon* (Tel Aviv: Hakibbutz Hameuchad, 2000).

Sharon, Ariel, *Warrior: an autobiography* (London: Simon & Schuster, 2001).

Shelah, Ofer and Limor, Yoav, *Captives in Lebanon* (Tel Aviv: Yedioth Ahronoth, 2007).

Shlaim, Avi, *The Iron Wall: Israel and the Arab world* (New York: Norton, 2000).

Siboni, Gabriel, 'The Military Campaign in Lebanon', in Shlomo Brom and Meir Elran (eds), *The Second Lebanon War: strategic perspectives* (Tel Aviv: Institute for National Security Studies, 2007).

—— 'Disproportionate Force: Israel's Concept of Response in Light of the Second Lebanon War', *Insight*, No. 76 (Tel Aviv: Institute for National Security Studies, 28 October 2008)

Talhami, Ghada Hashem, *Palestinian Refugees: from pawns to political actors* (Hauppauge, NY: Nova, 2003).

Van Creveld, Martin, *The Sword and the Olive: a critical history of the Israel Defence Force* (New York, NY: Public Affairs, 1998).

Voll, John Obert, *Islam: continuity and change in the modern world*, 2nd Ed. (Syracuse, NY: Syracuse University Press, 1994).

William, Arkin, M., *Divining Victory: airpower in the 2006 Israel-Hizbollah War* (Maxwell Air Force Base, AL: Air University Press, 2007).

Winslow, Charles, *Lebanon: war and politics in a fragmented society* (London: Routledge, 1996).

Yaniv, Avner, *Dilemmas of Security: Politics, Strategy and the Israeli Experience in Lebanon* (New York: Oxford University Press, 1987).

Index